Teaching for Justice
in the **Social Studies**
Classroom

Teaching for Justice in the *Social Studies* Classroom

Millions of Intricate Moves

Edited by

Andra Makler and Ruth Shagoury Hubbard

HEINEMANN · Portsmouth, NH

Heinemann
A division of Reed Elsevier Inc.
361 Hanover Street
Portsmouth, NH 03801-3912
www.heinemann.com

Offices and agents throughout the world

The author and publisher wish to thank those who have generously given permission to reprint borrowed material:

"Millions of Intricate Moves" by Kim Stafford. Copyright © 2000 by Kim Stafford. Used by permission of the author.

"Thinking for Berky" and "Peace Walk" copyright © 1962, 1998 by the Estate of William Stafford. Reprinted from *The Way It Is: New & Selected Poems* with the permission of Graywolf Press, Saint Paul, Minnesota.

"What Happened to the Golden Door? How My Students Taught Me About Immigration" by Linda Christensen. Copyright by Linda Christensen. Used by permission of the author.

"Collective Action: Speaking Up and Standing Together" by Sandra Childs. Copyright © 2000 by Sandra Childs. Used by permission of the author.

"The Human Lives Behind the Labels: The Global Sweatshop, Nike, and the Race to the Bottom" by Bill Bigelow first appeared in *Rethinking Schools,* Spring 1997. Subscriptions to *Rethinking Schools* are $12.50 per year, available from *Rethinking Schools,* 1001 E. Keefe Ave., Milwaukee, WI 53212: 800-669-4192; rsbusness@aol.com; www.rethinkingschools.org.

"Questions from a Worker who Reads" by Bertolt Brecht. Copyright © 1976, 1979 by Methuen London, Ltd. From *Bertolt Brecht Poems 1913–1956* edited by John Willet and Ralph Manheim. Used by permission of Methuen Publishing Ltd., London.

"Our Needs and Their Destruction—Oil Drilling in Nigeria: Engaging in the Struggle for Social Justice" by Sandra Childs and Amanda Webber-Welch. Copyright © 2000 by Sandra Childs and Amanda Webber-Welch. Used by permission of the authors.

Library of Congress Cataloging-in-Publication Data
Teaching for justice in the social studies classroom : millions of intricate moves / edited by Andra Makler, Ruth Shagoury Hubbard.
    p. cm.
    Includes bibliographical references.
    ISBN 0-325-00264-9 (acid-free paper)
    1. Social justice—Study and teaching (Middle school)—United States. 2. Social justice—Study and teaching (Secondary)—United States. 3. Social sciences—Study and teaching (Middle school)—United States. 4. Social sciences—Study and teaching (Secondary)—United States. I. Makler, Andra. II. Hubbard, Ruth, 1950–

HM671 .T43 2000
303.3′72′071273—dc21

00-031940

Editor: William Varner
Production: Merrill Peterson, Matrix Productions
Production coordinator: Elizabeth Valway
Cover design: Darci Mehall
Manufacturing: Louise Richardson

Printed in the United States of America on acid-free paper
04 03 02 01 00 RRD 1 2 3 4 5

We dedicate this book to our colleague Jim Wallace, who has been a teacher to many of the contributors to this book—including us. He continues to be a supportive, kind, and thoughtful critic, and a strong voice for John Dewey's vision of schools as laboratories for democracy.

CONTENTS

ACKNOWLEDGMENTS

We want to thank all the teachers who wrote chapters for this book for permitting us to further complicate their already busy lives with our requests for clarification, permission slips, meetings, revisions, and in some cases, more writing. We appreciate their willingness to open their classroom doors and discuss their struggles, questions, teaching materials, and hopes. We hope their honesty will encourage others as it has inspired us. It takes a special kind of courage to resist the push for standardized curriculum and high-stakes testing and teach in ways that encourage young people to grapple with important issues of justice. The authors of these chapters are models of such courage.

Grateful thanks to our editor, Bill Varner, for giving us free rein, nudging us gently, and providing good help whenever we asked. Bill's advocacy for the project from the beginning sustained us and permitted us to assure our contributors that this book really would happen. Also, a word of thanks to Brenda Power, who acted as matchmaker when we discussed the seeds of this project.

Finally, we thank our rather feisty students for challenging us to get on with this good work.

Introduction

Teaching from the Center of the Circle: "Doing Good Work"

Ruth Shagoury Hubbard

Opus, the Latin word that we apply to musical compositions, has the twin meanings of work and riches. We hear it in "operate" and "opulence." Good work enriches the world and also enriches the worker; it draws on our creativity, our ability to imagine actions before carrying them out, and our freedom to act on those images, guided by intelligence and skill.

Scott Russell Sanders

Teaching for justice is about fundamental changes in classroom practice. It's more than adopting a new up-to-date curriculum or adding innovative strategies to a teaching bag of tricks, more than a set of episodes to explore and "learn." It takes place in the classroom—and beyond the walls of the school, combining academic with experiential and community-based learning. Doing this good work is challenging, messy, complex—and it involves, as Kim Stafford reminds us in his opening chapter, "millions of intricate moves."

Reading the classroom tales of the authors of this collection helps make the intricacies involved in building toward an understanding of and a commitment to justice come alive. What these teachers generously offer us is a chance to open up the seams and see the inner workings of their classrooms, including their own questions, worries, inner struggles, and steps forward. We see "good work" in action— enriching the worlds of the classroom and the larger world—and enriching both students and teachers as well. What we see is the process of curriculum creation, teaching from the center of the circle.

Too often, teachers are pressured to become curriculum consumers of whatever canned curriculum or textbook their school, district, or state has bought into. Even when teachers have more freedom in their classrooms, it's difficult to move away from this mindset. It is tempting to adopt teaching lessons wholesale with each group of students whether the lessons are from a textbook or a teaching presentation at a conference. Even the most creative and inspiring lessons will fail if the epicenter of the circle is neglected: the students themselves. What works for one group of students, built from their needs and interests, cannot be cut out with a cookie cutter and fed to another classroom of very different learners. Theresa Kauffman explains with eloquence the seeds of her classroom curriculum with her eighth-graders: "I began to look for ways to engage these students in the circles of their daily life to show their own genius and to understand the world around them a little better in the process" (Chapter 10, this book). The classroom decisions that grew out of Theresa's discussions with her students would have a very different shape from those in David Molloy's classroom of middle school students (Chapter 11) just across the city.

This is not to say that there aren't wonderful materials to rely on and adapt for your students. Indeed, one of the main purposes of this text is to share the teaching materials, resources, and strategies that the authors have adapted or created. Theresa relies on Project Citizen materials; David, on cases to present at mock trials. At the end of each chapter, all the authors list resources that have helped their curriculum work in the content areas they write about.

Even more important than the resources themselves are the classroom stories that come alive in these pages. Through these stories, you can see the steps that dedicated educators take as they blend a powerful curriculum with the genuine voices and needs of their students. We hope you find practical ideas and strategies from the classroom stories in this book—"good work" that will help you "imagine actions before you carry them out." The uniqueness of your own classroom and community must ultimately guide the decisions you make as you use these ideas as a springboard for your work with students.

What *can* we learn when we take a close look at these classroom stories? Although your students have different names and life experiences from those of the adolescents who come alive in these chapters, we think you will see glimpses of students you have known, variations of the kinds of incidents that you can imagine happening in your own teaching. The stories may not share the particulars of your experiences, but they ring true. When we read a good novel, we relate to and learn from the universals that are at its essence. In a similar way, we can recognize the truths in the literature in this collection. You'll recognize students like Daneeka from Bill Bigelow's class (Chapter 5), who might bristle at your assignments, too. And although you may not know Cameron Robinson except through Bill's prose, Cameron's poem and its effect on Bill may call to your mind adolescents whose insightful poems or compelling metaphors have helped shape your perceptions.

One thing we do learn here flies in the face of teacher education lore: Beginning teachers *can* be innovators. Some of the chapters in this book were written by first-year teachers; Jessie Singer, Daniel Gallo, and Dirk Frewing. What do these educators have in common with some of their veteran colleagues? Certainly their passion and commitment to adolescents, to learning, and to their desire to teach toward an understanding of the complexities of the concept of justice. An important theme that cuts across the number of years in the classroom is the way these teachers bring the parts of their lives that are important to them into their teaching, drawing on their own creativity. They are unafraid to reflect on the personal experiences that shaped their own senses of justice. Kim Stafford is not alone when he writes of the "oblique but indelible stories" that helped frame his own convictions of not just *what* but *how* he would teach a sense of justice to his students. From beginning teacher Dirk Frewing's recollections of being awakened to the plights of migrant workers, to twenty-year veteran Linda Christensen's analysis of learning about "the other immigration," to the early genesis of this book in Andra Makler's interviews with teachers, these authors state their educational and *personal* reasons for the curriculum they teach. By their example, they invite you to do the same.

Their chapters offer other invitations as well. Through their stories, we can see what they place at the center of their teaching circles, themes that can inform others who wish to engage in the complex yet vital endeavor of teaching for justice: *Focus on inquiry, respect for the discipline, a repertoire of teaching strategies, and membership in a professional community.* We encourage you to see these stories, and the resources that follow, as the kind of spiraling outward that Voltaire describes when he writes, "The instruction we find in books is like fire. We fetch it from our neighbors, kindle it at home, communicate it to others, and it becomes the property of all." (quoted in Epel, 1998, p. 34.)

Focus on Inquiry

What can we understand about contemporary immigration laws by looking at these historical exclusions?

Linda Christensen

What happens when the theme of justice is introduced in a graduate-level course for teachers? What happens when the course is not educational theory or practice but subject matter specific; in this case, a cross-listed social studies and language arts course called *Vietnam and the United States*?

Michael Jarmer

Will multiple perspectives in the teaching of social studies provide students with a discourse and with tools to address issues of social justice?

Jessie Singer

How many of our graduates, we wondered, had the knowledge and understanding of poverty that would even begin to prepare them to serve this population?

Mary Burke-Hengen and Gregory Smith

How do you turn the situation in the Delta from a lesson about social *in*justice to a lesson about social justice?

Sandra Childs

Teachers in this collection frame their teaching around questions, wonderings, tensions. They wonder, "What can we learn from . . . ?" or "what will happen if . . . ?" These beginning queries often snowball into an avalanche of questions. "Having found 'the movement' to be one of the most compelling stories of recorded experience, I found the challenge of framing an exploration of its contours a daunting task," Daniel Gallo confides. "As I pondered, further questions emerged: Do the means by which justice is sought matter? Is it important for the actions of people to embody the vision of society that impel them to action? How should justice be sought after? With these questions swirling in my consciousness, we began our journey."

It can indeed be a daunting task to enter into "the work" of our classroom journeys with these questions still emerging, still swirling. This is counter to the notion of teachers having all the answers and working toward a predetermined outcome. But if the intent of curriculum creation becomes a cycle rather than an arrow, we can learn to welcome the messy but fascinating data that emerge. In a cycle where the evidence we collect from our students informs our teaching decisions, we become both more responsive to our students' needs and more efficient in our teaching, learning what works and what needs to be adapted. We become teacher-researchers, creating a culture of inquiry in our classrooms.

Respect for the Discipline

The notion of inquiry spreads outward to the students as well. Not only are they invited in as fellow researchers with their teachers, but the *methods* of inquiry of a particular discipline are also of paramount importance. This stance demonstrates a high level of respect for students' possibilities. For example, in Paul Copley's economics class, he teaches his students to think like economists and use the tools that economists rely on. Rather than being discouraged that his students often share the view that economics is indeed "the dismal science," Paul takes on the challenge by teaching them the basic ideas that frame the structure of "the distribution of goods and services." The ability to grasp market theory through a critical lens allows students to develop a more complex understanding of economic justice in a market economy. As Paul writes, "Once students learn some rules about market failure, they can begin to construct for themselves a vision of economic justice based on empirical evidence."

Russ Dillman and Geoff Brooks teach their students the tools of conflict resolution through the peer mediation program at their high school. The consequences of this mediation are real; the mediated solutions negotiated by the students are accepted by both the adolescents and adults at the school. Similarly, Theresa Kauffman expects her students to use the real-life strategies that are part of community organization and activism. And the students who engage in the mock trials that David Molloy describes need to research and prepare their arguments for the courtroom based on actual cases.

Historians rely on primary documents as they conduct historical research. Linda Christensen expects her students to conduct such "real" research: "not the scurry-to-the-library-and-find-the-closest-encyclopedia-and-copy-it-word-for-word kind of research, but research that made them ask questions about immigration policies, quotas, and personal stories that couldn't be lifted from a single text." She taught them to use the Oregon Historical Society's clippings file, photo files, and the rare documents room. And like adult historians, her students become "wonderfully devious researchers," finding sources in ancestors' letters and searching out local interviewees that their research led them to.

The subject area of social studies includes a wide range of disciplines: economics, history, government, sociology, anthropology, geography, political science. Furthermore, each discipline entails a way of thinking and approaching the information. Teaching toward justice in each of these areas requires helping students learn to use the tools that will take them deeper into the discipline. There is a long tradition of issue-centered education in the social studies disciplines, dating back to the 1940s. Maurice P. Hunt and Lawrence E. Metcalf (1955) published their work supporting teachers' efforts to discuss "closed areas" in their curriculum, and Anna Ochoa's work with Shirley Engle (1966) in decision making focused teachers and students' efforts on justice (see Allen, 1966, for a review). In the 1960s, curriculum materials developed by Donald Oliver and James Shaver focused on helping students to deliberate public issues and take a stand; many of the issues in these materials are issues of justice. Their jurisprudential inquiry model was exemplified in the Public Issues Series of curriculum booklets in U.S. and world history and contemporary issues published by the Social Science Education Consortium, of Boulder, Colorado, 1993–1998. The teachers in this collection carry forward this tradition into contemporary classrooms.

Repertoire of Teaching Strategies

Some of the tools and strategies described in these chapters are specific to the discipline, yet many cut across subject areas and invite students to make meaning through a range of literacies.

For example, these educators employ *writing strategies* as part of the expectations of the curriculum they teach. Mary Burke-Hengen and Greg Smith describe journal work as a way for their students to write their way to connection and understanding: The journals "were a place to relate and integrate personal experiences with poverty and to engage in constructing understandings about poverty and its causes and solutions."

Reflective writing appears in many of the classroom examples. Often, these teachers found it helped their students to begin at the center, with their individual voices and personal experiences. Daniel Gallo, for example, saw the power of using "I Am" poems to help students explore and express the emotional texture of a given moment in time.

Other teachers helped their students write their way to understanding through the use of interior monologues, as you'll notice in Sandra Childs' and Amanda Weber-Welch's chapter when the authors share pieces their students wrote as they tried on the minds of Ogani tribal women or Nigerian government officials. Jessie Singer also wanted her kids to use writing to get inside another person's experiences—in this case, the perspective of a person of Mayan descent on the morning a Spanish ship arrives on their shore. She found the students were able to capture distant people's worlds in voices other than their own.

In her social studies class, Jessie created a writing workshop to give her students a chance to write, get feedback on their drafts from her and each other, and take their pieces through a revision process to publication to be shared with a larger audience. You also see evidence of writing workshop and a range of genres in the classroom in Bill Bigelow's examples of descriptive paragraphs, work poems, letters, two-voice poems, and news articles. Linda Christensen's class generated poems and personal narratives, persuasive essays, and culture poems. A key element for these teachers' writing projects is the search for genuine audiences for their students' writing.

Linda also brings *literature* in a range of genres into her students' social studies curriculum. Her bibliography of resources for students to explore is rich: they read novels, poetry, essays, news stories. This is also evident in Michael Jarmer's graduate-level classroom, where the curriculum about Vietnam and the United States centers around novels and poetry written by authors from both countries. His goal is for the teachers who participate in his class to create places for adolescents where history and literature "speak to each other, and where justice is discussed, practiced, and made real for students." In these social studies classes, you'll also see a range of literature, from the novel *Things Fall Apart* to the compelling autobiography of Rigoberta Menchú, integrated as part of the curriculum.

The resources are not limited to the written word, however. Compelling examples of images through photography, film, and a range of media incorporate *visual literacy* into the curriculum as well. Jessie Singer's students not only viewed films, delighted in pictures, and perused art books and photographs, they were also encouraged to create paintings and collages as well as write essays or letters to the editor. Linda Christensen and Bill Bigelow's students not only watched films as a source of information, but they also learned to critique them, taking into account whose voices are heard—and whose are left out.

Role plays and drama are other teaching strategies you'll notice in many of these classrooms. Bill Bigelow created a transnational capital auction in his class; Sandra Childs and Amanda Weber-Welch used the 1998 World Economic Forum as a guide for their students to participate in a similar hearing on Nigerian oil and human rights. Although creating such complex role plays requires a great deal of preparation—and can be contentious and unruly in the classroom—teachers like

Bill, Amanda, and Sandra find the struggle is worthwhile. Working from these and other teachers' examples can help you bring an exciting strategy to your teaching repertoire.

Membership in a Professional Community

Doing the work together in the classroom weaves the bonds of community. It is often the negotiation, willingness to listen, share viewpoints and ideas, and honestly examine the process, blended together with working toward common goals, that form that strongest central core. Although acknowledging that rips in the fabric will need to be patched and mended, the teachers here who show you their teaching communities document what is possible through hard work. The students have learned to take on the minds and habits of the discipline, examine moral structures, take risks, give voice to their opinions—as Sandra Childs frames it, "speak up and stand together."

Teachers need the same community beyond the walls of the classroom, the same opportunity to work together for the long haul. Many of the teachers in this collection find community support through Portland Area Rethinking Schools— a local teacher activist group that meets monthly, sharing ideas and forming workgroups around specific areas, such as the globalization workgroup. The power of their work is well documented in this collection, with members such as Bill Bigelow, Amanda Weber-Welch, Sandra Childs, and Greg Smith in the globalization workgroup alone. Other teachers find groups that tie them to their professional affiliation bring the same kind of support and integrity to their work that we've described earlier. National teacher organizations such as the National Council for Social Studies and its state affiliates provide forums through national conferences, local gatherings, and a range of professional materials.

The Internet is also a way to access wider connections through listservs and websites. These often spark more personal connections—people with like minds who find ways to share the good work they are carrying out in their communities, schools, and classrooms. One of the best places to start is through the *History/Social Studies Web Site for K–12 Teachers* at: **http://www.execpc.com/~dboals.html**[1]

---

[1]Two good sources for social studies websites are Joseph A. Braun Jr. and Frederick Risinger (Eds.) *Surfing the Web, National Council for the Social Studies Bulletin* 96, and Barbara Cohen, 1997, *Social Studies Resources on the Internet: A Guide for Teachers* (Portsmouth, NH: Heinemann).

So, What does Justice Look Like?

As you'll see in the classroom stories that follow, justice has many facets. It looks more like hard work and struggle than distanced discussions of lofty ideas. It looks like rolling up your sleeves and digging in. It is indeed an intricate and complex dance of "millions of intricate moves," characterized by both tiny steps and bold gestures. Some of these gestures may worry teachers who question their role as political beings.

In his new book exploring literacy learning and the influence of social class, Patrick J. Finn takes on this issue, reminding us that "we engage in dozens of political acts and make dozens of political statements in our classrooms every day that support the status quo. We don't think of them as political because they are not controversial" (p. 178).

And Finn has a compelling retort to the question some educators might ask, "Will I get in trouble if I teach this way?": "'I'd get into trouble' is not an ethical reason why a professional does not make a professional decision. I'll agree it is the reason millions of professional decisions are made every day—that's why the status quo is the status quo—but we're talking justice here, not go-along, get-along" (p. 179).

The authors of the following chapters make hard decisions—ethical decisions—as they grapple with what it means to teach for justice. They do "the good work," aided by their knowledge, their commitment, their professional communities, and their belief in their students' possibilities. The educational landscape can and will change because of the choices teachers make about "what they do with their days." We hope this book will serve as an invitation to both toil and renewal, as Scott Russell Sanders (1997) so eloquently expresses it:

> Toil drains us; but good work may renew us, by giving expression to our powers. Work shapes our body, fills our thoughts and speech, stamps our character. The accountant bears the imprint from decades of vouchers as surely as the carpenter bears the weight from tons of lumber and the jolt from thousands of hammer swings. The plumbers' forearms are speckled with burns from molten solder, and the banker's face bears a crease for every foreclosure. Whatever else we make through our labor, we also make ourselves. So we had better choose carefully what we do with our days, and how we do it, and why. (p. 92)

References

Epel, Naomi. 1998. *The Observation Deck*. San Francisco, CA: Chronicle Books.

Finn, Patrick J. 1999. *Literacy with an Attitude: Educating Working-Class Children in Their Own Self-Interest*. Albany: State University of New York Press.

Hunt, Maurice & Lawrence Metcalf. 1955. *Teaching High School Social Studies: Problems in Reflective Thinking and Social Understanding* (2nd ed.). New York: Harper and Brothers.

Allen, Rodney F. 1966. "The Engle-Ochoa Decision-Making Model for Citizenship Education." In *Handbook on Teaching Social Issues,* ed. Evans & Saxe. *National Council for the Social Studies Bulletin 93,* Washington, DC: NCSS.

Oliver, Donald, & James Shaver. 1966. *Teaching Public Issues in the High School.* Boston, MA: Houghton Mifflin. Reprinted by Utah State University Press, Logan.

Sanders, Scott Russell. 1997. *Writing from the Center.* Bloomington: Indiana University Press.

1 *Millions of Intricate Moves*

Kim Stafford

If a sense of justice begins in childhood, how does it begin? Behind the playground scuffles and instructive betrayals that teach the honey of justice by the salt of injustice, what does a parent's own life vision provide? What language does a parent use to teach it, what intuitive silences, what oblique but indelible stories? My father, the poet William Stafford, had such quiet but indelible ways. And looking back into the story of our family's time, beyond my father's death in 1993 to my own childhood in the 1950s, I seek to understand how he and my mother shaped me.

Lately arrived in Oregon, our family was driving on a Sunday into the foothills of the Cascade mountains, somewhere near Scotts Mills, to find the place called Butte Creek Falls. The man who knew the way, Jim Stauffer, biology professor at Daddy's college, was in the car ahead. We were as we always were: Daddy driving, Mother in the front seat with him, baby Barbara between them, and in the back, right to left, Bret (maybe 9), sister Kit (maybe 5), and me (maybe 8 or so). And as we bounced through the forest on a bumpy gravel road, there came that feeling that all was right. Sword ferns splayed in their whorls in the shade of tall Douglas firs, sun-spangled coins of gold across the green world that now belonged to us. It was morning. We had seen our mother pack the big Hershey bar. And we were going to find a cave. Jim—or as we called him, Bim—said so.

Let that tramp down from the road where no trail led be all my childhood in one day—swishing through the ferns, losing my footing and tumbling into the safe, soft duff of Oregon, first hearing ahead the whisper of the falls, and then coming on it, grand, sudden thunder off a lip of basalt. And then the cave behind the falls, where we all went into the earth.

One of the strange things about having a writer for a father is the matching up of such an impressionistic memory with a poem by him that must be from that day:

Behind the Falls

First the falls, then the cave:
then sheets of sound around us fell
while earth fled inward, where we went.
We traced it back, cigarette lighter high—
lost the roof, then the wall,
found abruptly in that space
only the flame and ourselves. . . .

When men and women meet that way
the curtain of the earth descends and they
find how faint the light has been, how far
mere honesty or justice is from all they need.

I remember that darkness, and what is so strange about the overlay of the poem on my own memory is the way the word *justice* brings back to me the ride home. I had forgotten that, but my deepest mind had not: the ride home, kids drowsy, feet wet, my mother and the baby in Jim's car, and another man in the front seat by my father as he drove. That man, a stranger, saying to my father something I had never heard: "When a black person handles my food, I can't tell whether it is clean, because you can't see how clean the hands are."

The car went electric. I had so rarely heard my father scold anyone, even us kids. And I don't remember how he chose his words, but there was no question the passenger was being straightened out. Was he a student at the college, a professor? I don't remember. All big people were big people to us then. There was a silence. Words hung in the air. The green of Oregon was an arena for a major readjustment in the pistons and gears of human kinship. We must have driven in silence. Maybe I fell asleep at last.

I can glimpse the origin of my father's habits of mind when I gather scraps of the culture of his own family. Family letters from the 1930s and 1940s among my father and his sister and brother show a family culture tuned to notice prejudice, and ponder ways to advance inclusion. In 1943, for example, when my father was stationed in a California camp for conscientious objectors, he wrote to his brother Bob, the army air force pilot stationed in Texas, both reporting and inquiring about social issues:

The swinging, singing French pilots [reported in a previous letter home by Bob], with their verve and colorful background, should give a good flavor to the place [Bob's base near San Antonio]. Your report, Bob, of their feeling against the Italians and Germans checks, poignantly, with echoes we outsiders get through the papers, magazines, and radio. It seems there will be no oversupply of understanding for a while. Peg, I understand, became involved in a warm bridge club discussion about race problems recently. Well, wise as serpents and harmless as doves seems to be indicated, now as in bible times!

He goes on to say he hopes to get acquainted with some soldiers on the next forest fire job, as well as to report on contact with the "Mexicans and Negroes" he had met on the last fire. I see my father, like his brother Bob in the army and his sister Peg back home in Kansas, all three reaching out as they always had to make connection with people of all kinds.

In our many family moves those early years, we lived a strangely sheltered life, in some ways. In other ways, we were schooled to the variety of the world, and the inclusive necessity of human relations from a very early age. There is a story in the family about the first time my brother saw a black person. We were in a store, and my mother noticed little Bret staring, staring in fascination at a black child there in the aisle. Afraid he might say something inappropriate, she hustled him outside. On the sidewalk, she turned to him.

"Did you notice something about that little boy?"

"Yes, mother! He had gum!"

Gum, one of the great forbiddens.

By then my father had written one of his most compelling poems of dark anguish, "Thinking for Berky," a recollection of a girl from Kansas whose hard life brought him to the brink of his capacity as human witness. The poem begins with the girl, her plight:

> In the late night listening from bed
> I have joined the ambulance or the patrol
> screaming toward some drama, the kind of end
> that Berky must have some day, if she isn't dead.
>
> The wildest of all, her father and mother cruel,
> farming out there beyond the old stone quarry
> where highschool lovers parked their lurching cars,
> Berky learned to love in that dark school. . . .

But the person, the anguish such a tough life brings to a rememberer, soon has my father looking outward, for he is included in Berky's isolation in a tough world:

> There are things not solved in our town though tomorrow came:
> there are things time passing can never make come true.
>
> We live in an occupied country, misunderstood;
> justice will take us millions of intricate moves.
> Sirens will hunt down Berky, you survivors in your beds
> listening through the night, so far and good.

I want to know who is "we." Is it only Berky and my father? Is it my father's family, the small circle of our clan? Is it the few who have met in something like the cave under the earth, or as another poem tells it, those who have experienced "a deathless meeting involving a crust of bread"?

I suspect my father expected the "we" in this "occupied country" to be few, but clear-eyed kin. The "occupied country" I take to be mine—America, after World War II took something apart, something elusive and hard to name, but replaced by American patriotism as a kind of partisan retreat from vast inclusion. The Cold War was not *there* in a region of air between two superpowers, somewhere over the North Pole. It was *here*, in the night outside our house where sirens called to one another as they hunted down the quiet of the land.

You can look back now, back to my father's first writing that became "Thinking for Berky," early on a December morning in 1954, and see him begin to find his way from clumsy searching toward the poem:

> We all live in an occupied country;
> freeing will come with many intricate moves.
> Sirens will hunt down Berky from the quiet of our beds,
> in the night things are far that in the day will become good.

His passage from "freeing," to an interim version, "Freedom," and finally to "justice" that will "take us millions of intricate moves"—to my mind this is the journey he tried to create as a father for his children. Freedom is easy; any rebel can claim it. Justice is hard, for it requires the intricate cooperation of all kinds of people joined by negotiated agreement about human dignity. But the movement *toward* justice, the decision to direct one's life toward a just society on earth, this in my father's view is not hard. One morning he wrote,

> Once you decide to do right, life is easy. No distractions.

And that, I believe, was the working assumption that guided the household where I grew.

For there were stories in the family of "witness"—the overt though quiet declaration of a larger view. My father rarely spoke of such things directly, but for this very reason the few references were memorable. As a student at the University of Kansas in the 1930s he had taken part in a sit-in demonstration at the student union, to protest the exclusion of black students from the central seating area. Shortly after World War II, my parents invited two Japanese men to their apartment for lunch; they were evicted the next day. "I don't want no Japs in my place," their landlady said. "Better find another place yourselves." (The family lore records those two sentences verbatim, not as a judgment against the landlady, but as an example of how the war wrenched people loose from their native hospitality.)

And over the years there were demonstrations in the news, or locally and quietly, and sometimes my father took part:

"Peace Walk"

We wondered what our walk should mean,
taking that un-march quietly;
the sun stared at our signs—"Thou shalt not kill."

Men by a tavern said, "Those foreigners . . ."
to a woman with a fur, who turned away –
like an elevator going down, their look at us. . . .

But how do such values, held by adults, and articulated in rare conversations, poems, and teaching in the adult world, seep into the child's experience in ways that shape the conscience as it grows?

My short answer is this: My father enjoyed all kinds of people alive to experience, and honest in sharing what they knew. His was not a studied, an ethical devotion to justice. His was an appetite for learning that can only happen without restraint when all kinds of experience are available. Justice is a matter of yielding to delight in human variety.

When I was not yet two years old, my father wrote a poem about me that I never knew until it turned up in his papers after he died. This is truly a message from far away and long ago:

The open, easy way of Kim.
He doesn't worry or hide anything.
An event drops freely into his eyes
and is applauded before his conscience
knows it, by his startled hands.

No proportion is ever old.
"Is it true?"
Walking into that closed gong sound
the black horses lower their ears.
Whatever strokes their mane was already theirs.

We were living in Iowa then, in the Quonset hut of tin, while my daddy attended the first generation that gathered at the Iowa Writers Workshop. And here is the mystery: the earliest memory I can grasp is of my father there that winter, lovingly picking me up, and setting me on the counter. I have hurt my knee, and he is comforting me, lovingly touching my face. In the album, I see the place in black and white—the double sink where my brother and I took our baths side by side, the spare furnishings, the famous meals of pumpkin sauce straight from the can. "Nothing's too bad for the kiddies" was the family motto. But those details are not in my recollection, only the surge of devotion from my father that entered my body, the quiet elixir of his love.

When I asked my mother about this memory, after my father had died, she laughed and told me the "real" story.

"You know why Bill was so loving then? He had been carrying you outside, and when he slipped on the ice, he just threw you up in the air and caught himself from falling. You landed pretty hard, and he carried you inside to see if you were okay."

Why don't I remember falling, hitting hard on icy pavement? Why don't I remember his abandonment, his selfish instinct to save himself? I only remember his big hands on my face, his eyes looking into me.

I think that's one thing justice means, behind all the fine distinctions: We are here together. Things happen, and some get hurt. Together, we go on.

Other Poems by William Stafford

A short list of William Stafford poems that touch on our search for justice might include, among many others:

A Dedication

A Ritual to Read to Each Other

A Message from the Wanderer

At the Bomb Testing Site

At the Grave of My Brother: Bomber Pilot

At the Un-National Monument Along the Canadian Border

Entering History

Explaining the Big One

For the Unknown Enemy

Learning

Men

Objector

Peace Walk

Serving with Gideon

Thinking for Berky

Watching the Jet Planes Dive

These poems can all be found in *The Way It Is: New and Selected Poems by William Stafford*, 1998 (St. Paul, MN: Graywolf Press).

2

What Happened to the Golden Door?

How My Students Taught Me About Immigration

Linda Christensen

At Eureka High School, immigration equaled Ellis Island. We watched old black-and-white film strips of northern Europeans filing through dimly lit buildings. My textbooks were laced with pictures of the Statue of Liberty opening her arms to poor immigrants who had been granted an opportunity to "pull themselves up by their bootstraps" when they passed through America's door:

> Give me your tired, your poor
> Your huddled masses yearning to breathe free,
> The wretched refuse of your teeming shores.
> Send these, the homeless, tempest-tost, to me,
> I lift my lamp beside the golden door.

I felt pride at being part of a country that helped the unfortunate, including my own family.

Years later when I visited Angel Island in San Francisco Bay, I learned about another immigration that hadn't been mentioned in my high school or college texts. I walked through the deserted barracks where painted walls covered the poems of immigrant Chinese who viewed "Gold Mountain" through a barbed-wire fence. I felt angry that yet another portion of U.S. history had been hidden from me. Between 1910 and 1940, the "tired, poor, wretched refuse" from Asian shores were imprisoned on Angel Island before being accepted as "resident aliens" or rejected at the "golden door." As historian Ronald Takaki notes, "Their quarters were crowded and unsanitary, resembling a slum. 'When we arrived,' said one of them, 'they locked us up like criminals in compartments like the cages in the zoo.'"[1]

---

[1] Ronald Takaki, 1989, *Strangers from a Different Shore: A History of Asian Americans* (New York: Viking Penguin), 237.

Turning their anger and frustration into words, the Chinese carved poems on the building's wooden walls. Their poems stood in stark contradiction to the Statue of Liberty's promise:

America has power, but not justice.
In prison, we were victimized as if we were guilty.
Given no opportunity to explain, it was really brutal.
I bow my head in reflection but there is nothing I can do.[2]

All Europeans were legally eligible to apply for citizenship once they passed through Ellis Island, a right denied to immigrant Asians until the mid-1940s.

In 1995, California voters passed Proposition 187, which, if implemented, would deprive so-called illegal immigrants of health care and schooling. This initiative sparked my decision to teach about immigration—not just the traditional version—but the more dangerous and unspoken version that examines why large numbers of immigrants are discriminated against based on color, nationality, or politics. I wanted my students to read behind the media rhetoric that villified millions of human beings.

As a social justice educator, I consistently ask, "Whose voices are left out of our curriculum? Whose stories are buried? What can we understand about contemporary immigration laws by looking at these historical exclusions?" Ronald Takaki notes in the introduction to *Journey to Gold Mountain*, "[M]any history books have equated 'American' with 'white' or 'European' in origin."[3] I left high school with that equation. I didn't want to pass on the same misinformation to my students. To broaden their understanding of immigration as well as U.S. policy, they need to investigate how race, class, and gender shaped immigration policy. If the textbooks don't provide an answer, I must create the space for students to conduct the research.

Beyond these political reasons, I had personal and educational reasons to teach this unit. It was the last quarter of the year in Literature in U.S. History, a combined junior-level untracked history and English class that met ninety minutes a day for the entire year. The days had warmed up, and the students smelled summer. If I said the words *essay*, *interior monologue*, or *role play*, I could hear a collective moan rise from the circle and settle like stinky fog around my head.

For three academic quarters, my planning book had been filled with lessons attempting to teach students how to become critical readers of history and literature. They'd written essays, critiques, short stories, personal narratives, poems, and interior monologues analyzing their own lives as well as the history and contemporary issues that continue to deprive Native Americans of land and economic opportunities. They'd also reflected critically on the enslavement of Africans, starting with life

---

[2]Him Mark Lai, Genny Lim, & Judy Yung, 1986, *Island: Poetry and History of Chinese Immigrants on Angel Island 1910–1940,* (San Francisco, CA: HOC DOI), 58.

[3]Ronald Takaki, 1994, *Journey to Gold Mountain* (New York: Chelsea House), 10.

in Africa before slavery as well as forced immigration and resistance. We examined the literature and history of the Harlem Renaissance, the civil rights movement, and contemporary issues. They read and critiqued presidential speeches, historical and contemporary novels, and poems written by people from a variety of backgrounds. They were ready to do their own investigation and teaching—putting into practice their analytical skills.

Fourth quarter, I wanted them to conduct "real" research—not the scurry-to-the-library-and-find-the-closest-encyclopedia-and-copy-it-word-for-word kind of research, but research that made them ask questions about immigration policies, quotas, and personal stories that couldn't be lifted from a single text. I wanted them to learn to use the library, search for books, look up alternative sources, find the Ethnic NewsWatch, search the Oregon Historical Society's clipping files, photo files, and rare documents room. I wanted them to interview people and read novels and poetry that told the immigrant's story in a more personal way. I hoped that by doing this kind of thorough research, they would develop an ear for what is unsaid in political speeches and newspaper articles, would learn to ask questions when their neighbors or people on the bus began an anti-immigrant rap.

Setting the Stage for Research and Teaching

I started fourth quarter by outlining my goals and expectations. I do this each term, so students know what kinds of pieces must be in their portfolio at the end; for example, a literary essay comparing two novels, an essay exploring a historical issue, a poem that includes details from history, and so on. As part of the "opening of the quarter" ceremonies, I passed out an outline of their upcoming project. I wanted a lengthy deadline so students would have the opportunity to work the entire quarter on the project. I passed out the overview in Appendix A of this chapter.

Before students started their research, I modeled how I wanted their lessons taught by presenting Chinese and Japanese immigration. Although students who come through the Jefferson neighborhood network of feeder elementary and middle schools get at least surface background knowledge of Native Americans and African Americans, they appear to know less about Asian or Latino literature and history. In fact, students are often surprised that the Japanese and Chinese faced any prejudice.[4]

During the lessons on Japanese Americans, students examined Executive Order 9066 signed by President Roosevelt, which gave the military the right to force Japanese Americans from their homes and businesses into camps surrounded by barbed

---

[4]I have to thank my former student Mira Shimabukruro, who pointed out my own lack of attention to these groups, and Lawson Inada, professor at Southern Oregon State College, who served as my mentor in these studies.

wire and guard towers. Because these Japanese Americans, who included both "resident aliens" and U.S. citizens, were allowed to take only what they could carry to the "camps," they were forced to sell most of their possessions in a short period of time. Students read "Echoes of Pearl Harbor," a chapter from *Nisei Daughter* by Monica Sone, in which she describes her family burning their Japanese poetry and kimonos, breaking their Japanese records, destroying anything that could make them look like they cherished their Japanese heritage. Students wrote moving poetry and interior monologues imagining they were forced to leave their homes, businesses, and treasured possessions. "Becoming American" was written by Khalilah Joseph:[5]

> I looked into the eyes of my Japanese doll
> and knew I could not surrender her
> to the fury of the fire.
> My mother threw out the poetry
> she loved;
> my brother gave the fire his sword.
> We worked hours
> to vanish any traces of the Asian world
> from our home.
> Who could ask us
> to destroy
> gifts from a world that molded
> and shaped us?
>
> If I ate hamburgers
> and apple pies,
> if I wore jeans,
> then would I be American?

I created overheads and slides from the artwork in *Beyond Words: Images from America's Concentration Camps* (Gesensway and Roseman, 1987) a fascinating book of personal testimony and artwork produced in the camps: black-and-white drawings, watercolors, oil paintings, and pieces of interviews that give students a window into the lives of the imprisoned Japanese Americans. While I showed slides of the artwork, students I had prompted ahead of time read aloud excerpts from Legends from Camp by Lawson Inada, the poem "The Question of Loyalty" by Mitsuye Yamada, and segments of the internees' interviews that matched pictures on screen. With images and words of the prisoners in their minds, students wrote their own poems. Thu Throung's poem is called "Japanese Prisoners":

---

[5]Many of the student poems used in this article are printed in the literary magazine *Rites of Passage*. The magazine may be purchased through the Network of Educators on the Americas catalogue at **www.teachingforchange.org**

Guards watch us.
They wrap us around
in barbed wire fences
like an orange's meat
that never grows outside its skin.
If the orange's skin breaks,
the juice drains out.
Just like the Japanese behind the wire fence.

We watched and critiqued the somewhat flawed film *Come See the Paradise*[6] and talked about the laws that forbade Japanese nationals from becoming citizens or owning land.[7] Students read loyalty oaths imprisoned Japanese-American citizens were forced to sign. After learning about the "No No Boys"—Japanese-American men in the internment camps who refused to sign the loyalty oath—and their subsequent imprisonment in federal penitentiaries, students argued about whether or not they themselves would have signed the loyalty oath if they'd been interned.[8]

Students also looked at the number of immigrant Chinese allowed to enter the country, compared to European immigrants. For example, in 1943 when Congress repealed the Chinese Exclusion Act because of China's war-time alliance with the United States against the Japanese, 105 Chinese were allowed to enter Angel Island, whereas 66,000 English immigrants passed through Ellis Island.[9]

The Research Begins

During the same time period I presented lessons on Chinese and Japanese immigration, students started on their own projects. They had two 30-minute sessions the first week to discuss what they knew, itemize what they needed to find, and list the resources they had (people to interview, books at home, potential videos to use, outside resources such as Vietnamese, Russian, or Latino teachers or districtwide coordinators). During the following weeks while I continued my presentations on

---

[6]For example, like many films about an oppressed people, *Come See the Paradise*, features a white man in the lead. His Japanese-American wife is interned during the war. The film depicts Japanese Americans who are forced to sell their homes and belongings at unfair prices and follows them to the internment camps.

[7]The California Legislature passed the Alien Land Law in 1913. This law barred all "aliens" ineligible for citizenship from holding agricultural land.

[8]Jeanne Wakatsuki Houston & James D. Houston, 1973, *Farewell to Manzanar* (Boston: San Francisco Book Company/ Houghton Mifflin).

[9]Felicia Lowe, 1988, *Carved in Silence* (San Francisco: National Asian American Telecommunications Association).

Chinese and Japanese immigration, they were given varied amounts of time to conduct research: forty-five minutes to prepare for the library, a full day at the library, additional ninety-minute periods as we got closer to deadline, and so on.

At the end of each period of "research/preparation" time, students turned their information in to me so I could see if they had made headway, run into a block, or needed a push or help. During this research period, I moved between groups, listening in, asking questions, making lists of questions they raised but didn't answer, questioning literary choices when a piece was by a writer from the immigration group but didn't deal with any of the issues we were studying.

During this time, it was not unusual to see some of my students gathered around a television in the hallway outside my door or in the library as they watched and critiqued videos, looking for potential sections to show to the class. Travis, Roman, and Sophia, who conducted individual research projects, could be seen translating notes or cassette tapes for their stories. Sometimes they met to talk over stories or ideas for their presentation.

The group researching Mexican immigration had the most members—too many, really. They watched videos together and then split the rest of the work: Danica and Komar collected and read books to find a story; Shannon researched Cesar Chavez and wrote a profile to hand out to the class; Heather gathered information for a debate on Proposition 187 (a controversial 1995 ballot measure in California that sought to limit services to illegal immigrants); Stephanie and Stacey coordinated the group, collecting information from each subgroup, fitting research into a coherent lesson plan, and creating a writing lesson that would pull information together for the class; Rosa, the only group member fluent in Spanish, talked with recent immigrants in ESL (English as a second language) classes and the Latino coordinator to find speakers, videos, and stories to feed to her group.

Before I end up sounding like a movie script starring Michelle Pfeiffer, let me quickly insert into this idyllic classroom a word or two of other things you might see: kids whining and competing for my attention, *Right now;* students gossiping about a fight, a guess-who's-going-out-with . . . , an upcoming game, or a movie they saw last night; a sly student attempting to take advantage of the chaos to catch up on math or Spanish; the slippery students who said they were going to the library or to see an ESL coordinator, but who actually sneaked into the teachers' cafeteria for coffee or outside for a smoke. There were also two students who attended regularly and might have learned something through other people's work, but who produced no work themselves, and a few others who rode the backs of their group's work, contributing a little in spurts, but not making the sustained efforts of most students. The ESL coordinators and librarians and I developed an easy communication system regarding passes. I called students and parents at home to talk about their lack of work. Although the calls pushed the back-riding students, who then made some effort, I failed to bring the "slackers" into the research fold.

Besides the usual chaos a teacher might expect when turning over the curriculum to students, I simultaneously hit another problem. I'd set up immigrant groups that I knew would have some interesting and contradictory stories, because I was familiar with their history and literature. Although students did accept some of the groups I'd proposed: Mexican, Haitian, Cambodian, Irish, and Vietnamese, others argued vehemently that they be allowed to choose the immigrant group they would study. Our previous lessons on resistance and solidarity had certainly taken root within each of the class members, and I was the object of their solidarity. A few wanted to research their own family's immigration stories: Greek, Jewish, Macedonian, and Russian. Several African-American students wanted to study immigrants from Africa or from the African Diaspora. Most were happy to study Haiti, one of my original groups; one student chose to study Eritrea, because Portland has a larger population of Eritreans than Haitians. I agreed; in fact, he made an excellent choice. We ended our first rounds with the following research groups: Cambodians, Eritreans[10], Greeks, Haitians, Irish, Jewish, Macedonians, Mexicans, Russians, and Vietnamese. This first dialogue marked the end of my control over the history and literature presented in class. And I was nervous because I knew almost nothing about Greek and Macedonian immigration and not much more about the Russians.

Ultimately, the contrast between groups made for great discussion. In my class of thirty-one students, three had immigrated from Vietnam, one from Russia, one from Cambodia; several students were second-generation Americans from Greece, Ireland, Nicaragua, and Mexico; half of the class's ancestors had been enslaved Africans, and one girl's grandmother was the only surviving member of her family after the Holocaust. But I can imagine a more homogenous classroom where this might not be the case. In my high school English class over twenty years ago, twenty-nine students were white and one was black. Around Portland today, I can cite similar profiles. These ratios would have made me demand more diversity in the research if all students wanted to study their own heritage. I do think it is important to negotiate the curriculum with students, and I'm sure some students would be more interested in researching their own past than researching the past of others; but sometimes, in order to surface issues of race and class inequality, it is necessary to move beyond our personal histories.

Research Problems

Before beginning the unit, I spent time in the public library and the Oregon Historical Society (OHS) library, finding sources, articles, books, and practicing computer research programs before bringing my students across town. OHS officials were friendly and helpful, but told me that I couldn't bring the entire class to their

---

[10]The student studying Eritreans left school, so I will not report on his project.

library; I'd have to bring one or two at a time after school or on Saturdays. And they closed at 5 P.M.

In addition to limited library time, I discovered that the easily accessible research materials did not even have one critical page in their spines; they just restated the textbook version. Because I had initiated this project to teach about social justice, I wanted students to learn the "whole truth," not just a watered-down version that left out facts that might complicate the issues. I figured that part of research is getting lots of material and then deciding what is important to present so that others hear a fuller truth. But when I discovered that much of what students were reading only told one side of the immigration story—the same side I had learned in high school—I made an effort to put other facts in students' hands as well. We searched computer files of Ethnic NewsWatch and alternative news and magazine sources. Although many students dutifully read the computer-generated articles, most of these pieces were too academic or required extensive background knowledge to understand. If we had relied solely on these sources of information—either textbook or alternative—many students would have come away with material that they might have been able to cite and copy into a readable paper, but they wouldn't have understood much about the underlying political situations their immigrant group faced.

After the library research, I linked students with people or information that might provide facts and stories not available in the library. The Haitian group, for example, read articles, but hadn't comprehended what was going on: Who was Papa Doc? Baby Doc? What was the United States' involvement in Haiti? What was happening with Jean-Bertrand Aristide?[11] I distributed copies of the Network of Educators on the Americas (NECA) booklet *Teaching About Haiti,* which gave my students historical and political analysis they needed to make sense of the newspaper and magazine articles. The novel *Krik? Krak!* by Edwidge Danticat developed their personal connection; she gave faces and voices to the people on the boats, to those who lived in fear. The names in the newspaper became real: Aristide, the Tontons Macoutes, boat people, refugees. (The group's enthusiasm for the novel caught on. I'd purchased five copies, and there were arguments over who got to read *Krik? Krak!* after group members finished.)

Students became wonderfully devious researchers, using their own connections to gain information. They learned to find back doors when the front doors closed and windows when all the doors were locked. But sometimes these back-door, through-the-window–type researches posed another problem: What if personal history omitted vital historical facts and perspectives? Although I could help students who studied immigrant groups that I knew something about, I had little time to read and research the Macedonians, Greeks, and Russians. Travis was thoroughly confused when his research revealed a snarled web of history involving Greece,

---

[11]In December 1990 Jean-Bertrand Aristide was elected president of Haiti in a landslide victory. A military coup deposed Aristide's government in September 1991.

Bulgaria, and a historic trade route through the mountains. His research took him back to 146 B.C., when Rome conquered the kingdom of Macedonia, and forward to today. He wanted to know why his grandfather had immigrated. Instead of untangling the web of Macedonian history, he spent time with his grandfather, talking, asking questions, going through photo albums, relying on his personal relationships to decode the past. He arranged for a day at the Macedonian lodge where he interviewed men his grandfather's age about their immigration experiences. Because of my own limited knowledge of events in Macedonia, I let him. This was history via personal story—how much or how little of the history was included, I wasn't sure.

Likewise, when Meghan and I met one Saturday at the Oregon Historical Society, we discovered the letters that James Mullany, an Irish immigrant, wrote to his sister in Ireland in the mid-1800s. In one letter, he pleaded with his sister not to mention that he was Catholic: "Their [sic] is a strong prejudice against them here on account of the people here thinking it was the Priests that caused the Indian war three or four years ago."[12] Interesting. But in another letter he wrote of the Snake Indians who attacked a train of forty-five whites: "Only 15 survived but some of them died of starvation. . . . [A] company of soldiers . . . found them living of [sic] the bodyes [sic] of them that were killed by the [I]ndians."[13] Could we count these letters as historic evidence? Whose voices weren't included? What stories might the Snake Indians have told?

Students using voices of immigrants or novels to tell the history created a dilemma for me: What happens when personal narratives exclude the stories of large groups of other people or neglect important historical facts? When and how do I intervene? If students tell only their own stories or draw on personal testimonies, is that "inaccurate" history? As an English teacher who weaves literature and history together, who values personal stories as eyewitness accounts of events and who encourages students to "tell their stories," I began to question my own assumptions.

The Vietnamese group, occupying Tri's corner between the windows and closet, underscored my history-versus-personal-story dilemma. Their student-told account emphasized a pro-American stance around the Vietnam War, but said nothing, for example, of U.S. support for French colonialism, its creation of "South Vietnam," or its devastating bombardment of the Vietnamese countryside. How could I challenge the story these students grew up hearing from parents and elders in their community?

With Meghan's research, we'd studied historical accounts of Native Americans in the Northwest, so we knew that Mulany's letters lacked facts about land takeovers and Indian massacres. But I didn't have time to teach the unit on Vietnam that Bill

---

[12]Letters from James Mulany to his sister Mary Mulany, August 5, 1860 (Oregon Historical Society Mss. 2417), 10.

[13]Mulany, November 5, 1860, 14.

Bigelow and I developed when we taught the class together, so I also worried that the rest of the class would come away without an understanding of the key role the United States played in the Vietnam War, and without that understanding, how would they be able to critique other U.S. interventions?

I talked with Cang, Tri, and Thu and gave them resources: a timeline that reviewed deepening U.S. involvement in Vietnam and numerous readings from a critical standpoint. I also introduced them to the film *Hearts and Minds,* which features testimony from many critics of the war, as well as prominent U.S. antiwar activists such as Daniel Ellsberg. Without a sustained dialogue, this insertion seemed weak and invasive—more so than my talks with Travis and Meghan, because their research was at a greater distance from their lives. But I learned a lesson that lingers as a vexing teaching dilemma: Personal story does not always equal history.

The Presentation

Once presentation deadlines hit, students argued over dates and—who gets to go first, last, and so on. Our biggest struggle came around the issue of time. Students lobbied for longer time slots. The group studying Mexican immigration was especially ardent. They'd found great movies as well as short stories, informational videos, and a guest speaker from *Piñeros y Campesinos Unidos de Noreste* (PCUN) the local farm workers union, about working conditions and the boycott of Garden Burgers, a national veggie burger sold in stores and restaurants across the country.[14] They figured they needed at least a week, possibly two. We had five weeks left: four for presentations and a last sacred week to finish portfolios and evaluations. Rosa said, "Look how many days you used when you taught us about the Japanese and Chinese. Two weeks on each! Aren't the Latinos as important as the Asians?" They bargained with single-person groups, such as the Russians and Greeks, for part of their time.

A week or so before presentations, groups submitted detailed lesson plans. I met formally with each group to make sure all requirements were covered, but also to question their choices. During previous weeks, I'd read every proposed story and novel selection, watched each video, gone over writing assignments: I didn't want any surprises on their teaching day.

The power of my students' teaching was not in just the individual presentations, where students provided historical information in a variety of mostly interesting and unique lesson plans, but also in the juxtaposition of these histories and stories. Students created a jazz improvisation, overlaying voices of pain and struggle and tri-

---

[14]For more information on the boycott, write to PCUN, 300 Young St., Woodburn OR 97071, or call them at (503) 982-0243.

umph with heroic attempts to escape war, poverty, or traditions that pinched women too narrowly into scripted roles. Their historical research and variety of voices taught about a more varied history of immigration than I'd ever attempted to do in the past.

But the presentations were also like improvisation in that they were not as tightly connected and controlled as a rehearsed piece I would have conducted. There were off notes and unfinished strands that seemed promising, but didn't deliver an analysis that could have strengthened student understanding of immigration. Few students found research on quotas, few had time left in their presentation to engage in a discussion that linked or compared their group to another. The Haitian group, for example, tied our past studies of Columbus and the Tainos to modern Haiti but didn't develop the history of Duvalier or Aristide or the involvement of the United States.

Although presentations varied in length and depth, most gave us at least a look at a culture many students weren't familiar with, and at best, a strong sense that not only did racial and political background determine who gets into this country, but also how they live once they arrive.

The group studying Cambodian immigration arranged for our student Sokpha's mother to come to class, as well as a viewing of the film, *The Killing Fields*. Sokpha's mother told of her life in Cambodia, of hiding in the deep tunnels her father built to keep them safe from U.S. bombs, of her fear of snakes at the bottom of the tunnel that scared her almost as much as the bombs. She talked about the Khmer Rouge, the Vietnamese, and the United States. On her father's death bed, he said, "Go to America. Leave Cambodia." She did. Shoeless, nine months pregnant with Sokpha, and carrying a three-year-old on her back, she walked for three days and three nights from Cambodia into Thailand, dodging land mines that killed some of her fellow travelers. She also spoke of difficulties here—how her lack of language skills have kept her from finding a good job, her reliance on Sokpha, the breakdown of their culture, the Americanization of her children.

The group researching Haitians presented background history tying the modern struggle in Haiti with previous history lessons; their strengths were chilling descriptions of the refugees, their choice of story, their research into Haitian culture, and their writing assignment. Read aloud by a male and a female student, the two-voice story, "Children of the Sea," portrayed a political young man who dared to speak out against the Haitian government, writing to his lover as he rides a sinking boat in search of refuge in the United States. His lover writes of the increased military violence of the Tontons Macoutes who make parents have sex with their children and rape and torture suspected supporters of Aristide (as described by Danticat).

Cang, from the Vietnamese group, recounted Vietnam's history through a timeline. Thu's stories of escape and life in the refugee camps created nightmare scenes for her fellow students of drownings, rapes, and the difficulties of families who got separated. Tri pointed out the geographical settlements of immigrant Vietnamese and their induction into the United States. He talked about the struggle of the Vietnamese shrimp fishermen in the Gulf of Mexico, the attempts of the Ku Klux Klan to drive the fishermen out of the region[15], and the creation of Little Saigon in California, a space where the Vietnamese have forged a community inside the United States, not unlike many immigrants who came before them.

The student writing assignments generated excellent poems and personal narratives. After Sophia spoke about her mother's experiences, she said her inheritance from her mother was the strength to pursue her goals even when she faces opposition. Her assignment for the class: "Write about something you treasure from your family. It might be an heirloom, like a ring, but it can also be a story, a memory, a tradition, a personal trait. Write it as a poem, a personal narrative, or a story." Komar Harvey wrote an essay about his family's love of music:

> You can hear music on the porch before you enter our house. Tunes climb through those old vinyl windows and mailbox and drift into everybody's ears in the neighborhood. If you came during the holiday season you could hear the Christmas bells chiming through the static of that old crackling phonograph needle. You hear the rumbling voice of Charles Brown as if he were digging a hole up in the living room, "Bells will be ringing." . . . Nobody graces our door during those Christmas months without a little Charles ringing his bells in their ears.

After talking about his grandfather's struggles to get to the United States, Travis asked students to write a personal narrative about an obstacle they overcame in their lives. Cang wrote about his difficulty learning English in the face of classmates' ridicule. His narrative had a profound effect on students. I have not changed or corrected his language because it is part of the story:

> [After he left Vietnam, he was in the Philippines.] In 1989 we came to America. That's when I started to go to school. I went to all of the classes I had, but I felt the blonde and white-skinned people not respected me. They make joke over the way I talk . . . I'll never give up, I say to myself. . . One day I'm going to be just like them on talking and writing, but I never get to that part of my life until now. Even if I can understand the word, but still I can't pronounce it, if I do pronounce it, it won't end up right. Truly, I speak Vietnamese at home all the time, that's why I get used to the Vietnamese words more than English, but I'll never give up what I have learned. I will succeed with my second language.

The group who had researched Mexican immigration took several days for their presentation. They taught about the theft of Mexican land by the United States during the 1846–1848 war with Mexico, immigration border patrols, the effect of toxic sprays on migrant workers, the migrants' living conditions in Oregon. During this time, the students also initiated a debate on California's Proposition 187: Should the United States deny health and education services to illegal immigrants? Then the

---

[15]See the film *Alamo Bay,* which despite being flawed by having a white hero main character, does tell some of the story of Vietnamese immigrant fishermen.

presenters asked the class to write a persuasive essay taking a point of view on the question.

One day we watched the movie *Mi Familia,* about a "Mexican" family whose original homeland was in California. As we watched, we ate tamales and sweet tacos that Rosa and her mother-in-law lugged up three flights of stairs to our classroom. Then we wrote food poems that tied us to our culture. Sarah LePage's "Matzo Balls" is a tribute to her grandmother:

> Grandma's hands,
> wise, soft, and old,
> mold the Matzo meal
> between the curves of each palm.
> She transforms our heritage
> into perfect little spheres.
> Like a magician
> she shapes our culture
> as our people do.
> This is her triumph.
> She lays the bowl aside
> revealing her tired hands,
> each wrinkle a time
> she sacrificed something for our family.

Evaluation

On our last day, students overwhelmingly voted that immigration was the unit they both learned the most from and cared the most about. Komar, the first to speak, said, "I never realized that Cambodians were different from Vietnamese. Sokpha's family went through a lot to get here; so did Tri's, Thu's, and Cang's." Stacey, a member of the Haitian group, added, "I learned that the United States isn't just black and white. I learned that my people are not the only ones who have suffered in this country." Khalilah noted that she hadn't realized what research really meant until she struggled to find information about the Haitians. Others added similar points about various groups or presentations they learned from. Travis summed up the conversation by saying, "I didn't know anything about Proposition 187 or the discrimination immigrants have faced, because that wasn't part of my family's history. I didn't know that there was discrimination about who got in and who was kept out of the United States, and now I do."

I felt that students learned from each other about immigrants' uneven and unfair treatment. The Statue of Liberty's flame and rhetoric had met with a history, told by students, that dimmed her light. But they had also learned lessons that would alter their interactions with the "Chinese"—actually Korean—storekeeper at the intersection of Martin Luther King, Jr., and Fremont. At Jefferson, some of the most offensive scenes I have witnessed in the hallways or classrooms involve the silencing of immigrant Asian, Russian, and Mexican students as they speak their own languages or struggle to speak English. Throughout the year, Cang, Thu, and Tri's personal testimony during discussions or read-arounds about the pain of that silencing, as well as their stories about fighting with their parents or setting off firecrackers in their school in Vietnam, created much more awareness in our classroom than any lecture could have. I credit our study of history, for example, the Mexican-American War, as part of that change, but through this student-led unit on immigration, I watched students crack through stereotypes they had nurtured about others. Students who sat by their lockers on C-floor were no longer lumped together under the title Chinese; they became Vietnamese, Cambodian, Laotian. Students no longer mimicked the sound of their speech as a put-down. Latino students who spoke Spanish near the door on the west side of the building were no longer seen as outsiders who moved into the neighborhood with loud cars and lots of children, but as political exiles in a land that had once belonged to their ancestors. The Russian students who moved together like a small boat through the halls of Jefferson were no longer odd, but seekers of religious freedom.

Throughout fourth quarter, I tossed and turned at night questioning my judgment about asking students to teach such an important part of history—and the consequence that much history would not be taught. But after hearing their enthusiasm and their changed perceptions about their classmates, the world, and research, I put my critique temporarily on hold. Turning over the classroom circle to my students allowed them to become the "experts" and me to become their student. Although I lost control and power over the curriculum and was forced to question some key assumptions of my teaching, I gained an incredible amount of knowledge—and so did they.

References

Asian Women United of California. 1989. *Making Waves: An Anthology of Writings by and About Asian American Women.* Boston: Beacon Press.

Chin, Frank, Jeffery Paul Chan, Lawson Fusao Inada, & Shawn Wong. 1991. *Aiiieeeee! An Anthology of Chinese American and Japanese American Literature.* New York: Penguin Books.

Danticat, Edwidge. 1991. *Krik? Krak!* New York: Vintage Books.

Gesensway, Deborah, & Mindy Roseman. 1987. *Beyond Words: Images from America's Concentration Camps.* Ithaca, NY: Cornell University Press.

Harvey, Komar, Khalilah Joseph, & Sarah LePage. 1996. *Rites of Passage.* Portland, OR: Jefferson High School.

Houston, Jeanne Wakatsuki, & James D. Houston. 1973. *Farewell to Manzanar*. Boston: San Francisco Book Company/Houghton Mifflin.

Inada, Lawson Fusao. 1993. *Legends from Camp*. Minneapolis: Coffee House Press.

Kim, Elaine H. 1982. *Asian American Literature*. Philadelphia: Temple University Press.

Lai, Him Mark, Genny Lim, & Judy Yung. 1986. *Island: Poetry and History of Chinese Immigrants on Angel Island 1910–1940*. San Francisco: San Francisco Study Center.

Lowe, Felicia. 1988. *Carved in Silence*. San Francisco: National Asian American Telecommunications Association.

Okada, John. 1957. *No-No Boy*. Rutland, VT: Charles E. Tuttle.

Sone, Monica. 1979. *Nisei Daughter*. Seattle: University of Washington Press. (Originally printed in 1953 by Little, Brown.)

Sunshine, Catherine A., & Deborah Menkhart. 1994. *Teaching About Haiti* (3rd ed.). Washington, DC: Network of Educators on the Americas.

Takaki, Ronald. 1994. *Journey to Gold Mountain*. New York: Chelsea House.

Takaki, Ronald. 1989. *Strangers from a Different Shore: A History of Asian Americans*. New York: Viking Penguin.

Yamada, Mitsuye. 1976. "The Question of Loyalty." In *Camp Notes*. San Lorenzo, CA: Shameless Hussy Press.

APPENDIX A

Immigration Project

In this unit, you will work with a self-chosen group to study the history, politics, and stories of a past or contemporary immigrant group. You will conduct research in and out of the library. You will find and read poetry, novels, short stories, and watch videos in order to understand their lives and circumstances more clearly. During a presentation, your group will teach the history and stories of these immigrants to your classmates. Listed next are the questions your group needs to research, the criteria for your presentation, and a list of related individual tasks to complete on your own during this quarter.

Content Questions to Research

1. *Background history:* Why did this group come to the United States? What was happening in their home country that caused them to leave? Famine? War? Poverty? Political disagreements? Or was something happening in this country that encouraged their immigration?

2. *Treatment in the United States:* What kind of reception did this group receive in the United States? Any problems entering? Who else was coming at the time? Any quotas on the group? How has this group of immigrants been treated since their arrival in the United States? Give examples, tell stories.

3. *Where did these people find work?* Did their work pit them against workers of other racial or ethnic backgrounds? Were they able to find work that matched their occupations in their home country?

Lesson Plan

Each lesson plan must include the following:

1. *Story, movie, or speaker:* Bring the "voice" of the group to our class—either as part of the historical background information or as a way of showing us the group's culture and/or living situation.

2. *Background information:* Present the history of the people and their struggles (see content questions 1–3 above) as a lecture, a reading, a movie, a timeline, role play, or a series of stories.

3. *Class discussion:* After your presentation, plan some discussion questions that will explore the subject of immigration more thoroughly—relate it to previous presenters or past units of study, or link it to broader social issues.

4. *Written activity for class:* As a culminating activity about your group, give your classmates a writing assignment that grows out of your presentation. (For example, after reading and discussing the women's movement, you wrote a profile of a contemporary or historical woman's work for equality; after reading a critical scene in *Kindred*, you wrote an interior monologue from a character's point of view.)

Individual Tasks

1. *Short story:* Write a short story or play based on the lives of the people you researched. This is required of every student. You must include the following in your story:

   a. History—some background to let us know about this group.

   b. Dialogue

   c. Blocking—locating the characters in the setting as they speak—where are they? What are they doing as they speak?

   d. Description of character and place

   e. Flashback—revealing past action to shed light on present situation

   f. Interior monologue—the thoughts and feelings of a character from his or her point of view

2. *Final essay for the year:* Write about immigration using specific examples from your research and/or the presentations of your fellow classmates.

3. *Profile (extra credit):* Was there a person(s) whom we should know about from this group who displayed extraordinary courage or leadership? Profile this person somehow.

3

Collective Action
Speaking Up and Standing Together—the Story of Rachel and Sadie

Sandra Childs

Never doubt that a small group of thoughtful, committed citizens can change the world; indeed, it's the only thing that ever does.

Margaret Mead

It is almost September, and I have a decision to make. I stare at the fish on the dresser, swimming back and forth in its little bowl. I am mesmerized but no closer to making a decision. Before I brought the fish home, it lived on my desk in my high school classroom at Franklin High in Portland, Oregon. Every day my students would visit with the fish, insist I wasn't feeding it enough, and nag me about cleaning the bowl. The kids needn't have worried. I took good care of the damn fish. Fed it just the right amount. Washed its bowl thoroughly once a week. How else would you explain that it has survived almost an entire year? It was good to have it there on my desk, helped me think, kept me focused. But I wouldn't say I was attached to it. Rather, it was my obligation, my moral burden.

My three-year-old daughter, in contrast, is quite attached. That fish is the one thing she remembers from our visit to my school. Almost daily she would ask about her. She is thrilled I brought the fish home for the summer. The goldfish makes little bubbles. It is loud, like an old woman sucking her gums. My daughter jumps up from her resting spot next to me on the bed. "My Sadie! My Sadie!" she shouts, her face beaming with delight. She thinks of the fish as *her fish*. What would she say if she knew that Sadie was just another lesson during my *Night* unit in sophomore English? I stare at the fish and wonder what I am going to do.

———

Now it is Marvin shouting. "Sadie! Sadie! Rachel! Rachel!" He cries out, standing up to his full six feet two inches.

"Okay. That's a referral for you, young man. I told you, 'No Talking!'"

"But . . . But . . ."

"Sit down—or do you want to turn one lunch detention into two? "The boy falls silently back into his chair as I finish writing up the referral. I am sitting at the table in the center of my room, my teeth clenched against my own horror. A large stack of blank referrals sits off to one side and one completed referral rests in front of me. In the middle of the table sits the fishbowl with one fish in it. However, my kids are all focused on what is in front of the bowl—another fish, jerking and flopping in a tiny puddle of water, choking to death on the air we breathe. The expression "like a fish out of water" takes on new meaning for me. I try not to look at it. Instead I scan the room and check the clock. Three more minutes to go. Can I make it? Will the fish make it? Some students giggle. I let them know I am writing them up. Katrina groans and looks away. She gets a referral too. Terry puts his head down on the desk. Mckenzie glares at me in judgment. I look away. The fish has jerked itself to the edge of the table. What if it flops off? Can I take it? Can it?

Scott runs his hands through his hair, pressing his temples, as if the decision he is trying to make is hurting him. He looks like he might get up, but he doesn't. Instead he mutters, shaking his head, "She's killing the fish. She's killing the fish." I fill out a referral on Scott. The pile in front of me is growing, but not fast enough for me. The fish is now about to flop off the table and onto the floor already sticky with dried soda pop and mud from my students' shoes. I can't bear it another second. How can they? I hold my breath as I scoot the fish onto a piece of paper and drop it back into the bowl. It resumes its graceful swimming, and I silently ask for forgiveness.

I borrowed this lesson from Amanda Weber-Welch at Gresham High School in Gresham, Oregon, who borrowed it from Carol Kilpatrick at West Linn High in West Linn, Oregon. Amanda has done the fish activity for the last two years, but this was my first time. I tell the kids that I am fed up with their behavior (I act frustrated with them for a couple of days beforehand). They need practice in discipline. I act tough. I stay tough. I tell them that for the next ten minutes they must sit silently at their desks, looking straight in front of them, hands folded neatly. Anyone who makes a move or a sound gets detention or a referral. Then casually I scoop the fish out of the bowl and onto a table in front of the kids. And then I wait. It is said that fish can live for at least five minutes out of water. I can't risk more than two or three minutes. As kids move or shout, I write down their names and warn them again. Eventually either a kid saves the fish or I put it back. Then comes the discussion. I start with "Why did we just go through that? What am I trying to teach here?" At first some kids think it *is* about discipline, but they catch on pretty quick.

The activity has been used by other teachers over the years for a variety of reasons. One teacher I know used it to look at issues of private property. Should a person be able to do whatever he wants to *his* property no matter the consequences, no matter the morality? Are there higher values than the sanctity of private property?

The purpose of the lesson as I use it is to allow kids to look at issues of authority, resistance, and conformity as it applies to the Holocaust and to their own lives. I risk the life of a goldfish to invite kids to resist my authority for the sake of another living thing. In my classes this year no one takes that invitation. It is too close to the beginning of the year. The kids don't yet know what I am about. I am "an authority figure." In Amanda's class (she does the unit in the spring), someone always risks punishment to save the fish. Whether students do or do not save the fish, the activity is a powerful lesson. Its effectiveness in teaching kids the importance of standing up together for a cause is unparalleled. Travis writes,

> Then something life changing happened. I walk into class and we are all having our usual lively conversation about nothing important. Then Ms. Childs flips out on us. "Sit in your desk and be quiet for the rest of the period or I will keep you in at lunch!" My stomach instantly let out a grumble, almost like it was talking back to her. I thought the teacher had flipped her lid. "What am I gonna do?" Then I sat down and shut up. I followed orders. Exactly what I was supposed to do. Then out of nowhere she hastily takes the fish out of the bowl and plops it on the table. The fish starts to die right in front of us, and I'm thinking she is going to kill the fish. I tried to get the words out of my mouth but lunch was too important to me. Finally Ms. Childs put the fish back. She asked us why we did not help the fish. Everyone said because we would have gotten in trouble. This proved that if someone put fear into another person it gives them control.

Rose, in her final assessment for the year, writes,

> One activity that was an amazing experience was the fish. I sat at my desk, eyes glued to the fish and its emotionless face, wildly gasping for air. The thoughts that raced through my mind had only the message: SAVE THE FISH! But my feet would not respond. This activity gave me insight as to what the year would hold. It would be challenging, but fun. Keeping quiet was not an option. Participation was a must.

Rose "got it." If there was one thing I had hoped my kids got out of the lesson, it was that "keeping quiet is not an option," not when witnessing injustice, not when others are being persecuted. Of course it is always an option, and each person's decision to act or not act must be made according to his or her own value system, but I want students to have the chance to really find out why some people resist and some do not—to find out what keeps us from being social justice activists all the time. When I ask the kids why no one saves the fish, the responses are various and enlightening. Within this unit on Elie Wiesel's *Night*, an autobiographical narrative about the Holocaust, these literature students go beyond the theoretical to the experiential level of learning.

One student explains her reason for not getting up to save the fish. "You told us to be quiet. Not to move or make a sound. You had said you wanted us to practice obedience and discipline. You said we would get referrals for lunch detention.

My mother would die if I got in trouble. How could I explain it to her? It doesn't matter what the reason—you never disobey the teacher and you never get in trouble." The kids begin to get excited at the notion that I am teaching them to disobey. But through the discussion we clarify the difference between disobedience for self-serving reasons and resistance for a cause, for others.

Margaret defends her actions with "It was just a fish. Who cares?"

"I bet that's what some folks said about the Jews and the Gypsies! It's still a life!" shouts Terry.

"Ah, come on! You can buy another fish for fifteen cents at the store!" But Margaret is alone on this one. Kids start shouting in outrage.

One student insists he didn't see the fish flopping on the table, even though he was sitting front and center. The other kids refuse to believe him. I had the class examine his excuse. "Didn't many people claim they didn't know what was happening during the Holocaust? Are they telling the truth? Is it denial or fear?"

Joe explains that because I am the teacher, he assumes I would never do anything bad. He trusted me—even though it was the first month of class, and he didn't know me. But I was in charge so it must be OK. As one excuse after another fell from my students' lips, they quickly saw why many did not resist or stand up during the Holocaust, even if they weren't in favor of Hitler's anti-Semitic agenda. The condemnation they first felt for the generation of Germans/Europeans who did nothing melted into understanding.

———————

But it is not enough to let the kids leave the lesson simply feeling compassion for those who do not stand up. The purpose of the lesson is to help the kids see ways they can resist. To help kids deconstruct the ways in which society keeps us from standing up together. One student points out that if they had all stood up together—saved the fish and gone down to the vice principal to tell them what I had done, they wouldn't have gotten in trouble. I would have. "But we couldn't talk about it. How could I know you would go down to the VP with me? I barely know you," challenges Danai. The discussion shifts to what keeps us apart.

What if Danai insists in her year-end assessment, "Next time I would save the fish!" Would she really? What else can I do in my class to help her/them see that resistance is an option, that collective action is an effective method? We end the unit with stories of resistance, but none of these would be so powerful if students hadn't gone through the activity. Now they recognize how difficult it is to overcome fear, isolation, conformity, obedience, mistrust of others, and trust of the government. Now they know social justice is a risk that requires standing up together.

Ultimately the lesson itself echoes throughout the year and the curriculum, not only because the fish sits on the desk, reminding us of what we did and did not do. I do the lesson in two different periods. Sadie, the fish I torture in first period, survives. Rachel is not so lucky. She dies within a few days. I walk into the class to see her floating and Sadie swimming back and forth underneath her. This is not planned. What can I do? Should I run and get another fish so the kids won't know? I decide to turn this one-day activity into a two-day discussion. As kids file in, they notice right away that one of the fish is gone. I tell them what happened, and I ask the inevitable question "Who is responsible? During the Holocaust, was Hitler the only responsible party? What about the SS who carried out orders? What about the townspeople who turned away and did nothing? So here—who is responsible? Am I the only one? Or by not saving the fish are you also to blame?" The kids are quick to respond: some defend themselves, some blame me, some take on far more guilt than even I do (and that is plenty).

Finally Noah speaks. "Isn't that how we stay too divided to do anything? By blaming each other? We're not to blame, society is. We didn't save the fish because we were looking out for ourselves. We didn't think to act together because that isn't what is valued in our society. Instead we are taught to compete, to get ahead, to be number 1. Sure, once in awhile in a class someone talks about cooperation, but the rest of society isn't about that." What follows is a discussion on how society teaches isolation, mistrust, competition, and how we as members of society can change that. Ultimately bringing these issues out into the open, applying them to themselves and our own times, allows the kids the chance to see themselves in each other. At the end of the year Matt says, "We developed a bond. The whole fish thing changed how we saw ourselves, each other, and the world."

But is all that insight worth the life of a fish? How can I teach morality by committing an immoral act? So what if Travis writes, "It was the best lesson I have witnessed about human nature so far," What do I do when Katrina's parent calls to ask me not to ever teach the lesson again, but praises the lesson at the same time: "Katrina was really affected. I was disturbed too when I heard about it. But . . . I have to say, it is the most effective lesson I have ever heard about. Katrina has talked of nothing else. It has really made her think."

In the spring of this same school year, I am teaching a unit on the Holocaust to my global studies juniors. By now there have been rumors about what I had done, but I deny them. Ultimately I decide not to do the lesson. Not because I am afraid for the fish, but because I am afraid for my relationship with my students. I have known some of these kids for two years. My emphasis in the previous year has been on resistance and collective action. If no one stood up—would my whole teaching career be a waste? I am not brave enough to find out. And then there is Monica Anne. She is a compassionate and outspoken activist student who is deeply offended at the injustices of the world. We have grown close. She would be angry at me if I committed such an act, even in the name of teaching social justice. I decide I am not willing to risk her wrath. So instead of doing the activity, I merely tell them about it. The energy and discussion that follow are no less intense for not having put them through it. The fish sits in the middle of the desk. They know what I have done. They know what my classes have not done. We talk and talk. Even during the discussion Monica Anne weeps angry tears. Afterward, she realizes for her to be true to her values she must become a vegetarian—and she does. Still most of the kids are able to insist that *they* would have saved the fish. They never have the chance to put the image of themselves to the test. Just imagine if several had stood up! We could then have discussed how we can help others feel and act with that level of empowerment.

So now what am I going to do? I had hoped that writing this article would help me decide whether risking the life of a fish is worth a lesson for social justice. But I am still no closer to making a decision. If kids realize that social justice is a risk they can take together, is there a chance they will become change agents for a better society? Does this lesson mean that there's more of a chance they will stand up the next time they see injustice? But what am I teaching my students, and my daughter, if I kill a fish just to make a point? And what do I tell her if Sadie doesn't make it, the next time around? As a language arts and social studies teacher, an activist, a mother, a reflective human being—this kind of lesson forces me to examine my own moral structure. It forces me and the students to ask, What is it worth? Is my own behavior morally justified? Am I standing up for right? What am I really teaching here?

I get off the bed and lift my daughter up high so she can feed Sadie. She makes a little fish mouth and leans in toward the bowl. I shake my head and wonder, "What am I gonna do come September?"

4

Looking Through Layers
A Study of Guatemala

Jessie Singer

Getting Started

Before students can address questions of social justice, they must step inside complex issues of inequality and oppression and see them from multiple perspectives. Through planning a study of Guatemala for my first-year global studies class at the International High School in Eugene, Oregon, I realized I wanted to teach a way of seeing. To see a people and a place is to see them from different angles, some comfortable and familiar, others uncomfortable and cloudy. To see a people and place is to recognize injustice, but to go past it into the reason, history, and stories behind experience. The question I came back to throughout this teaching was, Will multiple perspectives in the teaching of social studies provide students with a discourse and with tools to address issues of social justice?

I chose to teach a unit on Guatemala for a variety of reasons. First, I lived in Central America after college, and I am continually intrigued with the history, culture, politics, language, and stories from this part of the world. Second, the study of Latin America was a curriculum expectation for the first-year global studies class I was teaching. Finally, Guatemala is ripe with the issues I was interested in exploring with my students. Present-day Guatemala is embedded in a history of oppression, inequality, violence, and instability. Guatemala is a country grappling with questions of how to create social justice for its people. To understand these questions, one must examine their roots.

Providing Historical Context

I taught parts of Guatemalan history that addressed how control and outside influence can lead to complex social and political divisions that are not easily erased. I wanted students to have a foundation for what people, culture, and life were like before conflicts involving nonindigenous peoples arose, so we focused on the history, culture, and folklore of the Maya in 2000–1000 B.C. I couldn't possibly explore the history of Guatemala in depth, but I knew students needed some historical context. I chose several important aspects that I believed would help ground them in their study and whet their appetite for more. I taught the Spanish conquest of 1500–1600s as a first conflict point. I jumped ahead in history to teach the "Liberal Revolution" of 1871–1900, when Guatemala's economy was restructured to benefit growers of new exports and to encourage foreign involvement and investment. We studied the years from 1944 to 1954, when a pattern of conflict and foreign control was interrupted by leaders committed to social reform. And finally, we studied the United States-backed coup of 1954, which paved the way for a series of military dictatorships and for social instability. My hope was that these periods of history would provide a context from which students could address issues of social justice in Guatemala today.

Storytelling

I once heard a writing professor tell how he was in a bustling room of people and announced, "I am going to tell you all a story," and the room fell silent. Stories and children's books catch students' attention and provide an accessible entry into new information. I began our Guatemala study with *People of Corn* and a Mayan creation story from The Popol Vuh. (pṓ pel vū́). As I read *People of Corn* (Gerson, 1995), retelling an ancient myth and describing the importance and meaning of land and food to the Mayan people, students took note of the things that stood out to them from the story. I asked if they could guess about the culture using only the brief glimpse that the story had provided. Jade blurted out, "There's bright color on every page, in the clothes the people wear and in the houses they live in. I'm guessing that color matters to these people." Victor said, "Corn is not just a crop or a food, it's where life comes from." Kyla added, "I am guessing that the Mayan people see land in a unique way." From this quick discussion, I could see that the children's stories had worked as a point of entry into our learning and thinking about the Mayan people.

The Popol Voh is a Quiche (kē chā́) Mayan creation myth. Students spent time with the meaning of this creation story and with the colors and words that go into retelling and learning it. I wondered if students would begin to see how these stories were more than entertainment or colorful tales; they provided a base for a belief system and history. I copied the first section of the Popol Vuh, "The Wooden People," which focuses on human creation, and cut it up into sections. Students illustrated the section of the tale they received. As I wandered the room and looked over students' shoulders, I heard conversations that surprised me. Ola shouted out, "This is fun . . . I feel like I'm in kindergarten again!" As she said this, Logan turned to her and asked, "If the gods created people out of wood and gave them no hearts, what did they expect? I mean, how can you be made of wood, have no heart, and be a caring person? I wonder if this is a story parents would tell their children to teach them how to be good?" Brooke said, "It reminds me of some of the stories in the Bible. They have a different way of telling it, but this is not that different from my creation myth." Shanna said, "I can't believe how many tries it took for the gods to get this right. You'd think they would figure it out the first time . . . I guess there's always room for improvement, even in gods." As students completed their illustrations, they hung them around the room in sequence, and we sat back as a class and read the myth along with its colors and pictures. While students enjoyed the playfulness and creativity of the task, they were clearly pondering the material more deeply, just as I had hoped.

Understanding the People

I spent one full class day telling the story of the Maya. The Maya were the first inhabitants of Guatemala's land and their culture, belief system, and narrative have not been erased. I realized that if my goal was to have students come away from this unit able to discuss and to grapple with questions of current inequalities and injustices, they would need to understand the perspective of Guatemala's indigenous people. Using notes from materials I had gathered on Mayan culture and history (see References at end of this chapter), I wove information into a story format. Teaching history through storytelling reinforces the narrative behind experience and brings facts, dates, and timelines alive for students. A storytelling format helps them view history in context. History can feel far away from fourteen- and fifteen-year-olds' daily lives. Stories appear to provide a point of entry for students to begin to understand a people and their time. As I told the history and students took notes, I showed color transparencies of some of the Mayan artifacts and ruins that have been found. After class that day, Soozey came up to me to say, "Thanks for the pictures, Ms. Singer. It really helps me to have something to look at. The pots and statues and ruins make it so I can tell that these people really happened."

Culture Groups

I wanted to get back to the sense that students were digging deeply into a culture and into their learning. Students spent the next two days in "culture groups." Each student chose a group that focused on a point of interest in the Mayan culture: society/nobility, religion/beliefs, the calendars, arts and crafts, architecture, music, feeding and nutrition, social habits and dress, and sculpture. I used *The Mayas, on the Rocks* by Javier Covo Torres, a text full of such information divided into separate chapters and written in cartoon form. The text provided a fun and accessible way for students to read and learn about these separate parts of the Mayan culture. Their task was to learn the information and then create a visual and oral lesson to teach the class. I told students that they were the teachers and that they had to think of interesting ways to get their information across in a quick and clear way. Each group found different ways of teaching. One presented a five-minute play to show what they knew of Mayan religion and beliefs, others drew posters advertising their food and cuisine, the calendar group created a calendar with Mayan symbols to explain to the class, and the architecture group drew examples on a transparency of the different structures created by the Maya. As each group presented, students created a mind map piecing together all the information their classmates were sharing.

Using Writing

Students became deeply embedded in their learning, and I began to push them to think about the idea of a "people's voice." Students began to use writing to get inside another people's experience. One of the perspectives I wanted to provide students with in their study was that of the affective domain in learning and living, where a people's voice, feeling, and experience are taken into account in understanding their historical and cultural context. For this, I chose an important series of events in Guatemalan history, and taught about the Spanish conquest of the 1500s. Once again, I told this history in a story format, piecing together dates and facts with narrative and description of the time and place. After a minilecture on what happened to the indigenous people in Guatemala when the Spanish arrived, students wrote an interior monologue from the perspective of a person of Mayan descent who awoke the morning a Spanish ship arrived on her shore. Students incorporated details from their learning of the Mayan culture into their monologues. I wanted students to have an idea of when the Spanish conquest of Guatemala took place. I was also interested in seeing if they could use the information they had been studying to capture the voice of another person whose entire way of life was about to be dramatically altered through an outside influence and conflict.

Shanna's monologue is a telling example:

After putting on my ex (a cotton cloth rolled up the waist), I ran back to the hut I shared with my family and started dressing for today's celebration. I was behind schedule, like always. The girls were already adjusting their headdresses, strapping on their xanabs and making up their eyebrows in any way they could. To the Maya, the eyebrows are the most beautiful part of a human. Everything must have eyebrows . . . I ran outside to join the other boys in our circle around the girls. Each of us had some eggs that we would crush over the heads of the people we admired. Then the dance began. The boys moved in one direction while the girls moved in another, crushing eggs as we went. I was just coming up to Yanab when a woman screamed and a commotion erupted at the beach. The music stopped and we all ran over to see what was the matter. It was a hurt monster in the water, sent from the gods. It was very big and must have been angry from being hurt. I looked up and saw many men taller than the tallest man in our village running all over the monster. I saw that the monster was made of wood. I heard screams and turned around. I saw women in the village laden with foods and liquors for trading. As I saw, I wept. I knew that we would give freely to these tall men and that they would take everything we had and leave us with nothing.

Interior monologues allowed students to get inside the history we had been studying and to show off the learning they had been doing of another culture, time, and place.

Questions of autonomy, freedom, and helplessness began to emerge within students' writing. Dagmara wrote, "With time came the diseases and soon most of my family was gone, killed by the white man's 'gifts.' I kept asking myself why this had happened? I kept wondering when it would be my turn to go? All I wanted was to go back to before the white men had come. All I wanted was to be free from pain, free from orders, and free to live like I had once lived." Students were seeing importance in the telling of history and experience. Lauren wrote, "Now that I have grown up, I realize the extent of the damage done by the Spanish. With their weapons and diseases, they killed 85 percent of my people, the Maya. Very few Maya survived this time in history, and even fewer wrote down what happened. That is what I have decided to do. I want everyone to understand how my people were treated."

Writing became an invaluable tool and outlet for our learning. My question, "Would multiple perspectives of Guatemalan history lead students toward a conversation about issues of social justice?" was answered through students' words. Their words began to capture voices other than their own. Questions regarding injustice, oppression, poverty, and resilience were not questions easily answered. Students began to understand that each of these issues is multilayered. Looking at a complex history, culture, and people through a variety of perspectives meant coming to a new place in our learning and it meant grappling with the meaning of social justice. The writing workshop (see p. 6) in my social studies unit gave students an opportunity to experiment with different perspectives within the same history. Eric Cook gave the following feedback about writing: "I think the written responses helped me a lot as a learner and speaker. They helped me get my head straight and get what I wanted to say together before I said it."

I wove writing workshop activities in and out of our lessons as we focused on historical information. We studied the difference in social class and daily life between the people of Spanish descent, the Ladino, and the people of Mayan descent, the Indio, within Guatemala. Students began to connect current social divisions to what happened in history. Victor said, "It makes sense that the people of Spanish descent are better off and own the majority of the land, they forced history to work out that way." We studied the importance of agriculture and economy within Guatemala and the Liberal Revolution of the late 1800s. We focused on the recent history and politics of Guatemala to further address the issue of foreign influence and control over the Guatemalan people. As I told students the story of Guatemala's United States-backed military coup in 1954, the train of military dictatorships and their brutality toward the indigenous population that followed, the involvement of multinational corporations in cultivating and ownership of the land, students wrote. Students were shocked by the U.S. role in the overthrow of a stable government. David wrote, "I am amazed at the involvement of the United States in this sad history. I have to admit that I am feeling ashamed to be from the United States as I learn about this." Soozey wrote, "The thing that baffles me most about the history of Guatemala is the fact that the United States actually supported brutality. We seem to be obsessed with money and our country's prosperity. I have a little secret that the government has not yet uncovered: Their prosperity is our prosperity, their pain is our pain."

Two-Voice Poems

Students were amazed at the power and influence of the United Fruit Company and multinational corporations in Guatemala's history. These companies and their economic hold on Guatemala, provided another perspective for students in their understanding of social inequality and the value placed on land within this country. I gave out articles and poems written by Victor Montejo and Rigoberta Menchú two famous activists and writers fighting for indigenous rights in Guatemala. Their voices provided yet another perspective to dive into and discuss. Students captured these two people's experience through two-voice poems. Andrew Karsek's poem shows how the poems helped students explore experience from the inside out.

Two Voices
My ground has been stolen
My ground has been stained with blood.
My family fought.
My family fled.

My family has been tortured.
I have been tortured.
My brother was killed by the army.
My town was killed by the army.
I watched my brother die.
I watched the innocent die.
I write for freedom.
I write to tell stories.
Mine is the story of many, the oppressed.
Mine is the story of a few, the escaped.
I made a stand.
I could do nothing.
I am one of the lucky.
I am one of the lucky.
I survived.
I survived.

Ursula Evans-Heritage wrote the following poem, also capturing the voices of Victor Montejo and Rigoberta Menchú:

Rezo por Guatemala
I, Rigoberta Menchú
I, Victor Montejo
have witnessed
unspeakable horror
the silencing
of a people
two voices
pray one prayer
for the dead
the disappeared
the tortured
the silenced
we cry
for the lost voices
we pray
for equality
for our land
for peace
we pray.

Poetry became a place where students begin to empathize with a certain segment of Guatemalan society. When I gave an opportunity for students to give me feedback, Jessica York wrote, "You allowed us to use poetry a lot in our learning. You let us do what we wanted to react to units and things we did. My dad was even surprised I was allowed to use poetry in a social studies class. I love being free to do what I need to do in my writing to understand the things we learned." In their words, equality, resistance, oppression, poverty, and rights became integral pieces to their questioning and seeing of Guatemala. As students immersed themselves in more and more information and variety of experience, their dialogue regarding issues of social justice grew.

Going Deeper

Through writing, I could see students begin to grapple with the questions of social justice within Guatemala and within their own country and culture, but I wanted them to go further in their thinking. It is one thing to learn of injustices in land distribution, wages, education, economy, and health care and to declare that they are wrong and should not exist. It is another to see that within injustice is a cloudiness that makes things hard to define and easily label as "good" and "evil." I wanted students to realize that in the acknowledgment of differing voices, experience, and values there is a kind of compassion. I decided to ask students to form a question that they could answer and debate in a mock hearing where voices from all parts of Guatemalan experience could be heard.

I spent a day providing students with statistics about Guatemala: poverty indicators, literacy rates for the Ladino people and the Indio, statistics on women, health care, and land use. In groups, students took the information and formed questions that they wanted to explore regarding Guatemala. After brainstorming, list making, and an informal vote, we decided to explore, as a class, the idea of land reform. The question students wanted to debate at their hearing was, Should there be land reform in Guatemala, and why? I prepared roles for students to study and research. I wanted to have voices from many different parts of Guatemalan society present in our mock hearing, so the following people and groups were chosen: the Catholic Church, the guerrilla movement, the military, Rigoberta Menchú (activist), Manuel José Arce (writer), Pedro Luís Ruíz (peasant), a laborer, an upper-class Ladino, the U.S. government, the United Fruit Company, an illegal drug cartel, a human rights reporter, and an expert on international law. Two students were assigned to each role and the remaining students were jury members who had to arrange the courtroom, create name plates for each participant, and work together to form a position based on the testimony.

I gave students a packet of information I had gathered through library research for the role that they were to play. This was time-consuming to create, but useful in giving students a head start into the study of their roles. Students had two class sessions to research their roles before writing a position statement. On the day of the hearing, a student convened our hearing with the question of land reform we were to debate. Each participant came up to a podium and presented their testimony as the jury and other listeners took notes and formed questions.

Julia represented the Rebel Armed Forces, one of the groups that make up the alliance of freedom fighters called the Guatemalan National Revolutionary Alliance. The following is an excerpt from her testimony, "Our groups began to organize in 1960. We recruit from the poor Ladinos and Indios alike, and from the poor we gain our strength. Again and again the army has tried to stop us, but they cannot succeed, because as long as the people suffer under corruption, they will join us to fight back against it for the well-being of all Guatemalans. In this position of strength and resilience, we make our demands. We fight for land reform, and by land reform we mean the distribution of property from the wealthy to the poor. We also demand a new government, one that is made up of equal representation from Indio and Ladino people, men and women. Only when these demands are met and we live in a country where the power is in the hands of the laborers, will we cease in our fight for liberty." In contrast to Julia's testimony from the guerrilla movement in Guatemala was the testimony from the armed forces presented by Jade Chamness and Caitlin Franke: "We are the armed forces. We work to ensure our people security and peace. We keep the 'elite' Guatemalans safe and consider ourselves to be society's guardian. We protect the established order from communists, socialists, rebellious workers and peasants, and all other left-of-center dissident groups and individuals. We do not support land reform. If the land reform agreement were to pass, Guatemala would become unstable and lose money in our agriculture and trade. We are here to make sure that control is kept within the right hands. Thank you."

As each testimony was heard, students were exposed to a variety of voices and perspectives on whether or not Guatemala should have land reform. When all the testimony was complete and the jury was excused to deliberate, I asked students to share their thoughts on the hearing before its completion. I wanted to informally assess where students were in their learning and understanding. Hands shot up. Karl blurted out, "Ms. Singer, there is no way on earth that these different groups would get together in the same room and listen to each other. No way! What we are doing is completely unrealistic . . . so why bother?" Chelsea said, "I found it interesting to hear people's voices and ideas even though I could guess by their role what their position on land reform would be." When the jury returned, they decided to propose a land reform agreement for Guatemala that took into account different perspectives. We then voted as a class to ratify the proposal.

After the hearing, students wrote what they thought of the process and what they came to in their learning. Tony wrote, "The hearing helped to show views of different groups, which is important to form an accurate opinion of the Guatemalan situation." Ursula shared the following, "As a person, it is usually hard for me to see what I have learned from something, I don't know why this is; I think I probably learn a lot without realizing it. The hearing illustrated to me that there are checks and balances (international law) that can work to change a repressive government.

I also learned that it is hard to know exactly what is just in some situations. In Guatemala, would justice be served if there were a land reform agreement? Or would it be just if the heads of the military who are responsible for so much killing, were put to death? Does Guatemala need an entirely new government? Can anything ever make up for the destruction of Mayan culture 500 years ago? What would it take for the Indians to finally be equal with the other racial groups in Guatemala? Is it even possible for everyone to be equal?"

Tanya wrote, "From hearing all the different organizations and groups speak, I find that politics is all about what benefits you the most. It could be for good or bad reasons, but mainly everyone wants what they will get the most from. I also see this happen in my life in the United States, where people will twist facts to get others to side with them. Inequality is an issue in Guatemala and probably in every other place in the world. I know that many places have come a long way and are much closer to equality among their people, but I think there will always be inequality in some way. What we can do is continue to learn about our past, and speak out against everyday injustices."

Ashley focused on the issue of fairness: "There is a huge range of people and opinions in Guatemala. There are so many voices, positive and negative. Now, having been involved in the hearing, I can see how it would be hard to consider any one side when dividing land. It seems as though there's no 'fair' way to divide anything." Suzanna Ryan-Zahara reflected on her new learning: "The hearing taught me about the different sides and opinions behind land reform, and it showed me a more personal side of politics and history. I also learned that people have less than I thought they had. I never even realized that people live on thirty-five dollars a month." Multiple perspectives in the curriculum *had* provided the language, information, and tools necessary for students to explore and grapple with issues of social justice. I had framed my unit around this teaching question, and the student reflections highlighted the importance of the varied voices and perspectives.

Culminating Project

As I read students' feedback, I decided not to guide students toward more information about Guatemala, but instead asked them to take what they had learned and apply it by creating a project defining social justice and connecting this definition to their own lives. This assignment was a culminating project for their study, and I wanted them to have a lot of choice and freedom within it. Students received a list of ideas they could choose from or use as a jumping-off place. The list included the following options: poetry, essay, narrative, letter to the editor, a painting, a song, a collage, a recipe, a play, or a journal. I also told students that if this did not work for them, they could come up with their own idea. Because of the reinforcement they had given me throughout the unit when I provided choice in assessment, students had freedom to choose the medium in which to define social justice. I was also curious to see if the path we had been walking on together in our studies had led them to a way of thinking that they could apply to other cultures or to their own.

Students' final projects were diverse, unique, full of voice, and surprising. Some students relied on visual presentations. For example, Emily Gaffney painted a picture of people screaming in flames, with the caption "With covered ears and dry minds society dies" within the flames. Forrest, a student who had begun the unit asking for dates and facts and a map, wrote the following in an essay: "Social justice is like love, it is a phantom, a fantasy of men and women. Like love, if you ask someone to describe it, you will get a sigh, and a reply that is indescribable. But like love, it does exist and like all things, it exists in degrees. It exists as a result of the minds of the people who make up a society. It exists as a result of priorities." Jessica wrote the following poem from the perspective of a person of Mayan descent in Guatemala:

> You ask us what we do to get along?
> How we live with such hate?
> What keeps us going?
>
> It is our art
> that keeps us going.
> We don't give up
> we paint, we weave, we sculpt.
> We do not give up our promise
> to win what has been taken from us.
> It is our music that keeps us going.
> We don't give up.
> We sing, we dance, and we play.
> We are neighbors, friends, family, and allies.
> We keep each other going.
> Our fear is put away.
>
> Soon we will overcome
> the pressures.
> We will pray
> We will believe
> and ultimately,
> we will soar.

Corey Barber returned to the format of a two-voice poem for her final project:

Resilience
In the face of opposition, I have fought
In the face of opposition, I have woven
a war of thousands
patterns of thousands
to stay strong
to recover

(both)
to survive.

Now, tell me again about social justice.
Remind me of what is in our hearts every moment, every day.
Yes, the equal distribution of all God's gifts
Yes, my spirit, tell me of equality in

Power
Wealth
Services
Opportunity
Land
Work
Education
Quality of life

Are we daydreaming?
Or are we living a nightmare?

Father used to tell me before I went to bed,
Grandmother would sing to me as I lay in her arms,

(both)
"The cry of the poor is not always just,
but if you don't listen to it,
you will never know what justice is."

Reflection

As a new teacher, planning and implementing this unit was exhilarating, refreshing, scary, and confusing. I have a firm belief that my work in the classroom is to create a microcosm of an equitable community. I work to build a learning environment where questions are raised even if not easily answered, where the places students are in their lives and in their learning are heard and respected, and where issues of equity are not placed on the back burner.

Looking back at my teaching of this unit, I realize the unease with which I walked away from certain discussions, writing, and sharing. Teaching that integrates ongoing reflection often left me feeling vulnerable and uncertain. I also realize how this reflection allowed me to experiment and take risks. When I teach this unit again, I want to take more risks. I want to listen more to where my students are in their learning, in their storytelling, and in their acceptance of new tools and ideas. I still think about Karl's comment when he said he was feeling ashamed of the United States after learning of our involvement in Guatemala. Is this a place I am comfortable leading and leaving my students? I wish I hadn't let that conversation end where it did. I wish I had asked Karl and his classmates to write and talk and think about his confession. What do we do as historians, writers, learners, readers, and humans looking back on difficult parts of the past? I wonder if a conversation would have led us down a path offering alternatives to injustice?

The mock hearing was a powerful way for students to rethink parts of the history, roles, and voices of Guatemala, but did it provide students with a firm sense that there is choice in the actions we take in this world? When Karl blurted out that "there was no way on earth these different groups would get together in the same room and listen to each other," I wish I had stopped to ask him why. If a gathering of voices from a hard and hurtful past seems unrealistic to students in the classroom, then how will it happen outside our four walls? With each time I teach this material or a unit like it, I will feel more comfortable in my purpose and less frozen by honest questions. Part of teaching with the premise that the classroom is a place to build and to work toward a more just society, is accepting students' perspectives in their learning and letting them guide and influence my curriculum. Each new group of students I teach will offer different questions and will lead me down new paths. I want to remember Forrest's definition of social justice. "It exists in degrees. It exists as a result of the minds of the people who make up a society. It exists as a result of priorities." Teaching social justice is a priority in my classroom.

References

Bertrand, Regis & Danielle Magne. 1995. *The Textiles of Guatemala*. London: Liberty Regent Street.

Brandow, Karen, & Thomas Reed. 1996. *The Sky Never Changes: Testimonies from the Guatemalan Labor Movement*. Ithaca and London: ILR Press.

Burgos-Debray, Elizabeth. 1983. *I, Rigoberta Menchú*. New York: Schocken Books.

Carmack, Robert, ed. 1988 *Harvest of Violence: The Maya Indians and the Guatemalan Crisis*. Norman: University of Oklahoma Press.

Covo Torres, Javier. 1987. *The Mayas, on the Rocks*. Yucatan, Mexico: Dante.

Edmonson, Munro S., trans. 1971. *The Book of Counsel: The Popol Vuh of the Quiche Maya of Guatemala*. New Orleans: Tulane University Press.

Gerson, Mary-Joan. 1995. *People of Corn: A Mayan Story*. Boston/New York: Little, Brown.

Gleijeses, Piero. 1991. *Shattered Hope: The Guatemalan Revolution and the U.S., 1944–54*. Princeton, N.J.: Princeton University Press.

Goldston, James A. 1989. *Shattered Hope: Guatemalan Workers and the Promise of Democracy*. Boulder/San Francisco: Westview.

Jonas, Susanne. 1991. *The Battle for Guatemala: Rebels, Death Squads, and U.S. Power*. Boulder, Co.: Westview.

Perera, Victor. 1995. *Unfinished Conquest: The Guatemalan Tragedy*. Berkeley/Los Angeles/London: University of California Press.

Schlesinger, Stephen, & Stephen Kinzer. 1982. *Bitter Fruit: The Untold Story of the American Coup in Guatemala*. Garden City, NY.: Doubleday.

Simon, Jean Marie. 1988. *Guatemala: Eternal Spring–Eternal Tyranny*. New York: Norton.

Turner, Wilson. 1980. *Maya Designs*. New York: Dover.

Resources on the Internet

Guatemala Human Rights and Sociopolitical Issues: www.mars.cropsoil.uga.edu/tropag/social.htm

Guatemala Historical Events: www.mars.crop

Latino Literature: Arte Publico Press, www.arte.uh.edu

Mexico and Central America: Resource Center on the Americas, www.americas.org

5

The Lives Behind the Labels
Teaching About the Global Sweatshop, Nike, and the Race to the Bottom

Bill Bigelow

I began the lesson with a beat-up soccer ball. The ball sat balanced in a plastic container on a stool in the middle of the circle of student desks. "I'd like you to write a description of this soccer ball. Feel free to get up and look at it. There is no right or wrong. Just describe the ball however you'd like." Looks of puzzlement and annoyance greeted me. "It's just a soccer ball," someone said. Students must have wondered what this had to do with global studies. "I'm not asking for an essay," I said, "just a paragraph or two."

As I'd anticipated, their accounts were straightforward—accurate if uninspiring. Few students accepted the offer to examine the ball up close. A soccer ball is a soccer ball. They sat and wrote. Afterward, students shared a few of these aloud. Brian's is typical:

> The ball is a sphere which has white hexagons and black pentagons. The black pentagons contain red stars, sloppily outlined in silver. . . . One of the hexagons contains a green rabbit wearing a soccer uniform with "Euro 88" written parallel to the rabbit's body. This hexagon seems to be cracking. Another hexagon has the number 32 in green standing for the number of patches that the ball contains.

But something was missing. There was a deeper, social reality associated with this ball—a reality that advertising and the consumption-oriented rhythms of U.S. daily life discouraged students from considering. "Made in Pakistan" was stenciled in small print on the ball, but very few students thought that significant enough to include in their descriptions. However, these three tiny words offered the most important clue to the human lives hidden in "just a soccer ball"—a clue to the invisible Pakistanis whose hands crafted the ball sitting in the middle of the classroom.

I distributed and read aloud Bertolt Brecht's poem "A Worker Reads History" as a tool to pry behind the soccer-ball-as-thing:

Who built the seven gates of Thebes?
The books are filled with names of kings.
Was it kings who hauled the craggy blocks of stone? . . .
In the evening when the Chinese wall was finished
Where did the masons go? Imperial Rome
Is full of arcs of triumph. Who reared them up? . . .

Young Alexander conquered India.
He alone?
Caesar beat the Gauls.
Was there not even a cook in his army? . . .

Each page a victory.
At whose expense the victory ball?
Every ten years a great man,
Who paid the piper?

"Keeping Brecht's questions in mind," I said, after reading the poem, "I want you to *re-see* this soccer ball. If you like, you can write from the viewpoint of the ball, you can ask the ball questions, but I want you to look at it deeply. What did we miss the first time around? It's not 'just a soccer ball.'" With not much more than these words for guidance, students drew a line beneath their original descriptions and began again.

Versions one and two were as different as night and day. With Brecht's prompting, Pakistan as the country of origin became more important. Tim wrote in part, "Who built this soccer ball? The ball answers with Pakistan. There are no real names, just labels. Where did the real people go after it was made?" Nicole also posed questions: "If this ball could talk, what kinds of things would it be able to tell you? It would tell you about the lives of the people who made it in Pakistan. . . . But if it could talk, would you listen?" Maisha played with its colors and the "32" stamped on the ball: "Who painted the entrapped black, the brilliant bloody red, and the shimmering silver? Was it made for the existence of a family of 32?" And Sarah imagined herself as the soccer ball worker: "I sew together these shapes of leather. I stab my finger with my needle. I feel a small pain, but nothing much, because my fingers are so callused. Everyday I sew these soccer balls together for 5 cents, but I've never once had a chance to play soccer with my friends. I sew and sew all day long to have these balls shipped to another place where they represent fun. Here, they represent the hard work of everyday life." When students began to consider the human lives behind the ball-as-object, their writing also came alive.

Geoffrey, an aspiring actor, singer, and writer, wrote his version as a conversation between himself and the ball:

"So who was he?" I asked.

"A young boy, Wacim, I think," it seemed to reply.

I got up to take a closer look. Even though the soccer ball looked old and its hexagons and other geometric patterns were cracked, the sturdy and intricate stitching still held together.

"What that child must've gone through," I said.

"His father was killed and his mother was working. Wacim died so young. . . . It's just too hard. I can't contain these memories any longer." The soccer ball let out a cry and leaked his air out and lay there, crumpled on the stool. Like his master, lying on the floor, uncared for, and somehow overlooked and forgotten."

Students had begun to imagine the humanity inside the ball; their pieces were vivid and curious. The importance of making visible the invisible, of looking behind the masks presented by everyday consumer goods, became a central theme in my first-time effort to teach about the "global sweatshop" and child labor in poor countries.

Teaching About the Global Sweatshop

The paired soccer ball writing assignment was a spur-of-the moment classroom introduction to Sydney Schanberg's June 1996 *Life* magazine article, "Six Cents an Hour." Schanberg, best known for his *New York Times* investigations of Cambodia's "killing fields," had traveled to Pakistan and posed as a soccer ball exporter. There, he was offered children for $150 to $180 who would labor for him as virtual slaves. As Schanberg reports, in Pakistan, children as young as six are "sold and resold like furniture, branded, beaten, blinded as punishment for wanting to go home, rendered speechless by the trauma of their enslavement." For pennies an hour, these children work in dank sheds stitching soccer balls with the familiar Nike swoosh and logos of other transnational athletic equipment companies.

Nike spokesperson Donna Gibbs defended her company's failure to eliminate child labor in the manufacture of soccer balls: "It's an ages-old practice," she was quoted as saying in Schanberg's article, "And the process of change is going to take time." But as Max White, an activist with the "Justice. Do It NIKE!" coalition, said when he visited my global studies class last month, "Nike knew exactly what it was doing when it went to Pakistan. That's why they located there. They went because they *knew* child labor was an 'ages-old practice.'"

My initial impulse was to teach a unit on child labor. I thought that my students would empathize with young people around the globe whose play and education had been forcibly replaced with the drudgery of repetitive work—and that the unit would engage them in thinking about inequities in the global division of labor. Perhaps it might provoke them to take action on behalf of child workers in poor countries.

But I was also concerned that we shouldn't reduce the growing inequalities between rich and poor countries to the issue of child labor. Child labor could be entirely eliminated and that wouldn't affect the miserably low wages paid to adult workers, the repression of trade unions and democratic movements, the increasing environmental degradation, and the resulting Third World squalor sanitized by terms such as "globalization" and "free trade." Child labor was one spoke on the wheel of global capitalism, and I wanted to present students with a broader framework to reflect on its here-and-now dynamics. What I share here is a sketch of my unit's first draft—an invitation to reflect on how best to engage students in these issues.

The Transnational Capital Auction

It seemed to me that the central metaphor for economic globalization was the auction: governments beckoning transnational corporations to come hither—in competition with one another—by establishing attractive investment climates, for example, by maintaining low-wage/weak-union havens and by not pressing environmental concerns. So I wrote what I called "The Transnational Capital Auction: A Game of Survival." I divided students into seven different "countries" each of which would compete with all the others to accumulate "friendly-to-capital points"—the more points earned, the more likely capital would locate in that country. In five silent auction rounds, each group would submit bids for minimum wage, child labor laws, environmental regulations, conditions for worker organizing, and corporate tax rates. For example, a corporate tax rate of 75 percent won no points for the round, but a zero tax rate won 100 points. (There were penalty points for "racing to the bottom" too quickly, risking popular rebellion, and thus "instability" in the corporate lexicon.)

I played "Capital" itself and egged them on: "Come on, group 3, you think I'm going to locate in your country, with a ridiculous minimum wage like $5 an hour. I might as well locate in the United States. Next round, let's not see any more sorry bids like that one." A bit crass, but so is the real-world downward spiral simulated in the activity.

At the game's conclusion, every country's bids hovered near the bottom: no corporate taxes, no child labor laws, no environmental regulations, pennies-an-hour minimum wage rates, union organizers jailed, and the military used to crush strikes. As I'd anticipated, students had breathed life into the expressions "downward leveling" and "race to the bottom." In the frenzied competition of the auction, they'd created some pretty nasty conditions, because the game rewarded those who lost sight of the human and environmental consequences of their actions. I asked them to step back from the activity and to write on the kind of place their country would become should transnational capital decide to accept their bids and locate there. I also wanted them to reflect on the glib premise that underlies so much contemporary economic discussion that foreign investment in poor countries is automatically a good thing. And finally I hoped they would consider the impact that the race to the bottom has on their own lives, especially their future work prospects. (That week's *Oregonian* carried articles about the Pendleton Company's decision to pull much of its production from Oregon and relocate to Mexico.) I gave them several quotes to reflect on as they responded:

> It is not that foreigners are stealing our jobs, it is that we are all facing one another's competition.
>
> *William Baumol, Princeton University economist*

> Downward leveling is like a cancer that is destroying its host organism—the earth and its people.
>
> *Jeremy Brecher and Tim Costello, authors,* Global Village or Global Pillage

> Globalization has depressed the wage growth of low-wage workers [in the United States.] It's been a reason for the increasing wage gap between high-wage and low-wage workers.
>
> *Laura Tyson, former Chair, U.S. Council of Economic Advisers*

Many global issues courses are structured as "area studies," with units focusing on South America, sub-Saharan Africa, or the Middle East. There are obvious advantages to this region by region progression, but I worried that if I organized my global studies curriculum this way, students might miss how countries oceans apart, such as Indonesia and Haiti, are affected by the same economic processes. I wanted students to see globalization as, well, global—that there were myriad and far-flung runners in the race to the bottom.

This auction among poor countries to attract capital was the essential context my students needed to recognize patterns in such seemingly diverse phenomena as child labor and increased immigration to the world's so-called developed nations. However, I worried that the simulation might be too convincing, corporate power depicted as too overwhelming. The auction metaphor was accurate but inexorable: Students could conclude that if transnational capital is as effective an "auctioneer" as I was in the simulation, the situation for poor countries must be hopeless. In the follow-up writing assignment, I asked what if anything people in these countries could do to stop the race to the bottom, the "downward leveling." By and large, students' responses weren't as bleak as I had feared. Kara wrote, "Maybe if all the countries come together and raise the standard of living or become 'capital unfriendly,' then capital would have no choice but to take what they receive. Although it wouldn't be easy, it would be dramatically better." Adrian suggested that "people could go on an areawide strike against downward leveling and stand firm to let capital know that they won't go for it." And Matt wrote simply, "Revolt, strike."

Tessa proposed that people here could "boycott products made in countries or by companies that exploit workers."

But others were less hopeful. Lisa wrote, "I can't see where there is much the people in poor countries can do to stop this 'race to the bottom.' If the people refuse to work under those conditions, the companies will go elsewhere. The people have so little and could starve if they didn't accept the conditions they have to work under." Sara wrote, "I don't think a country can get themselves out of this because companies aren't generous enough to help them because they wouldn't get anything out of it."

What I should have done is obvious to me now. After discussing their thoughts on the auction, I should have regrouped students and started the auction all over again. Having considered various alternative responses to the downward spiral of economic and environmental conditions, students could have practiced organizing *with* each other instead of competing *against* each other, could have tested the potential for solidarity across borders. At the least, replaying the auction would have suggested that people in Third World countries aren't purely victims; there are possible routes for action, albeit enormously difficult ones.

T-shirts, Barbie Dolls, and Baseballs

We followed the auction with a "global clothes hunt." I asked students to "Find *at least* ten items of clothing or toys at home. These can be anything: T-shirts, pants, skirts, dress shirts, shoes, Barbie dolls, baseballs, soccer balls, etc." and to list each item and country of manufacture. In addition, I wanted them to attach geographic location to the place names, some of which many students had never heard of (for example, Sri Lanka, Macau, El Salvador, and Bangladesh). So in class they made collages of drawings or magazine clippings of the objects they'd found, and with the assistance of an atlas, drew lines on a world map connecting these images with the countries where the items were produced.

We posted their collage/maps around the classroom, and I asked students to wander around looking at these to search for patterns in which kinds of goods were produced in which kind of countries. Some students noticed that electronic toys tended to be produced in Taiwan and Korea; that more expensive shoes, like Doc Martens, were manufactured in Great Britain or Italy; athletic shoes were made mostly in Indonesia or China. On their "finding patterns" writeup, just about everyone commented that China was the country that appeared most frequently on people's lists. A few kids noted that most of the people in the manufacturing countries were not white. As Sandee wrote, "The more expensive products seem to be manufactured in countries with a higher amount of white people. Cheaper products are often from places with other races than white." People in countries with concentrations of people of color "tend to be poorer so they work for less." We'd spent the early part of the year studying European colonialism, and some students noticed that many of the manufacturing countries were former colonies. I wanted students to see that every time they put on clothes or kick a soccer ball, they are making a connection, if hidden, with people around the world—especially in Third World countries—and that these connections are rooted in historic patterns of global inequality.

From here on, I saturated students with articles and videos that explored the working conditions and life choices confronting workers in poor countries. Some of the resources I found most helpful included *Mickey Mouse Goes to Haiti*, a video critiquing the Walt Disney Company's exploitation of workers in Haiti's garment industry (workers there, mostly women, make 28 cents an hour; Disney claims it can't afford the 58 cents an hour workers say they could live on); a CBS *48 Hours* exposé of conditions for women workers in Nike factories in Vietnam, reported by Roberta Baskin; an article, "Boot Camp at the Shoe Factory Where Taiwanese Bosses Drill Chinese Workers to Make Sneakers for American Joggers," by Anita Chan writing in the *Washington Post*, Nov. 3, 1996; *Tomorrow We Will Finish*, a UNICEF-produced video about the anguish and solidarity of girls forced into the rug-weaving industry in Nepal and India; and an invaluable collection of articles called a "Production Primer," collected by "Justice. Do it NIKE!" a coalition of Oregon labor, and peace and justice groups.[1]

I indicated earlier that the advantage of this curricular globetrotting was that students could see that issues of transnational corporate investment, child labor, worker exploitation, poverty, and so on were not isolated in one particular geographic region. The disadvantage was that students didn't get much appreciation for the peculiar conditions in each country we touched on. And I'm afraid that after awhile, people in different societies began to appear as generic global victims. This was not entirely the fault of my decision to bounce from country to country, but was also a reflection of the narrow victim orientation of many of the materials I had available.

I was somewhat unaware of the limits of these resources until I previewed a twenty-five-minute video produced by Global Exchange, *Indonesia: Islands on Fire*. One segment features Sadisah, an Indonesian ex-Nike worker, who, with dignity and defiance, describes conditions for workers there and what she wants done about them. I found her presence, however brief, a stark contrast to most of the videos I'd shown in class that feature white commentators with Third World workers presented as objects of sympathy. Although students generated excellent writing during the unit, much of it tended to miss the humor and determination suggested in the *Islands on Fire* segment, and concentrated instead on workers' victimization.

---

[1] [Many of the articles listed here may be found on websites mentioned in the Resources section at the end of this chapter; for a full listing of global sweatshop resources, see *Rethinking Globalization: Teaching for Justice in an Unjust World*, available from Rethinking Schools (800) 669-4192; **www.rethinkingschools.org** Eds.]

Critique Without Caricature

Two concerns flirted uncomfortably throughout the unit. On the one hand, I had no desire to feign neutrality—to hide my conviction that people here need to care about and to act in solidarity with workers around the world in their struggles for better lives. To pretend that I was a mere dispenser of information would be dishonest, but worse, it would imply that being a spectator is an ethical response to injustice. It would model a stance of moral apathy. I wanted students to know that these issues were important to me, that I cared enough to do something about them.

On the other hand, I never want my social concerns to suffocate student inquiry or to prevent students from thoughtfully considering opposing views. I wanted to present the positions of transnational corporations critically, but without caricature.

Here, too, it might have been useful to focus on one country in order for students to evaluate corporate claims—for example, "Nike's production can help build thriving economies in developing nations." I'd considered writing a role play about foreign investment in Indonesia with roles for Nike management as well as Korean and Taiwanese subcontractors. (Nike itself owns none of its own production facilities in poor countries.) This would have provoked a classroom debate on corporate statements, where students could have assessed how terms such as "thriving economies" may have different meanings for different social groups.

Instead, I tried in vain to get a spokesperson from Nike, in nearby Beaverton, to address the class; I hoped that at least the company might send me a video allowing students to glean the corporate perspective. No luck. They sent me a public relations packet of Phil Knight speeches, and their "Code of Conduct," but stopped returning my phone calls requesting a speaker. I copied the Nike materials for students, and they read with special care the Nike Code of Conduct and did a "loophole search"—discovering, among other things, that Nike promises to abide by local minimum wage laws, but never promises to pay a *living* wage; they promise to obey "local environmental regulations" without acknowledging how inadequate these often are. Having raced themselves to the bottom in the transnational capital auction, the frequent appearance of the term "local government regulations" in the Nike materials might as well have carried a sticker reading "weasel words."

Writing "Work Poems"

I reminded students of our soccer ball exercise, how we'd missed the humanity in the object until we read Bertolt Brecht's poem. I asked them to write a "work poem" that captured some aspect of the human lives connected to the products we use everyday. They could draw on any situation, product, individual, or relationship we'd encountered in the unit. As prompts, I gave them other work poems that my students had produced over the years. Students brainstormed ways they might complete the assignment: from the point of view of one of the objects produced, or from one of the workers; a dialogue poem from the point of view of worker and owner, or worker and consumer (see example in Jessie Singer's chapter, this book); a letter to one of the products, or to one of the owners (such as Oregon-based Phil Knight, CEO of Nike). Cameron Robinson, a student in my class, expressed the essence of what I was driving at with the assignment:

Masks
Michael Jordan soars through the air,
on shoes of un-paid labor.

A boy kicks a soccer ball,
the bloody hands are forgotten.

An excited girl combs the hair of her Barbie,
an over-worked girl makes it.

A child receives a teddy bear,
Made in China has no meaning.

The words "hand made" are printed,
whose hands were used to make them?

A six year old in America starts his first day of school,
a six year old in Pakistan starts his first day of work.

They want us to see the ball,
not to see the millions of ball stitchers.

The world is full of many masks,
the hard part is seeing beneath them.

As we read our pieces aloud (I wrote one, too), I asked students to record lines or images that they found particularly striking, and to note themes that recurred. They also gave positive feedback to one another after each person read. Sandee wrote, "I liked the line in Maisha's paper that said, 'My life left me the day I stitched the first stitch. . .' I like Antoinette's paper because of the voice. It showed more than just pain, it also reflected a dream"—an ironic dream of a sweatshop worker who wants to flee her country for the "freedom" of the United States. Dirk had written a harshly worded piece from the point of view of a worker for a transnational company; it drew comment from just about everyone. Elizabeth appreciated it because "he used real language to express the feelings of the workers. As he put it, I doubt that the only thing going through their minds is 'I hate this job.'" As a whole, the writings were a lot angrier than they were hopeful; if I'd missed it in their pieces, this came across loud and clear in students' "common themes" remarks. As Jessica wrote, "One of the things I noticed was that none of the [papers] had a solution to the situation they were writing about." Maisha agreed: "Each paper only showed animosity."

I expected the unit to generate anger, but I hoped to push beyond it. From the very beginning, I told students that it was not my intention merely to expose all the world's abuse and exploitation. A broader aim was to make a positive difference. For their final project, I wanted students to *do* something with their knowledge— I wanted to give them the opportunity to act on behalf of the invisible others whose lives are intertwined in so many ways with their own. I wasn't trying to push a particular organization, or even a particular form of "action." I wanted them simply to feel some social efficacy, to sense that no matter how overwhelming a global injustice, there's always something to be done.

The assignment sheet (seee Appendix A) required students to take their learning "outside the walls of the classroom and into the real world." They could write letters to Phil Knight, Michael Jordan, or President Clinton. They could write news articles or design presentations to other classes. I didn't want to force them to urge a particular position if they didn't feel comfortable with that kind of advocacy, so in a letter they might simply raise questions to an individual.

They responded with an explosion of creativity: three groups of students designed presentations for elementary school kids or for other classes at Franklin; one student wrote an article on child labor to submit to the *Franklin Post*, the school newspaper; four students wrote Phil Knight, two wrote Michael Jordan, and one each wrote the Disney Company, President Clinton, and local activist Max White.

Jonathan Parker borrowed an idea from an editorial cartoon included in the "Justice. Do It NIKE!" reader. He found an old Nike shoe and painstakingly constructed a wooden house snuggled inside, complete with painted shingles, and stairway. He accompanied it with a poem that reads in part:

> There is a young girl
> who lives in a shoe.
> Phil Knight makes six million
> she makes just two.
>
> When Nike says "just do it"
> she springs to her feet,
> stringing her needle
> and stitching their sneaks.
> With Nike on the tongue,

the swoosh on the side,
the sole to the bottom,
she's done for the night . . .

When will it stop?
When will it end?
Must I, she says,
toil for Nike again?

The "sculpture" and poem have been displayed in my classroom, and have sparked curiosity and discussion in other classes, but Jonathan hopes also to have it featured in the display case outside the school library.

Cameron, a multisport athlete, was inspired by a *Los Angeles Times* article by Lucille Renwick, "Teens' Efforts Give Soccer Balls the Boot," about Monroe High School students in Los Angeles who became incensed that all of their school's soccer balls came from Pakistan, a child labor haven. The Monroe kids got the L.A. school board there to agree to a policy to purchase soccer balls only from countries that enforce a prohibition on child labor.

Cameron decided to do a little detective work of his own, and discovered that of the five Portland schools he checked, 60 percent of the soccer balls were made in Pakistan. He wrote a letter to the school district's athletic director alerting him to his findings, describing conditions under which the balls are made, and asking him what he intended to do about it. Cameron enclosed copies of an article describing the students' organizing in Los Angeles—hinting further action if school officials didn't rethink their purchasing policies.

One student, Daneeka, bristled at the assignment and felt that regardless of what the project sheet said, I was actually forcing them to take a position. She boycotted the assignment and enlisted her mother to come in during parent conferences to support her complaint. Her mother talked with me, read the assignment sheet, and—to her daughter's chagrin—told her to do the project. Daneeka and I held further negotiations and agreed that she could take her learning "outside the walls of the classroom" by "visiting" online chat rooms where she could discuss global sweatshop issues, and describe these conversations in a paper. But after letting the assignment steep a bit longer, she found a more personal connection to the issues. Daneeka decided to write Nike about their use of child labor in Pakistan as described in the Schanberg article. "When I was first confronted with this assignment," she wrote in her letter, "it really didn't disturb me. But as I have thought about it for several weeks, child labor is a form of slavery. As a young black person, slavery is a disturbing issue, and to know that Nike could participate in slavery is even more disturbing." Later in her letter, Daneeka acknowledges that she is a "kid" and wants to stay in fashion. "Even *I* will continue to wear your shoes, but will *you* gain a conscience?"

"Just Go With the Flow"

At the end of the global sweatshop unit, I added a brief curricular parenthesis on the role of advertising in U.S. society. Throughout the unit, I returned again and again to Cameron Robinson's "masks" metaphor:

The world is full of many masks,
the hard part is seeing beneath them.

I'd received a wonderful video earlier in the year, *The Ad and the Ego*, that, among other things, examines the "masking" role of advertising—how ads hide the reality of where a product comes from and the environmental consequences of mass consumption. The video's narrative is dense, but because of its subject matter, humor, and MTV-like format, students were able to follow its argument as long as I frequently stopped the VCR. At the end of part 1, I asked students to comment on any of the quotes from the video, and to write other thoughts they felt were relevant. One young woman I'll call Marie, wrote in part, "I am actually tired of analyzing everything that goes on around me. I am tired of looking at things at a deeper level. I want to just go with the flow and relax."

I'd like to think that Marie's frustration grew from intellectual exhaustion, from my continually exhorting students to "think deep," to look beneath the surface—in other words, from my academic rigor. But from speaking with her outside of class, my sense is that the truer cause of her weariness came from constantly seeing people around the world as victims, from Haiti to Pakistan to Nepal to China. By and large, the materials I was able to locate (and chose to use) too frequently presented people as stick figures, mere symbols of a relationship of domination and subordination between rich and poor countries. I couldn't locate resources—letters, diary entries, short stories, and so forth—that presented people's work lives in the context of their families and societies. And I wasn't able to show adequately how people in those societies struggle in big and little ways for better lives. The overall impression my students may have been left with was of the unit as an invitation to pity and help unfortunate others, rather than as an invitation to join with diverse groups and individuals in a global movement for social justice—a movement already underway.

Another wish-I'd-done-better that may also be linked to Marie's comment is the tendency for a unit like this to drift toward good guys and bad guys. In my view, Nike *is* a "bad guy," insofar as it reaps enormous profits as it pays workers wages that it knows full well cannot provide a decent standard of living. They're shameless and they're arrogant. As one top Nike executive in Vietnam told Portland's *Business Journal*, "Sure we're chasing cheap labor, but that's business and that's the way it's going to be"—a comment that lends ominous meaning to the Nike slogan "There is no finish line." My students' writing often angrily targeted billionaire Nike CEO Phil Knight and paired corporate luxury with Third World poverty. But corporations are players in an economic "game" with rules to maximize profits and rewards and punishments for how well those rules are obeyed. I hoped that students would come to see the "bad guys" less as the individual players in the game than as the structure, profit imperatives, and ideological justifications of the game itself. Opening with the Transnational Capital Auction was a good start, but the unit didn't consistently build on this essential systemic framework.

Finally, there is a current of self-righteousness in U.S. social discourse that insists that "we" have it good and "they" have it bad. A unit like this can settle too comfortably into that wrong-headed dichotomy, and even reinforce it. Teaching about injustice and poverty "over there" in Third World countries may implicitly establish U.S. society as the standard of justice and affluence. There is poverty and exploitation of workers here, too. And both "we" and "they" are stratified, especially by race, class, and gender. "We" here benefit very unequally from today's frantic pace of globalization. As well, there are elites in the Third World with lots more wealth and power than most people in this society. Over the year, my global studies curriculum attempted to confront these complexities of inequality. But it's a crucial postscript that I want to emphasize as I edit my "race to the bottom" curriculum for future classes.

Enough doubt and self-criticism. By and large, students worked hard, wrote with insight and empathy, and took action for justice—however small. They were poets, artists, essayists, political analysts, and teachers. And next time around, we'll all do better.

References

Brecht, Bertolt. 1987. *Poems 1913–1956 Bertolt Brecht.* Ed. John Willet & Ralph Manheim. New York: Routledge.

Chan, Anita, 1996 (May 3). "Where Taiwanese Bosses Drill Chinese Workers to Make Sneakers for American Joggers." *Washington Post:* C1.

Renwick, Lucille. 23 December 1996. "Teens' Efforts Give Soccer Balls the Boot." *Los Angeles Times*. Available online at the *LA Times* website, **http://www.latimes.com** ($2.00).

At their request, some of the students' names used in this article have been changed. EDS.

Resources

Readers/Articles/Curricula

American Federation of Teachers, International Affairs Department. 1996. *Child Labor: A Selection of Materials on Children in the Workplace.* 555 New Jersey Ave. NW, Washington, DC 20001–2079 (e-mail **iadaft@aol.com**) (single copy, $1). Includes a number of articles that could be useful with students, such as "Child Labor in Pakistan" by Jonathan Silvers, and "Six Cents an Hour," by Sydney Schanberg. (Also ask AFT-IAD for its "Children Without Childhoods," a nine-page supplement.)

Brecher, Jeremy, & Tim Costello, 1994. *Global Village or Global Pillage: Economic Reconstruction from the Bottom Up.* Boston: South End Press. 237 pp., $14. (South End Press, 116 Saint Botolph St., Boston, MA 02115; website **http://www.lbbs.org/sep/sep.htm**). Provides a helpful wider framework to consider the "race to the bottom" but also focuses on grassroots responses worldwide. I used the book as a source of examples and quotations to share with students.

Collection of articles on Nike, "Justice. Do It NIKE!" 1996. *A Nike Production Primer* P.O. Box 219231, Portland, OR 97225. (503) 292-8168; e-mail **maxw@rain. com** ($10 contribution requested, includes postage.) I found this an invaluable resource, both for my own background knowledge and for articles I used with students.

"It's the Global Economy, Stupid: The Corporatization of the World." 1996. *The Nation* magazine. (July 15–22. Special issue.) Short articles provide a broader context for thinking about global sweatshop and child labor issues.

Milton Meltzer, 1994. Transnational Capital Auction." From his book, *Cheap Raw Material: How Our Youngest Workers Are Exploited and Abused.* New York: Viking. Available from Bill Bigelow, 2814 NE Mason, Portland, OR 97211. Free. Please include a stamped (55 cents) self-addressed envelope.

Videos

CBS News. *48 Hours* segment, "Nike in Vietnam." First aired October 17, 1996. (About 20 min.) Available from CBS News, $29.95 plus shipping; (800) 338-4847. Focuses on an incident in a Nike factory in Vietnam where a Korean supervisor beat women, who make 20 cents an hour, on the neck and head with a shoe; and Nike's response. Roberta Baskin talks with Vietnamese women and Nike public relations people, and weaves a stark contrast of exploited workers and willfully ignorant company officials.

Global Exchange. *Indonesia: Islands on Fire.* (25 min.) (See below for address, phone, and website.) Because this video focuses mostly on repression and resistance in

Indonesia, and includes just a brief section on the role of transnationals such as Nike, it would be useful only if a teacher decided to concentrate on Indonesia as an example of the social consequences of investment choices. But that's also the video's strength—that it locates sweatshop practices in the context of a particular society.

National Labor Committee. 1996. *Mickey Mouse Goes to Haiti.* (approximately 20 min.) 275 7th Ave. (15th floor), New York, NY 10001 (212) 242-3002). Depicts working and living conditions of Disney workers in Haiti. Responds effectively to the argument that it's all right to pay workers in poor countries less because it costs less to live. (The National Labor Committee also distributes *Zoned for Slavery*, focusing on conditions for Gap sweatshop workers in Central America, which I have not seen, but has gotten excellent reviews from other teachers. It includes extensive interviews with young workers and family members who describe the impact sweatshop labor has on their lives.)

NBC, *Dateline* segment, "Toy Story." (About 25 min., first aired December 17, 1996.) Not commercially available. Examines child labor in Indonesia and China. Reporter Stone Phillips poses as a U.S. toy manufacturer and "auctions" his toy business to sub-contractors who can produce items most cheaply.

UNICEF, 1994. *Tomorrow We Will Finish.* (26 min.). UNICEF. Distributed by Maryknoll World Productions (800) 227-8523). More than 150,000 girls between five and sixteen years old toil in 2,000 carpet factories in Nepal. This is the story of Suri and her friends. My students found it very compelling, in large part because it concentrates on telling just one girl's story.

Organizations/Web pages

Campaign for Labor Rights, 1247 "E" St. SE, Washington, DC 20003 (e-mail **clr@igc.apc.org**; website **http//www.compugraph.com/clr**). Publishes a very useful newsletter ($35 a year) filled with audiovisual resources, fact sheets, and updates on campaigns to support worker organizing around the world. Via e-mail, they also distribute updates on Nike and other CLR campaigns. CLR's web page is excellent, and includes lots of links to other resources, as well as a new "teaching ideas" page.

Global Exchange. 2017 Mission St., Rm. 303, San Francisco, CA 94110 (800) 497-1994; **http://www.globalexchange.org**. Engaged in hosting global "people to people" projects, including leading "reality tours" to Third World countries, managing "fair trade" stores, and publishing resources on global justice issues. Membership, $35; free quarterly newsletter.

Jobs With Justice. 501 Third St., NW, Washington, DC 20001-2797; **http://www.labornet.org/jwj/**. A national labor, community, and religious coalition organized to fight for the rights of working people. Throughout the country JwJ has coordinated solidarity efforts with workers here and abroad. Their website lists local JwJ chapters.

National Labor Committee. 275 7th Ave., 15th floor, New York, NY 10001 (212) 247-3002. One of the most prominent groups working to expose and eliminate sweatshops worldwide.

The Network of Educators on the Americas (NECA). P.O. Box 73038, Washington, DC, 20056-3038 (202) 238-2379; e-mail **necadc@aol.com**; website **http://www.cldc.howard.edu/~neca/**). Distributes classroom materials from a critical perspective on global issues. Call, write, or e-mail for their excellent (and free) "Teaching for Change" catalogue.

Nike Boycott Homepage (**http://www.saigon.com/~nike/**). At this website, I found several of the articles that I used with students. Also available here is the recent report by Thuyen Nguyen of the Vietnam Labor Watch about conditions at Nike factories.

Nike: Fair Play? (**http://www.xs4all.nl/~ccc/nike.htm**). This website, based in The Netherlands, includes many articles about conditions at Nike plants, and recent strikes in Indonesia and Vietnam.

Nike, Inc. (Consumer Affairs Division) (800) 344-6453). Nike has an automatic fax line (when the system answers, press 1 then 3) and will fax you an annual report/ company history (Document #650), and Nike manufacturing policies (Document #500).

Sweatshop Watch. 720 Market St., Suite 500, San Francisco, CA 94102 (415) 391-1655. A coalition of unions, community groups, and legal advocates focusing especially on domestic sweatshop issues. Publishes a quarterly newsletter ($20/year).

UNITE! (Union of Needletrades, Industrial and Textile Employees). 1710 Broadway, New York, NY 10019-5299 (212) 265-7000. Involved in fighting sweatshops abroad and in the United States.

APPENDIX A

Child Labor/Global Sweatshop: "Making a Difference" Project

The project you choose is up to you. The major requirement is that you take your learning about Nike—the "global sweatshop," child labor, conditions for workers in Indonesia, China, Vietnam, Haiti, and so on—outside the walls of the classroom and into the real world. Some examples:

1. Write a detailed letter of opinion or inquiry to someone connected with these issues—for example, Phil Knight, Michael Jordan, President Clinton, U.S. labor unions, the Disney Company, the governments of China, Vietnam, or Indonesia, and so on. In this letter, you can either make a strong point and back it up with evidence from class and your own research, or you can raise important questions. However, if you choose to raise questions, you still need to indicate lots of information that you know about the issue.

2. Write an article for the *Franklin Post*, the *Oregonian*, or some other journal or newsletter.

3. Prepare testimony for the Portland School Board, or some other agency or office.

4. Design a presentation for classes at Franklin or one of our feeder schools (Kellogg, Mt. Tabor, and so on) to teach others about these issues.

5. Become involved with a group that is trying to make a difference around these issues. Write up your reasons for choosing this group and what you hope to accomplish.

6. Produce a rap, audiotape, video, or other visual display on these issues. (You also need to accompany this with an essay explaining and defending your point of view.) Or write a skit to perform or a story to share.

7. An original idea that my teacher brain was too dull to come up with.

Other Considerations:

1. You may work in a group if required by the nature of your project—for example, presenting to other classes or giving testimony before the school board. But I will need to see evidence that each member of the group has participated.

2. You must use at least five different sources in your project. At least two of these must be sources you found on your own.

3. The final draft of your project must demonstrate clear ideas and support, and it needs to be "correct." No spelling, grammatical, or other errors on the final draft. (People outside of schools are always looking for ways to make students look ignorant; let's not give them any ammunition.)

4. Remember to go deep with this. Point out specific conditions that need changing, but also remember to talk about the deeper *causes* of these problems.

6

That Hard Thing

Getting Inside the Social Protest Movements in United States History

Daniel Gallo

Either we are "the people," with all the redemptive, responsible meanings of that identity, or we are unfaithful to everything that has been purchased with the blood of our forebears—everything, especially the awesome responsibility of helping to provide leadership for the re-creation of this nation. Can our students grasp the profound meaning of this emergence? I think so.

Vincent Harding

These words, found in Vincent Harding's *Hope and History,* helped me to understand the gravity of teaching about the civil rights movement. His words played heavily on my mind as I sought to frame an exploration of its textures. Such a powerful story, with such powerful messages about justice, identity, and differing philosophies, carries with it the possibility for a meaningful and transformative experience in the classroom. Knowing that the movement could start a fire in the imaginations of my students, I sought to frame an exploration that would mine its deeper meanings.

Last spring it was time to face the civil rights movement from a perspective that I had never explored it: that of a teacher. Having always found "the movement" to be one of the most compelling stories of recorded experience, I found the challenge of framing an exploration of its contours a daunting task. What was most important to know about? How would the content most intensely intersect with students' lives? What broader lessons should students draw out of the material presented to them in our journey? I was interested in how students would interpret differing notions of social justice and the means by which people have sought to realize their visions. How would they define social justice? Is it equality under the law? Freedom of expression? The embrace and affirmation of differing identities? As I pondered, further questions emerged. Do the means matter by which justice is sought? Is it important for the actions of people to embody the vision of society that impels them to action? How should justice be sought after? With these questions swirling in my consciousness, we began our journey.

My first stab at getting to students' perceptions of social justice proved futile. I asked students to define social justice. Many students stalled and became frustrated. Perhaps it was the abstract nature of my question and the lack of any vivid experience from which to make meaningful statements. I noticed students scurrying for dictionaries immediately, perturbed by the fact that "social justice" as a concept was not neatly defined by Webster's. Being a resourceful lot, many defined "social" and "justice" and then worked to amalgamate the two definitions. Within the first few minutes of my ill-conceived dive into realms of abstraction, I realized I had made a classic rookie mistake: I hadn't put students at the center of the exploration; I hadn't worked at creating an affective experience that would evoke the type of intense expression I knew they were capable of. Thankfully there was always Tuesday to dust myself off and move into journal entry number 2.

Having recently observed some remarkable language arts teachers, I had seen the power of using "I am" poems in helping students to explore and express the emotional texture of a given moment in time. My hope was that students would define social justice through a series of explorations of injustice, that they would "feel" their ways into more powerful and evocative spaces. As I prepared for Tuesday's class, I looked in our textbook (Gary Nash's *American Odyssey*[1]) and found a stunning picture of Elizabeth Ann Eckford. Eckford was one of the nine African-American students who were "integrated" into Central High School in Little Rock, Arkansas, in 1957. In the photo she walks through the street, books in hand, face stoic, with three middle-aged European-American women following close behind, their faces full of rage. As a class we had talked about the types of discrimination present in the south, the overt Jim Crow segregation, and the importance of the U.S. Supreme Court cases *Plessy v. Ferguson* and *Brown v. Board of Education*. It was time for us to go "inside" and explore the ways in which an individual would experience the weight of racism present in America at that time. The picture offered us the perfect opportunity.

My only requirement for the journal entry was that students begin the poem with "I am Elizabeth Ann Eckford" and then explore what they perceived to be the reality of the moment the picture was taken. As the students' words flowed, I was struck by their power. Rokeisha, a withdrawn African-American student who had difficulty with certain grammar constructions, offered one of the most powerful poems:

I am Elizabeth Ann Eckford one of nine students
I woke up this morning wondering what the day would bring for me
Scared that the white air would kill me
Why, how why would I feel this way because of what the man said to me the
    other day?

---

[1] Gary B. Nash, 1997, *American Odyssey: The United States in the Twentieth Century* (New York: Glencoe/McGraw-Hill).

Pain run through me like dirty water on a rainy day
It stop at my heart and lay
And I say why mother do I have to go today?
Why not tomorrow or another day?
So I span on my black and white dress and am be on my way
To fight for my rights and future that you have today

Rokeisha's words stressed the movement as a process. She saw the bravery, the confrontations, the struggle with fear as part of a progression toward the realization of a broader goal. Kira also echoed this sentiment with the lines "I am doing something new, something my ancestors never had the chance to do. I am doing something for myself, my friends, my people." Vanessa focused on the gravity of the moment by emphasizing the fear: "'Lynch her! Lynch her!' they yell calling for my blood. I am but a single student, one out of two-thousand, yet today, all of their eyes are on the color of my skin and their minds, on my blood."

Through their expressive poetry the students told me what their vision of social justice was. They saw social justice as the inverse of dehumanization by injustice. In expressing their empathy for Elizabeth Ann Eckford, the students identified the strains of injustice and the ways in which an individual was affected by it. Students expressed the lack of humanity afforded to Eckford by her tormentors. Implicit in their poetry was the realization that no person should be made to endure what Eckford was made to endure. In addition to expressions of empathy for the injustice Eckford suffered, I realized that the poems were also laden with testaments to sacrifice, strength, and collective action against injustice. Their words were compelling.

The view that social justice was a process—a work in progress—was also evident in the way class unfolded. As we delved further into the story of the integration of Central High, we read Daisy Bates' retelling of the events as a participant. Before we began our collective reading, I warned the students that the piece contained some inflammatory language. Bates' retelling of events includes many racial epithets that were slung at African Americans during those trying days of 1957. Kyle, a somewhat shy European-American student who sat in the back corner, offered to be the first reader. He read steadily but came to a sudden stop at the first use of the word "nigger." All the students could sense the tension in the seconds that he paused. The students all had texts in front of them and were reading along. We all knew what the next word was. A few students looked up at him.

I believe that Kyle faced a number of issues in that moment. What was the right thing to do? In many pieces of student writing I found European-American males to be baffled by the "n" word. If it was a derogatory word used by slave "masters" in a bygone era, why did African Americans use it as a term for each other in the hallways of Grant High School? Why was it inappropriate for European-American students to use the word, but seemingly appropriate for African-American students to use it among themselves? It seemed that the gravity of these questions rested on Kyle's shoulders. He took a deep breath and read the word that followed, skipping

Personal Experience

the derogatory slur. Kyle established an important precedent in that moment. From then on, readers of all backgrounds simply passed over the word and read the words that followed. Kyle's decision brought our class to an important unstated understanding: It was important that we understood painful epithets in their historical context but equally important that we not release them into the air of the classroom. Kyle's sensitivity proved a gift to us all.

Having explored the events in Little Rock, we journeyed to Montgomery, Alabama, and the infamous bus boycott. It was important to me that we embrace the strength of Rosa Parks and at the same time debunk the myth that her act was spontaneous. Looking through student reflections on Parks' contribution to the movement, I was struck by a phrase spun by Wyatt—a nineteen-year-old rapper and street artist extraordinaire. He wrote that Parks offered "politically visual discrimination." I find an eloquence in that statement in that he expressed, in his own way, the importance of visible symbols or "mileposts" in the struggle for justice. If we look toward Parks, that is indeed what she offered—the image of a respected African-American woman suffering injustice under the political and social realities of her time. Moving from the story of Rosa Parks, we talked about the conditions that the Montgomery bus boycott sought to change and the economic pressure that it created. Our discussion led us inevitably toward a meeting with the bus boycott's charismatic young leader, Martin Luther King, Jr.

Facing the reality that I had a finite amount of time to spend on the civil rights movement, I thought long and hard about what students needed to know about King. In the end I decided that his philosophy of nonviolence, rather than an extensive look at his biography, would be most compelling for students to explore. It would offer us our first exploration of a means or course of action by which a group sought to realize their vision of social justice. We undertook a class reading of King's "Pilgrimage to Nonviolence,"[2] taking time to break down and understand each tenet of his philosophy. Knowing that this philosophy would be alien and abstract to many of the students, I asked them to work in groups on creative projects that would embody the tenets of nonviolence advocated by King. Students could draw pictures, write poetry or rap songs, create icons, or make an infomercial—anything to get them wrestling with King's notions. "Maybe they'll enjoy it so much they won't realize they're learning," I mused. After allowing a day for them to work at their creations it was time for them to present to the class.

The most frenetic presentation was from a group that created an infomercial "selling" nonviolence. Although I was concerned that allowing students to present the material in that way would commodify the ideas and obscure the difficulty of the practice of nonviolence, the exuberance of the students eased my anxiety. It struck me that the group that created the infomercial represented the mosaic that King dreamed of seeing in our schools. Kevin, an African-American student whose

---

[2]"Pilgrimage to Non-Violence," 1984, in *The Sixties Papers,* ed. Judith Albert. (New York: Praeger).

parents were from Ethiopia, Mayumi, a Japanese-American student, and Brett and Johan—both European Americans—all laughed together and approached the project with verve. It touched me to see this high-functioning group breathing life into the ideas of nonviolence.

"Hang up those boxing gloves, it's time to get spiritual," barked Johan with the panache of a home shopping network salesman. Kevin followed: "Fighting is in the past. Step into the twentieth century by loving your opponent instead of fighting him." Their commercial proceeded with a group of products designed to help people practice nonviolence. There was a helmet that symbolized the acceptance of suffering, boxing gloves designed to knock the evil out of people rather than striking the person, a bracelet that would magically awaken shame in the other party, and a Bible to help people be "spiritually active like a mutha." Although helmets and boxing gloves—symbols that could have led to misinterpretation—were obviously not present in the marches, boycotts, and sit-ins that the students had been studying, the presentation illuminated a sensitivity to the ideas of nonviolence.

The other presentations contained elements of the six central tenets of King's essay, but many of them simply paraphrased or parroted back King's words without the personal interpretation I was seeking. It was a couple of weeks later, through reading student journals, that I began to see the ways in which students had made sense of King's writings on a personal level. Tiesha, a young woman whose eyes seemed to glow more intensely during our discussions of the movement than they had earlier in the year, wrote,

> I feel that nonviolent protest is the best way to achieve a goal or get what you want. Nonviolence is more than just a method, it is a commitment emotionally and spiritually, a way of life. Many think of nonviolence as doing nothing or being a coward but this is in fact for the strong. You must be aware and understand mentally what is going on. You use nonviolence as a form of reverse psychology to awaken a sense of moral shame in your opponent, to make him realize what he is doing is wrong. Booker T. Washington said, "Let no man pull you so low as to make you hate him." When he brings you that low he has taken you to a point of working against your goal. He drags you to the point of defying creation and becoming depersonalized.

Tiesha, like many students in the class, found King's assertion that violence is dehumanizing to resonate with her own sensibilities.

Simi, whose writing had captivated the class on more than one occasion, wrote,

> I believe that nonviolence is definitely the best way to get social justice. When you say that these people have no right to treat us badly, you must show them how to treat you. When you use violence against violence, you become the enemy. By not using violence you show other generations that violence isn't always needed.

Her statement "When you use violence against violence, you become the enemy" was perhaps the most evocative rendering of the belief that people surrender their humanity when they become violent. Kyle, writing of the protestors of the early civil rights movement, stated, "They stood for what they believed in without adding hate to the world, they didn't ask for one thing and then go around and do it. They showed to others that they are not the ones that carry the evil inside them." In these writings students expressed the moral import of nonviolence. They saw non-violence as a way of maintaining spiritual high ground and providing an important example for the future.

I had entered the unit wondering whether students would consider important the actions taken to achieve a vision of justice. In their reflections on King's philosophy of nonviolence, most students expressed the belief that it was important that the actions of individuals reflect the world they are endeavoring to create. Through their reflections, I felt that they came to understand the idea present in Gandhi's oft-quoted statement that we must "be the world that we envision." Students also acknowledged the challenges that this path toward justice presents.

Through our discussions and writings I found that students also understood the difficulty of practicing nonviolence in the face of violent aggression. Jordan wrote, "I can't imagine lying on the ground, just trying to protect my head , as I was slowly and steadily kicked to near death." The sacrifices made by the protestors and the level of discipline required to not strike back were also present in Cam's writing. In a journal entry moving for its honesty and perceptiveness, he wrote, "Based on what I have learned it seems easy for me to say that nonviolent protest is the best way to achieve social justice. However, I do not think that I, personally, am capable of such self-control at this point in time. It would seem much easier to me to be violent as a means of showing my unhappiness."

When we moved from studying nonviolent protest through text and discussion to watching a video that showed the violence of the period, some interesting dynamics entered. Teaching for Tolerance's *A Time for Justice* is a short documentary that was created to produce an intense emotional response in the viewer. In our classroom it produced the desired effect. The scenes of brutality during a sit-in at a lunch counter evoked an air of tension in the students. As the angry mobs pulled demonstrators off their stools, beating them savagely, I could see students nodding sadly, looking away, not wanting to face the violence. I paused the tape after the lunch counter scene and checked in with the students to see how they were doing.

Kyle spoke first: "I can't believe people did that to each other." Measuring the room I sensed that other students were also in disbelief. A long silence fell over the room. Looking to my right I noticed that Melvin and Jamal—two African-American males—were clearly uncomfortable. Writhing in their seats, they looked toward me, their eyes burning with anger. "There's no way I would sit there and let somebody do that to me," Melvin said with a firmness that brought out his rage. Jamal, his deep eyes focused on me, nodded in agreement, "How could they just sit there and do nothing?" "Do nothing" hung in the air for a while. I thought about

Seeing both sides of issues

King's "Pilgrimage to Non-Violence,"[3] which advocates being passive physically and active spiritually. I thought of the words of Gandhi (quoted by King) that if you are a coward it is better to fight than to use nonviolent methods. In the moment I felt mute, I could feel the gravity of my color.

As a European American I felt that I needed to be careful in the space we were occupying. I felt that if I were not sensitive in the way I responded, Melvin and Jamal might interpret my explanation as advocating a passivity toward the oppressors that Melvin and Jamal found weak, compromising, and damaging to African Americans. Would they understand my invitation to revisit the spirit of King's writings? Kyle broke the silence: "They are doing something...they're keeping the high ground . . . I mean, look at those other people, they look stupid beating up on people that don't fight back." Many in the class nodded. I looked to Melvin and could see the wheels turning. That exchange proved to be one of the most rewarding of our exploration as students respectfully challenged each other while they were expressing strong feelings. It also brought me joy to see that students were thinking about many of the notions that we had explored—they knew what sacrifices were made, they knew the difficulty of practicing nonviolence, they understood the tenets of nonviolence, and they soon came to the next part of our journey: victories and "the schism."

We spent a brief amount of time studying the march on Washington and King's famous speech. We then explored the meaning of the Voting Rights Act and Civil Rights Act of the mid-1960s. Our conversations were about local, state, and federal victories. It was an important time to ask, What did we gain? How was society transformed? What remained to be done? In order to lay the groundwork for the ruptures in the movement that occurred in the mid-1960s through the early 1970s, I asked students to characterize the types of gains that the movement had made to that point. We slowly arrived at the collective understanding that the movement had gained acknowledgment of civil rights for African Americans, or rights that pertained to people's relationship to governmental or legal institutions. As students discussed the importance of the Civil Rights Act of 1964 and the Voting Rights Act of 1965, they emphasized the importance of the gains that were made. As we turned our attention away from the early civil rights movement, we moved to the Mississippi march of 1966, in which the call to "black power" began to define different ends and means for many in the struggle for social justice.

I had not anticipated the ways in which students would interpret the shift in the focus of the movement that occurred in the mid-1960s. In their responses I came to see that students felt that justice existed not only in acts of Congress but also in the freedom of individuals to assert and express their identities. Two documents framed our understanding of the differences between the early, southern

[handwritten margin note: Purpose of Civil Disobd. and Passive Resistance]

---

[3]"Pilgrimage to Non-Violence." 1984.

[handwritten note: What different branches of Social Studies?]

Daniel Gallo ■ 81

civil rights movement and the black power movement that emerged later—Stokeley Carmichael's "What We Want"[4] and the Black Panther Party for Self-Defense's Platform and Program.[5] Both documents assert that African Americans were unjustly denied not only civil rights but economic and social rights that would help them to gain power and foster a distinct identity. The Black Panther party sought to "center" itself in the struggle against oppression by including a segment of the Declaration of Independence in its platform and program. Rather than seek assimilation into the "mainstream" of American life, Carmichael and the Panthers asserted that their distinct identity and struggles were not unlike earlier struggles in American history.

Student responses to both pieces demonstrated that they understood the ways in which the black power movement differed from earlier movements. I also found that the discussion we had about rights had paid off in that students could identify the extent of newer demands. Kyle offered what was perhaps the most intense characterization of the new demands. After writing of the ways in which the black power movement "upped the ante," he closed his journal entry with "You can't eat the Bill of Rights." Like Kyle, many students saw the addition of economic rights and the call for black power and autonomy as important distinguishing factors of the movement. Sarah wrote, "Stokeley Carmichael thought that the movement was not going anywhere or helping anything. He and the Black Panther party wanted concrete things, with no room for compromise." Just as Sarah had, many students clearly heard the voice of the black power movement. Dylan wrote, "Stokeley's action said, 'Give me my rights or I'll take them.'" Students seemed to feel that injustice should be met with an immediate remedy.

A critical part of understanding the black power movement involved looking at the strong assertion of a distinct African-American identity. We looked at the rise of black identity in the period, at the donning of dashikis and the embracing of Afro hairstyles. We listened to the words of James Brown in "Say It Loud, I'm Black and I'm Proud."[6] Students seemed energized by the call for a strong identity, by the black power movement's refusal to have its dreams defined as acceptance into white middle-class society. The rejection of assimilation and the forging of a distinct identity—along with increasing demands—all captured the students' attention.

While watching a segment of the documentary *All Power to the People,* I was struck by how strongly the Panthers called out to the imaginations of my students. During an interview with the animated Bobby Seale, students sat in rapt attention.

---

[4]Stokeley Carmichael, 1984, In "What We Want," *The Sixties Papers,* ed. Judith Albert. (New York: Praeger).

[5]Black Panther Party for Self-Defense Platform and Program, 1984, In *The Sixties Papers,* ed. Judith Albert (New York: Praeger).

[6]James Brown, 1984, "Say It Loud, I'm Black and I'm Proud." 1984, *In Search of Color Everywhere: A Collection of African-American Poetry,* ed. Ethelbert Miller. (New York: Stewart, Tabori & Chang).

When Seale told of the first armed Panther patrol in Oakland, California, and the first "clack, clack" of shotguns in a staredown with a white officer making an arrest, I heard voices in the back of the room: "Oh, man, that's tight!" "Yeah!" I wondered if it was simply the romanticization of violence that called to the students or whether the Black Panther mission had captured them. The shotguns, berets, leather jackets, and sunglasses fit so snugly with contemporary renderings of adolescent cool that I found myself uncertain of the meaning of their enthusiasm.

Many students wrote that they thought the pinnacle of achievement during the civil rights movement came from the Panthers and the black power movement. David wrote, "The civil rights movement didn't start to make extreme progress until it got violent, but the violence came at the right time." When I noticed so many journals with similar assertions, I asked the class to give me examples of advances that were made when parts of the movement embraced violence as a means by which to realize their vision. Although students could have mentioned the education programs, soup kitchens, medical assistance, or escort services for the elderly that the Panthers provided in the late 1960s and early 1970s as examples, none of them explained their statements. Once again, I started to speculate. I wondered if the advancement they were talking about was the assertion of black African-American identity. It's possible that students who are themselves struggling to foster a distinct identity find a resonance in the Panthers. Perhaps they saw the struggle to broaden the American mosaic, to include a distinct vision of African Americans in the center of social, economic, and political life, as a move toward social justice.

In our three-week exploration of the civil rights movement, we traced the contours of the early civil rights movement and of the call to black power. We studied nonviolence and sought to understand its underpinnings. We also looked at the frustrations with the early civil rights movement and the rise of new identities out of that frustration. As I reflect on our time together I believe that most students found something much deeper than a collection of events now three decades past: They found compelling ideas. One student's words, written at the end of his journal, called out to me. Dylan, a student often "off task" or absent, blessed me with these words at the end of our time together

> Eliminate hate. Moral high ground. Spread love around. This is probably the coolest thing I've learned all year. These concepts are holy to me. I think the ability to act passive physically and strong spiritually will bring immense power and control and love.

At the end of our year together I found that I agreed with Dylan: The unit on the civil rights movement was the coolest thing we learned all year. As historian Vincent Harding had told me in a midnight read, it is critical that students understand the transformations that occurred in American society during this time and the ways in which the movement brought people to articulate their visions of a more just society. After our study of the movement, I found that my deepest hope was that my students were out in the world doing the same.

Scope of
Unit

Reference

Harding, Vincent. 1991. *Hope and History: Why We Must Share the Story of the Movement*. Mary Knoll, NY: Orbis Books.

7 Social Justice and Vietnam
A Conversation Around Literature, History, and Teaching

Michael Jarmer

This Is How it Begins

What happens when the theme of justice is introduced in a graduate-level course for teachers? What happens when the course is not educational theory or practice but subject-matter–specific, in this case, a cross-listed social studies and language arts course called "Vietnam and the United States"? It strikes me that the study of justice may seem most at home in a social studies curriculum, but this course gave me an opportunity to explore how the two disciplines could speak to each other in ways that would make the theme of justice more vivid, more complex, and more relevant to my students' lives and work. Further, it gave me the opportunity to explore with teachers and teachers-in-training the question of what role justice should play in our curriculum and classrooms.

Having taught "Vietnam and the United States" only one other time, this was not the way I had previously framed the course, nor was it a lens through which I was in the habit of asking students to look at the material. But certainly it was something we must have talked about. Even if we never used the words "social justice" in our discussions, dealing with subject matter as powerful as the Vietnam War specifically, and war in general, it must have been impossible for us to avoid issues of morality, ethics, what was right and wrong, just or unjust about the war. I was sure of it. But I was equally sure that I was going into this particular study with only these kinds of vague recollections and cloudy theories about how the theme of social justice came into play through my class on Vietnam. I was working with a clean slate. And I was nervous. Happily, what I discovered most of all is that, with very little prodding on my part, the theme of justice would poke its gnarly head out at almost every turn. And later when I did prod, the theme was taken up enthusiastically, rigorously, and with various, fascinating results and implications for the study of the Vietnam War, for our teaching, and for the students' learning.

It's wonderful how these things turn out. You're presented with a problem, and when you face the thing once and for all, even if with the foggiest notions about how to proceed, things begin to happen. I walked into class on the first day, without having revised my syllabus to "appease" the theme, or without having devised some great project that would sufficiently touch on the target, and simply shared with the teachers who were my students, as I had asked them to do, what my own personal learning goals were for the class. I told them that my learning goal was to do some thinking and writing about social justice in the context of the Vietnam War, and that I would like to enlist their help with that. I expressed my misgivings about how to move forward; I figured that on this first day, I would just plant some seeds, and then later I'd come back to water.

A Snapshot of the Class

I'd like to tell you a few things about these students before I describe the stewardship of the seeds I had planted. Lewis & Clark is a private liberal arts school with graduate departments in teacher education, counseling psychology, and administrative education. Classes tend to run small and are highly personalized. In this particular session, my class load was seven! I had one student from administrative education, four new students and one finishing up in the masters of arts in teaching (M.A.T.) preservice program, and one more in the M.A.T. inservice program. The administrative education student and the M.A.T. inservice student had significant teaching experience under their belts. But only the administrative student was old enough to have "experienced" the war in any way. Fred graduated from high school in 1973 just as Nixon was withdrawing American troops from Vietnam in large numbers. Fred did not serve; he just missed the draft, but as a high school and college student he was involved in the peace movement. The only other student with significant ties to Vietnam was a young preservice M.A.T. student named Ben. On an earlier quest to travel the world, Ben and his traveling companion found themselves in Vietnam and liked their experience there so much they stayed four months.

Outside of Ben's incredibly tangible Vietnam experience, the class, with the exception of Fred, knew little about the American war experience in Vietnam outside of what they gleaned through a reading here and there, a tiny exposure to it in high school history perhaps, and through the prevalence of Hollywood Vietnam films from the 1980s. The class, I think, was ripe for this conversation about justice. There were enough holes in their awareness and knowledge about our war in Vietnam so that they had not made up their minds. They did not come to class, it seemed to me, with opinions or beliefs that would cloud a discussion about justice in Vietnam. It was important to me, as we were tackling a controversial and emotionally charged body of work, that the forum for discussion was both open-ended and open-minded. And because I believe that this particular history and this kind of literature is often poorly represented in many high school curriculums, I believed that a good, safe experience here would make more likely their competent and comfortable use of the material in their own schools.

Finally, a "Plan"

So I had introduced on the very first day of class the idea of looking at justice, particularly social justice, in the context of the Vietnam War. I had asked for their help, but as I have said, I did not know how I would approach the subject with them or what kind of help I wanted. Initially I agonized over this. I feared being too directive, or narrowing the lens of our study, or putting an artificial thematic structure over our work together. I wanted them to learn from their understandings and constructions of justice, not from prodding them into my own. And personally, I wanted to travel along with them, to make my own discoveries, deepen my own understanding.

Without a preconceived plan about how to take them to this discussion, what actually happened was that I taught the course as I had planned to teach it, and I put aside about two and half hours at the end to explore the justice theme. Fortunately, though, it was my perception that students were intrigued from the beginning by the idea. They seemed sincerely engaged by the proposition. Perhaps it is that justice is simply a topic with some intrinsic value to most folks, perhaps even more so to people in the teaching profession. But initially, I think, they were fascinated by the seemingly incongruous pairing: Vietnam and justice. When we think about Vietnam, it may be our natural tendency to think only about the dearth of such a thing as justice. So would this conversation simply turn to a kind of laundry listing of atrocities and outrages and crimes against humanity? Would we find "justice in Vietnam" an oxymoron? Or would we discover other kinds of justice, outside of the purely legal kind, somewhere along the way? For whatever reason, the students seemed ready to tackle this theme, and I would realize fairly quickly that questions about ethics, about what is right and wrong and fair would come up again and again without any real direction from the teacher. And this helped me come away with the first of the many little learning nuggets I would glean along the path: If you present students with material that is rich in posing questions and raising issues of justice or ethics or morality, the conversation naturally turns in that direction. And/or: If you plant the seeds, that is, simply tell students you are interested in a particular issue, they may rise to the occasion in an effort to help or to share in the endeavor.

Justice Rears its Head: The Work in Literature Circles

It was as if the writers I had chosen for the course had come to my rescue. They knew I was struggling. First up were Bao Ninh (1993) and Tim O'Brien (1991). By a fortunate accident, the two literature circle study groups chose *The Sorrow of War* and *The Things They Carried* respectively, offering two complementary pieces of the same puzzle, the perspective of the foot soldier or "grunt" in Vietnam, one North Vietnamese, one American.

I'd like to begin by discussing Sheila's work, an experienced teacher moving from the French language classroom to the language arts classroom. She was in the Tim O'Brien literature circle, working through the short story collection *The Things They Carried*. Her first paper in response to that text seemed to me a wonderful place to begin the conversation about justice. It was from a more personal point of view, the idea that justice is a thing that begins within each individual, and she saw several examples in O'Brien's collection. Sheila chose to write about the conflict between "popular opinion and personal integrity," focusing on several stories where the protagonists were put in situations where the struggle between what was right for them personally butted up against societal expectations, or pressures put on them by the war in general or by fellow soldiers specifically. She wrote about the external pressures experienced by the narrator of "On the Rainy River," a young man on his way to Canada to escape the war who ends up returning home and serving in Vietnam because he was afraid not to. "It had nothing to do with morality. Embarrassment, that's all it was" (O'Brien, 1991, p. 62). Sheila found another powerful example in the character of Norman Bowker, who is haunted by his father's expectations. She wrote, "Bowker punishes himself for not winning the Silver Star, preoccupied by an imaginary conversation with his father about the medals he won, and the one he did *not* win." Sheila was noticing the ethical dilemma in the situation: the societal pressures perceived by these young men prevent them from making moral choices. Sheila made some giant connections between the choices these soldiers must make and the choices that all of us must make. She concluded,

> For O'Brien and the other soldiers he writes about, the struggle between outside pressure and personal conscience is profound. So profound in fact that it haunts them years after the decisions were made. The Vietnam War amplifies that struggle, but it is one that every human being must fight at one time or another. Indeed one of the lessons we may learn from reading *The Things They Carried* is that we must do our best to live consciously."

In discussing both O'Brien stories, Sheila was exploring the way guilt and shame worked on these veterans of the war, a statement, I think, about the psychological and emotional injustice of the Vietnam experience.

The group that tackled Bao Ninh's *The Sorrow of War* found its connection between justice and Vietnam more directly in the text. I asked the groups at the end of their study to prepare a presentation through which they would share what they had learned from their novel. Included as part of that presentation was a short reading from the text, to give their classmates a feel for the sound and style of their novel. Fred chose to read the following passage:

> The wind of war had stopped. The branches of conflict had stopped rustling. As we had won, Kien thought, then that meant justice had won; that had been some consolation. Or had it? Think carefully; look at your own existence. Look carefully now at the peace we have, painful, bitter, and sad. And look at who won the war.
>
> To win, martyrs had sacrificed their lives in order that others might survive. Not a new phenomenon, true. But for those still living to know that the kindest, most worthy people had all fallen away, or even been tortured, humiliated before being killed, or buried and wiped away by the machinery of war, then this beautiful landscape of calm and peace is an appalling paradox. Justice may have won, but cruelty, death, and inhuman violence have also won.
> Just look and think: it is the truth.
> Losses can be made good, damage can be repaired, and wounds will heal in time. But the psychological scars of war will remain forever. (Ninh, 1993, p.193)

Bao Ninh was speaking directly to us about the paradox of "winning" the war for the North Vietnamese, and the shallow nature of the justice that was served for them. But Ninh was speaking on a more personal level to Fred, who shared with me that throughout the reading, he was having revelations about his own history with the war as a result of his interaction with Ninh's novel. It was helping to relieve some of the residual guilt he had felt throughout his entire adult life for not serving in Vietnam. Reading about how the "enemy" had no more enthusiasm for the struggle than Americans had, perhaps, gave him a perspective he needed to make sense of his own resistance; his peace efforts had been validated. Some personal justice for Fred: a coming to terms with the past, an acceptance of his own history, and forgiveness.

In terms of "personal justice," the group studying Le Ly Hayslip's *When Heaven and Earth Changed Places,* during our second round of literature circles, found a wellspring of redemption, spiritual growth, forgiveness, and reconciliation coming from the experience of a woman whose life in Vietnam during the war had been a living hell. I was struck, listening to their presentation, by how profoundly moved they all were by this memoir. It seemed to them to be a fitting and healing place to conclude the study of Vietnam, with a woman who, after the ravages of the war on her homeland, on her family, and on her own physical and spiritual well-being, immigrated to the United States, and returned to Vietnam ten years later to reunite with her family. Ben wrote in his paper, aptly titled "Hope": "In the end, when her family unites at Tinh's house, Bay Le [Le Ly Hayslip] comes full circle and experiences a sense of closure. Maybe this is an aspect of social justice: the feeling that old ghosts have been dealt with and unclosed loops connected. From here, our lives may begin a fresh path." For their presentation, Ben's group read their own "remix poems" inspired by the book. Ben's poem "Circles," about the earlier reunion of Le Ly and her mother in a modernized hotel in Vietnam, echoes what he wrote about in his paper:

> And I hope you and your son
> Will learn charity and forgiveness
> Through my example.
> Remember, Bay Ly, it's easy
> To be charitable when
> You're powerful and rich;
> It's more difficult when you're needy
> But that's when it counts the most.
> I sowed kindness, and you can see
> The crop we harvest.
> One word of forgiveness
> Brings back nine gentle favors.

Rather than floating from one literature circle group to another as an observer, I decided, mostly because I could not stand to disengage myself from the "action," to participate each time in one of the groups as an equal member. I chose whichever group had three members, so that the two literature circles would have an even number of participants. I'm glad I made that choice; it put me in the position of doing the same work my students were doing and changed my status in the classroom from one of being the expert to being just another traveler or learner. It is the kind of status I wish I could experience more often in a high school setting. But alas, my teaching with adolescents has not evolved to that point yet. But I digress. This is all a way of moving into my own thoughts about the novel I read with my second literature circle group. We found yet another take on justice emerging from the classic 1955 Graham Greene novel, *The Quiet American,* in which an English journalist expedites the demise of a young gung-ho American Office of Strategic Services (OSS) man who is in over his head and doing far more harm than good in a country he knows little to nothing about. My job in our literature circle presentation was to provide a thematic overview of our novel. What follows is what I said, in part, about that:

This book is about two forces: One is a force that works on the very best of intentions and causes irreparable damage. Pyle [the American O.S.S. man] is that force, and he represents, foremost, America's involvement and (from hindsight) subsequent defeat in Vietnam. It is clear he has no business there. It is clear he knows nothing about this place. It is clear he is in way over his head. And Fowler [the English journalist] realizes how dangerous he really is. "Innocence is a kind of insanity" (Greene, p. 213). And Fowler represents another force. He represents another kind of innocence—the innocent bystander, the objective reporter, someone who is disengaged from life and the war. He's just doing his job and has no stakes in the outcome. But he is, despite his nihilism, a highly moral individual, and he is forced, "in a moment of emotion," to take a stand against Pyle and to make the ultimate moral choice. He sets Pyle up for assassination.

Justice is served in this novel on a few different levels for the hero. In a time and place in which social justice is not often forthcoming, where political and military alliances between France and the United States prevent both countries from holding each other accountable, Fowler, by cooperating with "the enemy" and setting up Pyle, takes justice into his own hands. In doing so, he learns what it means to allow oneself to "get involved." The perfect moral dilemma. The same dilemma found its way into our "justice" discussion later on, when Jerry, a young beginning teacher, presented us with a hypothetical situation not unlike Fowler's: If you had the opportunity to "off" Hitler, knowing what you know now about what would happen in the world if you didn't, would you do it? When social justice takes a hiatus, we find examples of individuals whose personal ethics spur them into action.

The Justice Discussion

I warned the class a few days in advance. I told them that I was setting aside an hour on each of the last two days. During that time we'd have a final pow-wow on the theme of justice as we saw it connected to our study of the Vietnam War. I asked their permission to record the conversations. I asked them to do a little bit of thinking over the theme before they arrived. I suggested, but did not require, that they do a little log writing in preparation. As we approached the last two days of class we had a significant amount of reading under our hats—the novels and memoir we covered in our literature circles and Stanley Karnow's book *Vietnam: A History*. We had traversed enormous ground. We had learned much together. But justice? What would we have to say about justice? My plan was to start with a working definition of justice, and then more specifically, to do a little brainstorming about what we perceived as being just and unjust about the war in Vietnam. Then I hoped to move to a more general and philosophical discussion about relevancy. Was the theme or concept of justice a crucial one in our curricula, and why? And finally, to get more specific again, how can we approach the topic of justice in the context of this kind of history, where, on the surface, justice seems to be intangible? As of this writing I'm beginning to see how that may be an important way of studying something we value, by looking carefully at its absence in a particular time and place! My ultimate goal, though, since we were all in the education game together, was to arrive at a place in the conversation where we were talking about how the issue of justice in our classrooms could intersect with the lives of our students.

Justice? What Justice?

First, we had to define the animal and see if we could agree about what justice was. I think Carol was the first to speak. "I don't think it exists," she said. There was an awkward moment or two. And then we realized that despite whether or not we thought it exists, we were still looking to define it. There was some talk immediately following concerning "law," how laws are made, and how we entrust our elected officials to vote into law bills that are "just." Garrit defined justice as "a loose collection of moral norms that are enforced, in part, by the courts." There was then a discussion about the intersection and/or separation of the personal perception of justice and the public perception—what is just behavior to an individual may not be just behavior according to law. To confuse matters, "There are unjust laws," someone said. Jerry said that "Our vision or definition of justice depends on our interpretation of the social contract." Another person brought up that time-honored notion of the impartiality of justice: "Justice is blind." And back again to the conflict between the personal and the social, Ben added that he thought all justice originates in the individual. Looking back at this paragraph, it's clear we were a long way off from consensus on the matter. In the end, I read to them Webster's offering, and it seemed, happily, that even in our haphazard approach, we had touched on most of the issues raised by this dictionary definition. This is not to say that arriving at the dictionary definition was our goal; we just needed a place to start, a jumping-off point.

We then transitioned into a brainstorming session in partnerships in order to come up with examples of justice specific to what we had learned about the Vietnam War. I think the list they came up with is interesting enough for inclusion here. If an item was mentioned once, I added it to the list. A tally mark indicates each successive mention of the same item. It's helpful to remember there are only seven students and myself represented here, four partnerships—so an item with three tallies indicates that it was chosen by every group:

Injustices in Vietnam

Economic disparity regarding the draft—|||

Civilian casualties/peasant casualties—||

Diem's rigging/interference in South Vietnam elections—||

Corruption of South Vietnamese government

Obstruction of the truth

Peasants caught in the middle, harassed by both sides—|

Peasants forced to make choices based on survival, not on true belief or real loyalty

Bay Le (Le Ly Hayslip) excommunicated unfairly by Viet Cong

Free elections promised by Geneva Convention never occurred—|

Manipulation of media by U.S. government and military

Illegal bombing of North Vietnam and Cambodia

Diem's murder—|

The strategic hamlet program

Communist government's land reform programs

Millions of deaths for essentially political ends

Lack of justification for U.S. involvement in Vietnam

The rape of Bay Le (Le Ly Hayslip)

Soldiers' fragging (assassination) of superior officers

The My Lai Massacre—perpetrators went unpunished

Veterans mistreated on their return—no effort made to reintegrate them or provide them with essential services

Nixon's covert activities—Watergate—|

Due process circumvented

Violence against protesters in United States—at the Democratic National Convention/Kent State

Imposition of democracy and other Western principles on Vietnam

Manufacturing consent after Gulf of Tonkin incident

President given indiscriminate powers to wage war without congressional support

Justice in Vietnam

Nixon's resignation—|||

America's awareness of its own limitations, both morally and militarily

Lessons learned from Vietnam have shaped U.S. foreign policy

Effectiveness of public protest—||

Media became openly critical of government

Out of the My Lai trials: the concept that an officer has a moral and legal obligation to refuse an immoral or unethical order gained prominence

Success of the Communists to unify Vietnam and become independent—||

The way that guilt or conscience has worked on those involved (especially government officials)

Reunion of Bay Le's family (Le Ly Hayslip)

Diem's murder—|

Diem's overthrow

One-year tour of duty for an American officer

The end of imperialist rule in Vietnam

Mandarin societal structure a thing of the past

One particular item of interest for us was the inclusion of the murder of South Vietnamese President Ngo Dinh Diem on both lists. There was some controversy in the room, I remember, concerning this item. Diem was ineffectual and corrupt. But the U.S. government put him there, and rather than finding some "just" way or *truly* democratic way of removing him from office, the evidence suggests that they conspired, at first to instigate, later to allow, his violent overthrow. They neglected to warn him or to provide safe passage for him when they knew his overthrow was imminent. It goes back again to the hypothetical situation Jerry presented us with during these discussions. Is violence justified to prevent other violence? Jerry, through the course of the reading and thinking he was doing about this topic, finally came to the conclusion that it was not. "I'm turning into a Gandhi," he said in our discussion. "Two weeks ago I thought that yes, violence can be just." He had changed his mind, "especially after Hayslip," he said, citing the epilogue in *When Heaven and Earth Changed Places* as having the greatest impact on his thinking. And some final words on the subject from Jerry's last log entry: "Something has happened in my thinking in the last few weeks that has made me aware of the 'slippery slope' that violence represents. If you take a utilitarian argument toward justifying violence as I would have—you must eventually arrive at the point where you end up splitting hairs as to the value of a human life—Is one good guy worth more than a bad guy?—How much is an innocent worth?—Is it worth killing innocents to get a bad guy to save other innocents? It becomes pretty screwed up." No one else was very convincing on the other side of the argument. Diem's murder helped no one. It made no positive contribution other than paving the way for other equally ineffectual and corrupt puppet leaders in South Vietnam.

A final word about generating these lists: My initial assumption was that students would have a difficult time thinking of examples where justice prevailed in some way in Vietnam. As is evident from the list, I was mistaken. Sure, there were less overall examples of this than there were of its opposite, but they found them nevertheless. Some of those items are stretches. I am not sure that a one-year tour of duty constitutes any kind of "justice." Perhaps it is in our nature to right the wrongs of history—to find, in our most challenging or desperate moments, glimmers of hope and of justice. No piece of history, even the most horrific, is devoid of goodness and dignity altogether.

Reflections on Justice in our Own Classrooms: a Conclusion

After this initial defining and brainstorming session, the question I posed was exactly this: Is the concept of justice an important one in our curricula? Jerry said, without hesitation, "Absolutely. . . . it's where we should start." After a general nod of agreement spun around the room, the subsequent responses set us going into a kind of tailspin that took us far away from Vietnam, but really, to the heart of the matter as far as teaching goes, into our classrooms and into our students' lives.

Jerry went on to talk about the challenges of working with a diverse student body and the demands on teachers to spend more time with some students than they do with others. "Justice does not mean equality," he said. And then he posed the suggestion that we must "teach justice from the actual interactions between people."

I think it was Ben who considered the teaching of justice to be a kind of awareness raising: "Kids need to realize there are discrepancies." Garrit came back at that with a warning about the dangers of a gloom-and-doom approach. "Just to tell students that society is unjust—I don't think you're telling them anything new," he said. And he went on to suggest that a classroom that teaches justice is one that models democratic principles. "When the behavior is modeled, when they feel like democracy *works*, then they feel encouraged to take it to the next level."

And Fred, from his experience as an administrator in an inner-city school, passionately argued that he deals with justice in the classroom every single day. Fred talked about the importance of a nurturing environment. "Create a classroom where you have self-directed learners, where kids are allowed to do appropriate and personalized work. They will progress."

I concluded then that the teaching of justice has a lot to do with the way we set up our classrooms and the way we treat individual kids. I made an effort here to bring the discussion back to Vietnam somehow. I posed a second question: In the context of the Vietnam War specifically, or a study of any war or any historical tragedy, how do we ask our students to approach the concept of justice in a way that will make some kind of significant impact on their learning and on their lives?

Ben talked about how the study of war gives us very concrete examples of justice. "You're going to have winners and losers," he said, and he talked about the importance of having students study both points of view. Only by looking at multiple perspectives can students determine for themselves what is right, or, as Ben put it, "What is reality?" I imagine that Ben, like many of us often do, was thinking of justice in terms of who is victorious when the smoke clears, as if the act of "winning" was some determination of which side was "right."

Sheila warned against the study of justice in war becoming a discussion about who wins or loses. She wanted something deeper; she wanted students reaching some understanding. She wanted students to go beyond the catalogue of corruption and into envisioning the world that they wanted to live in, and learning how to bring that vision of the world into reality by their own actions. "I'm going to exemplify the way I want the world to be. If everyone did that, we'd be okay."

Matt, with his understanding about how much horror is inherent in *honestly* teaching the content of the Vietnam War, expressed some real misgivings and fear about approaching these controversial and disturbing realities in a classroom of young people. "How do I accurately teach them what happened? How many things am I going to have to omit because it's not appropriate for kids to know that little babies were gunned down, or that North Vietnamese soldiers burned with liquid petroleum until there was no flesh and bone left to burn. What type of things are appropriate? And that was the truth; that is part of understanding what was just or unjust about the Vietnam War. Justice is historical, it's about action, and it's also about controversy, it's about the issues we don't agree on, it's about debate—and I see a big problem in honestly doing that in the classroom."

It was a huge issue. And a good place, I think, to conclude. Matt was worried about students' misunderstandings, he was worried about accidentally leading students to inaccurate or misinformed conclusions. And I think he was worried about being too heavy-handed, or too directive, too political perhaps. "You really have to be careful about what you say."

Jerry, the young intern about to embark on his first job in an alternative city school, and no stranger to controversy, helped us, finally, with this dilemma: "I don't think you need to be too careful. If you are in this game, you better have your ideas and your feelings on things pretty well straight, and you might as well just accept the fact that as a teacher you're going to have to teach from who you are and what you believe. You're not teaching them to *be* what you are, but you need to be able to *own* statements. 'Jeremy, I understand your position; in fact, I understand how you're justifying it because I've seen other people with that argument before. I, personally, don't feel that way, but as your teacher it's my job to tease your thoughts out a little further, to grow you. That is my job, so I'm going to ask you to think about this,'" Jerry gave us a pause, a place for that important question, followed by this directive for Jeremy: " 'Now, write a paragraph!'"

I was happy with the results of our discussion. It was one of those moments in a classroom—no consensus was reached, no huge problem was collectively solved, no prescription or recipe was found for all of us to walk away with; but even so, we felt a sense of the ideas buzzing, and of the importance of the talk, and that we shared together a commitment to pursuing a line of inquiry about social justice in our classrooms. As a result, whether these teachers teach the history and literature of the Vietnam War or not, hundreds of adolescents will benefit from their experience, their wisdom, and their thoughtfulness. Their classrooms will be places where history and literature speak to each other, and where justice is discussed, practiced, and made real for students. And I was thinking about justice even in our last moments together: we had finished our last literature circle presentations, Le Ly Hayslip had done much to help us on our way to healing the wounds left by the legacy of the Vietnam War, and finally, Ben performed for us a song he had written, inspired by his travels to the actual place we had been reading about and agonizing over throughout our four weeks together. "Hooray, Vietnam," he was singing, a celebration of what was good and intact in both that country and ours. Even that is a powerful kind of justice.

References

Butler, Robert Olen. 1993. *A Good Scent from a Strange Mountain*. New York: Penguin.

Erhardt, W. D. 1985. *Carrying the Darkness*. Texas: Texas Tech University Press.

Greene, Graham. 1992. *The Quiet American*. New York: Modern Library.

Hayslip, Le Ly, with Jay Wurts. 1989. *When Heaven and Earth Changed Places*. New York: Doubleday.

Herr, Michael. 1978. *Dispatches*. New York: Avon.

Huong, Duong Thu. 1994. *Paradise of the Blind*. New York: Penguin.

Karnow, Stanley. 1997. *Vietnam: A History*. New York: Penguin.

McNamara, Robert S. 1996. *In Retrospect: The Tragedy and Lessons of Vietnam*. New York: Random House.

Ninh, Bao. 1993. *The Sorrow of War*. New York: Pantheon.

O'Brien, Tim. 1991. *The Things They Carried*. New York: Penguin.

Sheehan, Neil. 1988. *A Bright Shining Lie*. New York: Random House.

8

Students in the Soup Kitchen

Mary Burke-Hengen and Gregory Smith

If you are poor, there are many things you do not take for granted. The shape of your shoes may have been determined by a sibling or an earlier, more prosperous wearer. Choice in food may mean whether to eat what's on the menu of giveaways for the day or be hungry. If you are young and living in a stable but poor situation, your right to a free and public education means that you must go to a place where your smell may cause others to move away from you and where you will spend most of the day learning about people, events, and ideas that do not honor or even seriously include you. If a tooth becomes infected, it will likely be pulled, but if you are depressed—an almost invariable result of poverty—your withdrawal will scarcely be noticed. If you are poor, you are expected to be invisible, and that is as true in schools as it is in stores, churches, and office buildings. You are a symbol of failure in the society, the reminder that not everyone makes it, or can make it, and that not everything works as promised; in a class society, the "trickle down" stopped two rungs above you. For a child of poverty, food and shelter must be attended to before school is attended, and school may be a place where shame and distancing make learning difficult or impossible.

Few teachers are prepared to empathize with the experience of poor children. Those who have not been poor themselves cannot know how education seems like a luxurious extra when survival is tenuous, or how difficult it is to concentrate on anything other than food when hungry, or what it is like to be an outsider to a myriad of assumptions about life: that a parent or parents have enough energy to notice their children, that they can afford any of the things commonly advertised to children, that your family has never been part of the group who, so the story goes, through hard work and patriotic purpose formed this country into a great land of opportunity. What poor children know as reality is that they are worried about getting their needs met, that everything must be fought for as well as earned. Small medical conditions become crises, and anger often circles around looking for the match of another humiliation before exploding in a fire that they fear may consume them at the hands of a parent. Teachers who have not lived these realities too easily disregard the sheer difficulty of showing up to school and fail to understand clearly that their job is to find their strengths and talents even when these are buried in a crust of defensiveness or tied to a bundle of worries.

During the spring of 1998, we discussed our thoughts and feelings about how well poor children were and were not being served by the Lewis & Clark Teacher Education Program. How many of our graduates, we wondered, had the knowledge and understanding of poverty that would even begin to prepare them to serve this population? We both agreed that there were no more books we wanted to add to reading lists, no discussions that we believed would result in needed changes. The "insufficiency of abstractions" became a theme of our discussions. We began to craft a class that would take interns into places in Portland where they could experience some aspects of "living poor."

Making the Abstract Personal

At the heart of our effort to develop in students a sense of direct connectedness with people experiencing poverty was a coupling of personal encounters in local shelters or soup kitchens to readings or films that challenge common assumptions about the poor and the safety nets provided by our society to support them. Because our society tends to brush the poor to the margins of our consciousness as well as our communities, we wanted to help students overcome the common tendency to see the poor as threats or as unaesthetic intrusions into the well-ordered opulence of urban life. In the past, people in smaller communities could not help but interact with individuals and families who had few resources and prospects. Today, it is easy to insulate ourselves from the "unfortunate" or the "ugly." And by isolating ourselves from those who would benefit from our support, we lose the capacity to identify with their needs in ways that might lead to generosity or advocacy.

The Dalai Lama in his book *Ethics for a New Millennium* (1999), suggests that ethical thinking and behavior are grounded in a sense of interconnectedness. Because we have the capacity to grasp our relatedness to others, we seek to protect them from harm and preserve their happiness. In another context, Stephen J. Gould (1991) has argued that we cannot love what we do not know. For us, the willingness to work for social justice is based on the capacity to care. From this course about hunger and homelessness, we wanted our students to begin to know the poor as people with stories not so different from the stories of people they loved. Our hope was that from this experience of relatedness they would come to advocate for poor students in the way they would advocate for those already within their circle of care.

Schools remain one of the last hopes for many impoverished families. Although the odds are against poor kids making it in school, those who do, acquire knowledge and capacities that will allow them to create opportunities denied to their parents. Teachers can be instrumental in this process, but their attitudes and assumptions often prevent them from establishing the positive relationships that generally undergird successful learning. Their often unconscious judgments, distaste, condemnation, or fear serve to block students from discovering and realizing their own potential. We wanted to unsettle our students in ways that would lead them to question the stereotypes they held about the poor and develop a willingness to dismantle whatever personal hesitancies might prevent them from becoming closer to children who at the outset might appear unlikable or unapproachable. We wanted them to begin to reach across to the other before they judged and attempted to correct.

We did not know how to accomplish any of these goals. We did know that we felt a profound distance from the community in our own work at Lewis & Clark College. The nature of our responsibilities tended to isolate us and prevent us from interacting with the people we most wanted to serve. A class that made service to the community part of those responsibilities would meet our own need for interconnection and meaning. We hoped that by participating with our students in work that linked us to street kids and impoverished adults, we might uncover ways to enhance our own capacity to care and respond.

Since the course was being offered for only one semester hour of credit, students would anticipate no more than 15 hours of class meetings—not much time to realize our intentions. Knowing, however, that all the participants in this course had full academic plates and internships in local schools or mental health agencies, we understood that we could not ask much more from them than this. We scheduled the class to meet for five 3-hour blocks on Fridays between September 11 and December 11. The course would begin and end with whole-group meetings, the first of these providing an opportunity for everyone to meet one another and become oriented to how the class would operate, and the last, a chance to come together to share our observations and look toward the future. In between these bookends, students would volunteer in groups of 3 to 12 at five local organizations willing to accept our services.

Our first class meeting had to accomplish a variety of tasks in a very short period of time. We needed to establish enough contact with students so they would feel confident about our capacity to guide them as they encountered people and places we knew, for at least some, would be unfamiliar and potentially frightening. We also needed to be able to explain the logistics of the class and expectations for participation in off-campus experiences where one of us might not always be present. In conjunction with this, students had to sign up for groups and volunteer slots that fit their schedules and the schedules of the participating agencies. Finally, we wanted to have everyone share an experience with regard to hunger and homelessness that would unsettle some of the beliefs about poverty we suspected a proportion of students probably carried with them. We felt that this piece of the first lesson was crucial because so much of the success of this class rested on the understandings about hunger and homelessness students would construct as a result of their work in the field.

We began the first class by dividing our twenty-six students—large by Lewis & Clark graduate school standards—into two groups. Each of us took one group and spent approximately fifteen minutes with introductions. We asked students to talk for no more than sixty seconds, indicating the professional program they were involved with, their reasons for taking the class, and any prior experience they had had with people who live on the economic margins of our society. These last two questions were very helpful in revealing students' intentions and their own level of experience working with the poor. Greg Lawler, for example, mentioned growing up on the edge of the Yale campus in New Haven in an area frequented by homeless people. His parents regularly provided them with food and assistance, priming Greg from childhood on to reach out to those with less than himself. Other class participants were completely new to this kind of work and saw the course as a valuable opportunity to become more knowledgeable about the life circumstances of some of their students or clients.

On regrouping, we dealt with some of the practical business of the class: passing out the syllabus and having students sign up for groups that would visit different clusters of sites on varying dates throughout the fall semester. We then showed the made-for-TV film *Hidden in America*. As mentioned earlier, we believe that the desire to advocate for the rights and welfare of others is predicated on the ability to identify with them and their needs. In the absence of such identification, people easily turn from those who might benefit from their assistance. The movie provided a way to establish the open and compassionate perspective we hoped students would bring to their time at the different volunteer sites. It depicts the experience of a family in Seattle that is experiencing hard times. The father, played by Beau Bridges, had worked in the automobile industry in the Midwest but had been laid off during the downsizing and automation that was prevalent in the early 1990s. After he lost his job on an assembly line, his wife was diagnosed with cancer. Caring for her during her illness exhausted all of the family's resources. After her death, he and his two children, a girl and a boy on either side of the cusp of puberty, move to the Pacific Northwest. A high school dropout, the only work he can find is as a part-time short-order cook in a fast-food restaurant. His earnings are not enough to both house and feed his family, and his daughter's health begins to suffer. The family eventually is forced to seek help from a food bank, something the father had told his son was an option only for losers. Nearly destroyed by these events, the father, by force of desperation and will, convinces a building foreman on a construction project that he should be hired. The movie ends with information about the number of hungry children in the United States and suggestions for citizen involvement.

Following the film, students broke into small groups to discuss their responses. A pivotal observation was that the film did not show educators involved whatsoever with the plight of this family, even though the daughter was clearly ill and the son, probably no more than thirteen years old, was cutting classes regularly to earn money to supplement his father's limited income. This observation provided a useful closing point, because it was the rectification of this lack of attention to impoverished students by teachers and counselors and their subsequent failure to advocate for and support them that we hoped to address through the course.

Out of the Classroom/Into the Community

During the next next three months, students incorporated into their coursework and internships three volunteer experiences with people who were encountering events similar to those described in the film. The sites we visited were varied and provided different lenses on the nature of poverty in our community. The St. Francis Dining Hall is a well-established institution in the near southeast section of Portland. On an average night, volunteers and staff serve a single sit-down dinner to over 200 people. During the day, people are welcome to spend time with one another on the grounds around the church that helps support the dining hall. Another dining hall operated by the Salvation Army is located in Portland's Old Town; it provides two dinners for residents of its homeless shelter and other drop-in diners. People who take meals at the Salvation Army are expected to participate in a short service before the first meal in a chapel adjoining the dining hall. In these sites, class members helped with meal preparation, serving, and clean-ups. At the St. Francis Dining Hall, in particular, students had many opportunities before, during, and after meals to speak with other diners. The West Women's and Children's Center serves women and their children who require temporary refuge in a secured setting as well as displaced women who are building a new life and need support while they become financially independent. Because of confidentiality and safety issues, students were not able to interact with residents of the center; staff members, however, provided a comprehensive overview about those who seek their support as well as the number of women in crisis who must be directed to other facilities because the center is fully occupied. While there, we painted a central living area and helped with sorting donations and cleaning. The Greenhouse Drop-In Center and New Avenues for Youth offer education and refuge to homeless youth. Both the Greenhouse and the West Women's and Children's Center are supported by the Salvation Army. At the Greenhouse, our students interacted with homeless youth and participated in some of their classes. At New Avenues for Youth, staff arranged for us to join in designing and painting a mural that would be hung in one of the central halls of the facility.

In preparation for these visits, we asked our students to observe some general guidelines. Included with these were the need to dress informally but appropriately, avoiding shorts or any tight clothing. We also asked them to think about topics they might wish to discuss in a respectful manner that would help them learn about hunger and homelessness. We suggested that they rely on comments that invite expansion and agreement or disagreement rather than direct questions. We also reminded them that some of the homeless or low-income people they spoke with might have mental or emotional disturbances, and that all would be likely to be under enough stress to make their contacts with them feel awkward. Despite this, we urged students to offer eye contact and a willingness to engage in conversation. Finally, we encouraged people to make the most of the experience, suggesting that they would not damage anyone by trying to converse. We reiterated the importance of keeping confidentiality and being prompt so as not to create any inconvenience for the institutions that were welcoming us.

To extend the meaning of these volunteer experiences, students discussed assigned readings each time we gathered. Together, we read selected chapters from Jonathan Kozol's *Rachel and Her Children* (1988), fact sheets from the National Coalition for the Homeless (see NCH's website, **www.nch.ari.net**), a chapter entitled "Dumpster Diving" from Lars Eighner's *Travels with Lizbeth* (1993), *The End of Work* by Jeremy Rifkin (1995), Robert Kates and Sara Millman's "On Ending Hunger: The Lessons of History" (1990) and much of Peter Medoff and Holly Sklar's detailed review of the link between governmental and economic policy and poverty in *The Streets of Hope* (1994). These readings combined personal narratives with more formal sociological analysis. In their written and oral reactions, students were especially moved and angered by Kozol's novelistic account of his interviews with homeless families. They were struck by the exploitive nature of apparently charitable institutions and questioned the legitimacy of conventional responses to hunger and homelessness. Others were impressed with Eighner's description of the amount of sustained labor required to survive on the streets. At the end of the semester, students valued Medoff and Sklar's well-documented account of the impact of corporate downsizing and governmental cutbacks on the poor. Medoff and Sklar's book provided information about the broader social context that can lead to poverty and offered students data they were able to bring to conversations about hunger and homelessness they reported having with skeptical friends and family members.

One of the differences between teaching in a classroom and teaching in the community is that planning can only go so far. The unexpected and serendipitous can come to play much larger roles in contributing to the learning of both students and teachers. At one of our first visits to the St. Francis Dining Hall, for example, a number of events served to underline and extend some of the themes we, as teachers, hoped students might encounter during the course. This particular evening was the last time one of the staff members would share a meal with the diners; she was going to return to Chicago after several months in Portland. A number of diners sought her out after this announcement and shared gifts and words of encouragement and thanks with her. The strength of community among the "regulars" at the dining hall was clearly evident, as was the generosity of spirit that existed among these people. Later, after we had helped with cleanup, two homeless people who volunteer at St. Francis in exchange for small lockers where they can keep some of their gear, joined us during our debrief. One gentleman talked about the value of having a dog when you are sleeping on the streets, because the dog will bark out a warning if a stranger approaches. He shared chocolates with all of us. Another regular, Mary, spoke at length with us about her own story and her decision to live on the streets because of the freedom this has offered her. Her narrative suggested that although living without a home can be filled with difficulties, people who find themselves in this situation can also exhibit intelligence, energy, and determination. What happened this evening served to dispel stereotypes about who the homeless are and what their lives are like.

New Avenues for Youth offered a different kind of experience. This program provides a drop-in center, job training and placement opportunities, and GED classes for young people who live on the streets. The week before our visit, a young man who had found his way to New Avenues had been able to obtain a job at a local department store thanks to a suit of clothes and the encouragement given to him by program staff. The mural painting project mentioned earlier offered a setting in which informal conversations among our students and New Avenues students could occur as they created something together. What emerged from this experience was knowledge about the interests, commitments, and talents of the adolescents who sat around the mural with us. They took genuine delight in their work, designing and executing sections of the mural with care. They also demonstrated an interest in coordinating their efforts and making something that would please other people at the center. Although little of a profound nature was shared during the time we and our students spent at New Avenues for Youth, our hours there showed us that these young people were not very different from high school students anywhere. Given the degree to which local merchants have tended to see these same individuals as little more than threats to their business, our opportunity to make something with them confirmed their value as people. Painting a mural drew out our commonalities, affirming what we shared rather than what was different.

At out final meeting of the class in mid-December, we shared what they had learned as a result of these community-based experiences and formulated plans for what they might do to address issues related to hunger and homelessness wherever they found themselves after being hired as teachers and counselors during the coming year. We had asked students to bring two things to class. The first was an artifact that spoke to them or served as a metaphor for their experiences at the different sites. The second was a "found poem" drawn from Medoff and Sklar's *The Streets of Hope*. We had instructed students to go through the book and find eight to twelve lines that addressed issues of concern to them and then to rearrange the lines, adding their own words until the poem made a statement they felt strongly about. Class opened with a "museum style" viewing of the artifacts and a poetry reading.

Students also came to class prepared to discuss and develop potential responses to two of the following issues related to hunger and homelessness:

- Caring for people who are mentally or physically challenged

- Caring for women and children who are victims of domestic violence

- Caring for people who suffer from drug and alcohol addiction

- Caring for the working poor

- Providing adequate medical care for low- and no-income people

- Providing sufficient low-income housing

- Providing adequate employment opportunities and compensation

- Providing the right kinds of job training and occupational counseling

We gave small groups a significant block of time during the final class to explore topics of their choice and develop a list of recommendations to share with everyone else. In addition, we had invited a retired political scientist and hunger/homelessness activist from Eugene to act as a discussant for these different proposals.

Students chose to consider four of the possibilities. With regard to ways to support the working poor, they suggested that addressing the following issues would provide some immediate assistance to people in these circumstances: affordable day care, after-school programs, provision of a sliding fee scale for public transportation, low-interest loans at community banks, earned income credits, and subsidized vocational education for youth and adults. Members of this group recognized, however, that deeper issues would need to be addressed to rectify the problem. As a society, we would need to examine rising housing costs, the inadequacy of worker rights, and the increase in part-time as opposed to full-time work; we would also need to challenge and alter policymakers and decision makers' inaccurate concept of a livable wage. Two groups considered ways that women and children who are the victims of abuse could be supported. Among their more than twenty recommendations were the following: educating doctors, police, and other caregivers about the cycle of abuse and how to be sensitive to women and children in this situation; counseling for women and children who are experiencing domestic abuse as well as counseling for abusers; establishing effective restraining orders and tougher laws to contain and prevent abuse; job training for women who have been forced by their partners to leave their homes; publicly funded child care and health care; and pressuring the media to avoid the production of programs that degrade women or promote their inequality. Other groups this evening addressed the issues of low-income housing and support for mentally or physically challenged people.

All the groups demonstrated the capacity to recognize structural factors that contribute to economic distress and the way systemic and attitudinal changes among the more affluent could contribute to a reduction of homelessness and hunger in our own community. They realized that truly addressing elements of our common life that lead to these conditions will require more than charity, as important as this may be. The achievement of social and economic justice in Portland and elsewhere demands a more careful examination of our own priorities and our tacit assent to corporate and governmental policies that exclude a proportion of the population from resources they need to live decent lives. What will be necessary is a shifting of blame away from the poor themselves to the institutional factors and common attitudes that lead to their marginalization.

Writing Our Way to Connection and Understanding

Integral to this work was the use of journals. Through journals, we could know what students were thinking throughout the course, and we could respond with thoughts of our own. As mentioned earlier, the journals consisted of responses to class activities, our participation at the various agencies, and readings. They were a place to relate and integrate personal experiences with poverty and to engage in constructing understandings about poverty and its causes and solutions. We responded with questions and thoughts of our own about the content of the comments. In all the writings, a level of honest personal sharing is noteworthy. Often we felt ourselves privileged as readers/responders, fortunate to have the opportunity to learn what others thought on topics we cared so deeply about ourselves. We were always anxious to read what our students had to say (to themselves as well as to us, because journals are often a way to conceptualize what is not yet fully known) and never more than after the last meeting. Did a transformation take place? What would they say about what they had experienced and come to know?

Ben Keller provided an overview as part of his ending statement: "When I first signed up for this Hunger and Homelessness course, I was not fully aware that our class would be meeting at homeless shelters. As an individual I had never really thought about volunteering my time in this manner, not out of fear or gross 'disillusion,' but rather a veiled naiveté. Having to work in a homeless shelter or food kitchen was a direct confrontation [with] my abilities to grapple with our community's larger issues of poverty and immediate response to people with needs. . . . I honestly don't feel that most people feel proud about participating in a society that penalizes people for being or becoming poverty stricken. I *do* feel that most people (including myself sometimes) do not realize or dare confront their desires for comfort over the realities of necessity."

Some participants responded to their volunteer experiences and to the course as a whole with broad swaths of understanding and change of thinking. Some chewed on old ideas laid against new experiences and understandings, and some painted word pictures with details of the things we did and experienced in the course. Amy Brodie's thoughts at the time centered on food: "It is funny how most of my memories of working in this Hunger and Homelessness class involve handling food: cutting, sorting, serving, cleaning up food. One of the hardest things about serving was the rationing required. Only one scoop, one serving, one donut. I think more about my own meals now—I feel guilty if something goes bad and I wonder if it is only bad to me—perhaps not to someone who might find it after I have discarded it. I feel I came in direct contact with hunger."

Vinny Chau Chin also remembered food as central to her experience: "I cannot get over the image of the homeless person who sneaked in the food line to take an extra donut. How could I deny him the extra donut? After all, it would probably be his breakfast the following morning. I will never forget the look on his face after he had successfully sneaked in the line to get the extra donut. He was totally satisfied and he had accomplished an important task."

The open parameters of journal writing, the ongoing opportunity it provided for responding to experiences and integrating them with the readings plus the acceptance of a wide variety of responses provided enough flexibility in structure for participants to address what most mattered to them. In his summary writing, Jonathan Auld expressed his frustration with societal values: "Throughout this course, I found myself oscillating between sadness and anger. I feel both of these emotions simultaneously when I consider the homelessness in our country. We live in the richest, most productive country in the world and yet we still allow people to live in such terrible conditions. Sometimes I think that we are so concerned with 'doing what is best for me and my own' that we cannot or do not want to see that helping those in need may be what is best for us."

Although from the beginning we wanted to transform how people in the course thought about and related to poor children, we were surprised that some participants talked in their journals about teaching the ideas we had been reading about and discussing to their students. Nicole DeMango was intern teaching in a fourth-grade class during the time of the course and decided to introduce some of the issues of poverty to her fourth-grade class. "I taught them (her students) about human diversity, emphasizing that despite the many differences between people, there are many similarities. Eventually, we got into the topic of poverty. The students initiated a discussion about those who go hungry and don't have a place to live. I asked them to think about how these people might be similar to them. I wanted the children to see the poor as people just like them. We talked about the fact that we all have the same basic needs and we share some of the same emotions."

These were ripples and repercussions that took us beyond our original goals for the course and linked us in a broader way to society. People began to see hunger as a choice rather than a given, a choice that demanded examination and provided for the possibility of change. Elizabeth Peter expressed a commonly held view: "I was like the rest of the population when it came to views about homelessness. 'Why don't they get a job? I have to work for my money.' I never took the time to understand their world, therefore I feared the unknown. I never stopped to realize that these people are a lot like myself and I could end up like them."

Almost all the participants in the course reported some level of change in their thinking about the poor. Many expressed a desire to continue volunteer work at one of the soup kitchens or shelters. Some reported an increase of compassion and understanding for the poor and connection to them. One person convinced her relatives to make donations to the poor for Christmas rather than giving gifts. There were heated discussions with friends, and several people said that they enjoyed having suggestions of readings and the film we had shown at the first meeting to back up their arguments and convictions. Does this mean that the course participants will be better teachers, school psychologists, or school counselors in serving poor children? We cannot measure that change, but shifts in students' attitudes and beliefs suggest that their relationships with the poor will be entered into with less judgment and possibly more comfort and respect. Given the amount of time we had and the scope of our work together, we achieved a great deal.

Four themes emerged early in the ongoing journal entries. They were common to many of the writings:

- People are not poor through their own fault.

- I recognize and must reconcile my own good fortune.

- The sources of poverty make me angry because of their injustice.

- What are our responsibilities for the poor, what should we do to change things?

Supporting these ideas, especially the first one, were the conversations that many participants had with people who came to eat at the soup kitchens. This was perhaps the hardest part of what we wanted for the course, simple exchange of experiences and ideas between the people eating at the soup kitchens and us, the course participants. Many of these conversations offered reality and immediacy to the ideas we had been reading and thinking about. Now they became embodied in real people. Nothing else could have been as powerful.

Lodi Loder wrote, "We sat at one of the dining room tables, and she began to tell me her story. She called it her 'testimony.' I was amazed and curious at how open she was with me. She told me that in July she was at her 'bottom.' Like many, K. became homeless after a series of events. She said she was a workaholic and a drug abuser when her thirteen-year-old daughter moved out of their apartment. Everything from there went downhill."

After Michelle Erlander's first volunteer experience, she wrote, "I felt apprehensive upon my first visit at the Salvation Army. I worried about how I would appear to these people and that they would hate me and reject my meager attempts
to help as a rich, liberal Lewis & Clark student. After some time there, talking with
the staff and interacting with some homeless people, I came to understand differently.
These people didn't care about what I was wearing or where I'm from; all they care
about are their basic human needs/rights and fulfilling them. If I am moving to help
them, that is all that is important. Of course I am being general about "all these
people" and what they think, but I feel much more capable and sure of myself to
volunteer in the future."

It often felt easiest to make and serve food rather than relate to the people coming to eat. Mary, mentioned earlier, who worked and ate at the St. Francis Dining
Hall, helped make talk easier. Tracy Arensberg talked with several people there but
in his journal said, "While my talk with other folks gave me a window into the dining hall culture, it was our discussion with Mary that really personalized the whole
experience. She was so generous to allow us to ask questions and hear her stories.
I especially will not forget her descriptions of finding a place to sleep. Being awakened in the night multiple times and told to go elsewhere must invoke such feelings
of unwantedness in someone! I admire her wit and savvy, which I'm sure has aided
in her survival on the streets."

For Alyssa Kennedy, there was not one particular person or experience but
many that affected her thinking. She described her contacts with the poor in this way:
"The people are real. They are not 'messed up' or 'freaked out' but are actual people who happen to be 'down on their luck.' How true that phrase, 'down on their
luck.' This is the case more often than not, as they often have real life stories which
account for this fact. They are real people who have real faces and real lives. They
also have dreams and hopes . . . [and as with] us, those dreams and hopes may never
be realized. The major difference in this is that conceptual parts of the dreams and
hopes are so vastly different from our side of the spectrum to the other side, where
the hunger and homelessness is an issue."

Writing in her journal toward the end of the course, Sarah Colton said, "One
of the main issues that Medoff and Sklar address in *Streets of Hope* is that poverty is
largely blamed on the 'breakdown of the family,' which masks the growing reality
of dead-end jobs, falling wages, and higher shelter and living costs. Good, high-
paying jobs are becoming harder to find and harder to keep, minimum wage has
plummeted in value and fallen behind price inflation, corporations have been 'downsizing,' benefits and promotions have declined, and welfare programs remain un-
derfunded and underachieving."

For the last night of the class, we asked students to react to the ideas in *Streets
of Hope* by composing a found poem to share using lines from the book. These poems
can be written with a prior theme in mind before looking for lines. They can also
be a way to discover theme in that you look for eight to twelve lines that resonate

without knowing exactly why. Sarah's poem relates closely to the thoughts she had expressed in her journal:

The time is now
We can change if we open our minds and democratically
reorder our priorities.
It is time to stop the Scapegoating,
to start solving our shared problems.
All human beings deserve equal rights and dignity.
If we continue with all this
Separate but unequal
We will surely self-destruct.
True compassion is more than flinging a coin to a beggar.
We can change if we open our minds.
Good jobs at good wages . . .
Harder to find. Harder to keep.
It is fashionable to blame the supposed
        "Breakdown of the Family"
    and ignore
        The Breakdown in wages and Employment.
How quickly we spend money on prisons
Not schools.
Only a society that is hopeful about *all* its children has hopes for the future.
We are now faced with the fact that tomorrow is today.
Today . . .
while we still have a chance.
We can change
The time is now.

In his poem, Tracy Arensberg combined Medoff and Sklar's words with a response (Tracy's words are in quotes and and Medoff and Sklar's in italics) that helps explain our lack of progress in solving the problems of hunger and homelessness:

Wealth is being redistributed upward.
"My mutual fund did pretty well this year."
The United States is the poorest richest country in the world.
"I had a great time traveling in Mexico, it was so cheap."
Real wages are dropping because of global corporate restructuring, deunionization, the shift toward lower-paying industries, the lower value of the minimum wage, increased part-time work, upsized unemployment, and underemployment, automation, and other trends.
"After I receive my $20,000 master's degree, I will be able to work anywhere."
While the rich are getting richer, they are also getting stingier.

"But I'm just a student, I can't afford to donate."
Democracy cannot survive, much less thrive, in a world where people are secondary to corporate power.
"Fred Meyer has great prices on broccoli right now."
Since the time of slavery, Blacks have been systematically dispossessed of the fruits of their labor and denied government benefits, which helped many White Americans prosper.
"It's not like I've grown up overly privileged."
As bad as unemployment and underemployment are now, the situation is going to get much worse in the future, without a major change in politics.
"Once I'm earning a steady income I hope to build a house on some land, the city is too depressing for me."

Benjamin Lee's simple use of repetition in his poem imparted a feeling of what hunger and homelessness might feel like from the inside:

> Many poor families . . .
> . . . they live and live and live
> cutting back on food . . .
> . . . they starve and starve and starve
> living in dangerous housing . . .
> . . . they (are) scared, scared, scared
> some without heat . . .
> . . . they shiver and shiver and shiver
> or plumbing . . .
> . . . they thirst and thirst and thirst
> many do without health insurance . . .
> . . . they cough and cough and cough
> or reliable transportation . . .
> . . . they walk and walk and walk
> stresses arising . . .
> . . . they break up and break up and break up
> time to build the preventive foundation . . .
> . . . they build and build and build
> a change in course . . .
> . . . they change and change and change
> kids in futuristic splendor . . .
> . . . they grow and grow and grow
> Chaos or Community . . .
> . . . you choose and choose and choose

As we sat in a circle that last night of the class listening to our poems, we were surrounded by the artifacts of poverty and our encounters with it that people had brought to the class. Stale doughnuts, shoes splattered with paint from the work at the West Women and Children's Center, paintings and drawings of people lost in modern cityscapes or children held by caring adults—these are some of the graphic representations of what students rendered from their experience. Taking time to walk around and examine the objects heightened their impact and gave us an opportunity to add new images to our thoughts of the meaning of poverty in people's lives and the meaning of our experiences as volunteers. There were surprises and "Oh, yes, I remember that." We had all come with unique views to present of our encounters with poverty. That night it was clear that the course had impacted us all in profound ways.

Engaging in the Work of the World

As teachers, we finished this course pleased with the impact it had had on our students and on us. But even more significantly, we were surprised by what we discovered about teaching and learning. We had felt sure at the outset that choosing the transformation of students' social attitudes as a course goal ought to include experiences beyond the classroom. As educators deeply influenced by John Dewey, we wanted to meld practice and reflection. This is a goal we often seek to implement, but after teaching this course, both of us realized how seldom we achieve it. What made this class unique was the fact that our conversations with students were based on experiences all of us had shared, not on experiences only reported by others. We drew on background readings and films about hunger and homelessness, but we provided opportunities for students to encounter these phenomena themselves. In an effort to support our students' and our own emergent understandings about these issues, we also incorporated journal writing, more open-ended creative responses, and informal discussions. Students had multiple opportunities to think about and mesh what they had read with what they experienced.

What struck us was the degree of congruence that characterized students' responses at the end of the course. We had not gone into this experience with a clearly defined set of expectations about students' conclusions, nor did we ever try to direct them to preconceived viewpoints and attitudes. But in December we found that nearly all students had developed analyses about the causes of hunger and homelessness based on a broader understanding of the social dynamics that contribute to these conditions. Furthermore, as their recommendations at our final meeting demonstrate, this group of disparate people had developed a common commitment to finding ways to thoughtfully and humanely address these issues in their own communities.

What does this say about teaching and the way we might organize more courses so that they, too, could tap some of the transformative power we encountered in the Hunger and Homelessness course? It was easy enough to compose the course once we had talked through our beliefs about how social change is possible through education and shared our visions of how a good society operates. We easily came to points of consensus in our beliefs and attitudes through active listening to each other's ideas and experiences and discussion of a key question: How could we facilitate change in people's belief systems? If you believe that people are poor because of their own fault, then you respond in that way to them—we agreed that this is not the reason some people are poor. We did not see ourselves as do-gooders or benefactors; instead, we had between us a good deal of faith in the power of simple encounter. What we wanted for ourselves and participants in the class were the simple goals of interacting with people who were experiencing hunger and homelessness and the freedom for everyone to move as close to people in poverty as seemed appropriate. For example, we encouraged but did not require conversations with the people we served in the dining halls.

We began and ended our course strongly believing that experience needs to accompany theory and a hope that contact with the poor would result in enhanced caring and understanding as well as growth in our own students' commitment to serve the poor and to change the conditions that result in poverty. Kathleen Miller says best both what we hoped for the course and where as a group we came to at the end of our time together in what she called the "missing verse from Imagine":

If You Can Dream It . . .
Imagine there's no poverty
It's easy if you try
No homelessness
No hunger
And no one left to die
Imagine all the people
Living life with Dignity

References

Dalai Lama. 1999. *Ethics for the New Millennium.* New York: Riverhead.

Eighner, Lars. 1993. *Travels with Lizbeth: Three Years on the Road and on the Streets.* New York: Fawcett.

Gould, Stephen Jay. 1991 (September). Enchanted Evening. *Natural History*, 100 (9): 14.

Kates, Robert W. & Sara Millman. 1990. "On Ending Hunger: The Lessons of History." In *Hunger in History: Food Shortage, Poverty, and Deprivation*, ed. Lucile F. Newman. Oxford, England; and Cambridge, MA: U.S.: Blackwell.

Kozol, Jonathan. 1988. *Rachel and Her Children: Homeless Families in America*. New York: Random House.

Medoff, Peter, & Holly Sklar. 1994. *Streets of Hope: The Fall and Rise of an Urban Neighborhood*. Boston: South End Press.

Rifkin, Jeremy. 1995. *The End of Work: The Decline of the Global Labor Force and the Dawn of the Post-Market Era*. New York: G. P. Putnam's Sons.

Rifkin, Jeremy. 1995 (May–June). A Blueprint for Social Harmony in a World Without Jobs. *Utne Reader* Vol. 69: 53-63.

National Coalition for the Homeless. **http://www.nch.ari.net/** This website provides up-to-date fact sheets on a variety of issues related to homelessness, extensive bibliographies, and links to other sites that provide information about this topic.

9

Peer Mediation and the Color of Justice

Russell Dillman and Geoffrey Brooks

"You're just a bitch! I'm not hearin' that!"

"You don't ever hear anything, and you're the bitch."

Other students in the classroom back away in both confusion and amazement. What just happened here? Often the student-to-student conflicts that come up in classrooms, rest rooms, hallways, or the cafeteria seem to arise spontaneously. Typically these students are sent to the vice principal or dean of students for discipline or punishment. However, in this case of student conflict, the teacher exercised her option of referring these students to mediation. In fact, at Franklin High School in Portland, Oregon, where we have an active student mediation program, 85 percent of all student-to-student disputes are resolved through peer mediation.[1]

We are both teachers and program directors at Franklin High School. Geoff, an African American in his early fifties, is the student integration specialist. He also teaches African-American history for U.S. history credit. As integration specialist, one of Geoff's key responsibilities is to coordinate the peer mediation program at Franklin. Russ, a fifty-year-old European American, teaches social studies and is coordinator of the Law and Public Services Program at Franklin. The Law and Public Service Program was mandated by a former superintendent in an effort to encourage minority students to attend Franklin High School. In this chapter we will at times refer to ourselves by name to help the reader recognize which of us is speaking.

Geoff is the only full-time integration specialist in the Portland School District. His responsibilities include advocating for students of color: counseling, teaching, and coordinating schoolwide projects. Interestingly, the title "Integration Specialist"

---

[1]Peer mediation is the name of the program; conflict resolution is the process that is used. We will use the terms *peer mediation* and *conflict resolution* interchangeably in this chapter.

comes from a period in this district when the city schools were becoming more segregated by demographics, class, and ethnicity. The district wanted to attract white students to the inner-city schools to balance school populations. Given our personal experience, we're not sure that Portland Schools' integration model has benefited African-American students in the best manner. Portland's integration model was to use specialized programs in schools to attract nonwhite students to achieve racial balance. This model has had little success. Historically the burden of integrating schools has fallen on African-American children. The experience of one of Russ' African-American students exemplifies this. This young woman took the bus every day to school, which required her to leave home at 5:30 A.M. in order to arrive at school by 7:30 A.M. Asked how she felt about this, the student said she saw it as just another example of injustice in our society.

Justice and Peer Mediation

This student became one of our mediators at Franklin. In describing the mediation program, she said that it provided an opportunity for justice to all students and seemed to transcend racial barriers. Geoff knew very little about mediation before arriving at Franklin High School. He now believes that school mediation enhances personal and interpersonal communication skills in young people, thus empowering them to find justice on their own terms. Besides reducing student-to-student violence, Geoff has seen the program reduce the negative impacts of racism, classism, and genderism among the high school students with whom he works.

The power imbalance in schools is often abused by those in power. A curriculum that allows students to consider what their rights and responsibilities are as humans and as Americans under the Constitution is a paramount prerequisite to even beginning a discussion. Many student-to-student issues, such as conflicts around lockers, clothes, girlfriends/boyfriends, have the potential to erupt into larger problems. To have students consider not only their rights, but also their responsibility to others, both in and out of school, is very empowering to students. Of course, many of them want to run with the rights, but leave behind the responsibility piece.

An understanding of the lack of fairness in the U.S. judicial system becomes apparent to our students as they look at the Fourteenth Amendment's Equal Protection Clause in social studies classes. In a capitalist economic system, equity and justice cannot be gained within the system itself. Without socioeconomic equality (good attorneys cost a lot of money), people are not equal in their ability to gain legal justice. Justice does not always require equality, but it does require fairness. The concept of fairness is hard for students to truly believe in, until they are empowered in ways that allow them to participate in problem solving.

We believe power and conflict are concepts central to a discussion of justice. Conflict resolution programs in schools provide a venue in which power is more evenly distributed than historically has been the case in schools as well as the larger society. Further, such programs help students to recognize conflict as a normal and necessary part of human interaction and an avenue toward justice. School mediation programs offer this avenue because they allow resolution of conflict by the disputants themselves. Webster's International Dictionary defines justice as "an impartial adjustment of conflicting claims." By empowering students to negotiate differences through conflict mediation, we have seen them gain a sense of justice.

Who Owns the Solution?

Mediation programs in schools help students use a problem-solving paradigm to settle conflict, instead of having punishment inflicted on them for being involved in a dispute. The idea is to allow those who understand and are part of the conflict to actually solve the problem and thus avoid future disputes over the same issue. Although this is not always effective, it certainly provides a possible solution. More importantly, however, it empowers young people to try to reach what all parties see as a fair or just solution to their problems.

Traditionally, punishment or discipline has been used to prevent further disputes between students. In this model, the only motivating factor in preventing future disputes between these people is fear of wrath from teachers, administrators, and/or parents. Fear may work for some, but it certainly doesn't serve to solve the root problem or offer any true sense of justice. In the American justice system, we all learn that the way to deal with disputes with others is to take an adversarial stance. This is one reason for the backlog of litigation in the courts. The most competent attorneys, however, always attempt to negotiate settlement between the parties to reach justice. If negotiation is not attempted, a solution is imposed on the disputants rather than reached by them. In American society in general, and in schools in particular, solutions to problems are rarely made by those having the conflict, but by a third party deciding what is best. At times this may be perceived as just, but often it is not. Further, the solution is not "owned" by those with the problem; the problem has not truly been solved and probably will recur. The principle underlying mediation programs is to allow disputants to develop and thus "own" the solution.

Throughout the world, disputes arise over resources, perceptions, and values. Although this is somewhat simplistic, most disputes between people or groups of people fall into one of these categories. The same is true in schools. Students get angry with locker partners for keeping a messy locker. Teachers get angry with students because they may see a student as lazy or disruptive. Students get angry because someone looked at them the wrong way or gossiped about them. Students get angry with other students or staff members because of perceived intolerance for their beliefs, their lifestyle, or their cultural heritage. Some disputes over such issues are easy to resolve; others may never be resolved. Mediation programs allow students to air their grievances in a safe setting. We have found that the easiest conflicts to solve are conflicts over resources. This hardly seems plausible if one looks at conflicts in the world today. However, student resources take the form of gym shoes and disc players, rather than water or oil. Usually, disputes over perceptions or misperceptions can reach resolution. Conflicts that arise over values, however, present difficulty. This is because young people have often learned racism, ethnocentrism, homophobia, and so forth from a very young age. As adolescents develop their identities, they perceive their beliefs as the essence of who they are. To try to alter their belief systems through the mediation process is at best difficult if not impossible.

Intolerant beliefs are among the root causes of injustice in society. Despite deep-rooted and complex obstacles, the mediation process does provide opportunity for the disputants to consider their own values and the effect that those values have on themselves and others. For example, a conflict that arises over a racial slur and is dealt with through mediation requires the disputants to consider the source of the problem. Whether the problem can be resolved or not, mediation provides an avenue for discourse and subsequent introspection on the part of disputants and mediators alike. This discourse and introspection may help to lead to increased fairness in society.

We continue to discuss with students, staff, and administrators the value of including a course in mediation as part of the regular curriculum. In a recent speech to all Portland High School principals, Adrienne Armstrong, Franklin student body president and mediator, advocated for mediation programs in every high school. Some Oregon legislators have advocated for this as well. However, this is a time when funding public education is waning. Despite increased school violence, the climate is hardly ripe for such courses or legislation to become reality. Yet we both believe that mediation programs hold great potential for reducing school violence and instilling in young people a genuine sense of justice. When mediators are asked what justice means to them, the most common response is "being heard."

Implementing a Peer Mediation Program

In 1990, Russ, two other teachers, and an administrator traveled to Ohio and New York to observe law magnet programs in high schools. During this trip, the team noticed that a peer mediation program was an integral part of nearly every law program. After returning to Portland, Russ and the others began to design and implement the various elements of Franklin's law program. In 1991, Russ was asked by the principal to begin to construct a peer mediation program. Having little knowledge of how to implement such a program, he began by going through training in mediation at a local college workshop. He also contacted two professional mediators in the Portland area, who kindly volunteered to help with the initial training.

Russ solicited potential student mediators through the school's daily bulletin and by asking teachers to recommend students. Very few students responded to the bulletin request. Russ worked with the former integration specialist to talk to recommended students one-on-one. They selected student mediators who would reflect the racial, ethnic, and gender diversity in the school. The goal was to train twenty-five students. Many of the recruited students had been involved in conflicts at Franklin. In one instance a vice principal advised us that it was a mistake to include among the mediators a student known to have gang affiliations. Yet this student proved to be one of our best mediators.

In February 1992, Franklin held its first training. The training lasted two days at an overnight retreat, beginning with a diversity training exercise on the first night. Participants received guidelines for the mediation process and engaged in discussion and student role plays over the next two days. The retreat allowed students to bond as a "mediation team" and provided them with an opportunity to be both mediators and disputants during role plays. At the end of the two days together, students provided Russ with their school schedules and identified times they were available for mediation during the school day.

On return to school, the real work began. That work involved "selling" the program to faculty. Russ and the integration specialist attempted to persuade the staff of the program's merits at two different faculty meetings. (Luckily, tomatoes weren't available.) Finally, Russ decided to have four student mediators come to a faculty meeting to perform a short role play of a dispute and mediation. This five-minute skit convinced most of the faculty. This turning point showed us that students truly owned and could promote the program. The next step was to get student disputants to trust a different mode of solving their problems. Trained student mediators spoke to classes to make other students aware of the program. Gradually the student body and the staff began to take advantage of mediation as a means of problem solving.

At this point in the evolution of the Franklin Peer Mediation Program, Russ asked that coordination of the program be made part of the job description of the integration specialist. This was necessary because coordination of the program requires freedom from the time constraints of a full-time classroom teacher. During this period, Russ also was developing a philosophy that would provide the basis for a mediation program in an urban high school.

What Have We Learned from Franklin's Peer Mediation Program?

When asked to contribute a chapter to this book, we were both flattered and apprehensive. Our apprehension arose not only from time constraints, but more importantly, from wondering whether *we* truly had the expertise to talk about conflict and rights. One can never be an expert on resolving conflict in high schools or making a blanket statement about how students' perceive fairness or their rights in public schools, but we have gained some insight by both trusting our students and watching them. The students, our children, and life in general have served as our mentors. We came to realize that we could use our experiences with the mediation program to explore issues of justice with other educators.

For a mediation program to be truly effective in schools, adults must be willing to relinquish power to young people and to trust them. This sounds easy, but is probably one of the greatest obstacles in establishing such a program. We found it difficult to get administrators to trust students in conflict with each other to attempt to solve their problems through mediation. We also found that administrators were accustomed to dealing with conflict using a punishment model rather than a problem-solving model.

Student discipline in schools often takes an inordinate amount of administrators' time. When our own administrators agreed to allow us to design this program and empower students to deal with conflict, they soon realized that such a program was invaluable: Not only did they have time to deal with disputes that had escalated to violence, but there were fewer recurring problems between students. Another benefit was that students themselves felt that they were being treated more fairly. For example, following one mediation, a fifteen-year-old female student said, "I love the mediation program because I was trusted to try to solve my own problem before it got worse." Disputes rarely recur if those involved are empowered to arrive at their own mutually acceptable solution.

Logistic problems in establishing a school peer mediation program become obvious if one considers the normal schedule in a school day. Students often must be pulled out of classes, teachers must assent to these students' absence, a private space for the mediation to take place must be located, and so on. Such difficulties are not insurmountable. And, over time, the program itself becomes an accepted part of school routine. Once this happens, it is our experience that most students who use peer mediation to resolve conflicts do feel they are treated justly and with respect.

However, students are keenly aware that they still remain second-class citizens with regard to staff members. This is a generalization, and we have seen adults willing to relinquish power with regard to students and view them as equals. But few staff members have been willing to negotiate with students using the mediation process. It is difficult to teach about justice, and hard for some students to view justice with anything but cynicism, when they see adults continuing to use power rather than negotiation to solve conflicts. This is an issue we continue to grapple with.

Aside from resolving problems, we found many unanticipated benefits from the peer mediation program. As they worked through the peer mediation process, students involved in a dispute learned to listen to others, to try and look through the eyes of the other disputant or disputants, and acquired negotiation skills that they could use in their everyday lives. This opportunity to acknowledge other peoples' needs enhanced the possibility of resolution.

The students who train as mediators, however, may gain the greatest benefit. They too learn to listen, not take sides, and try to assist in communication without offering their own opinion. This is a skill we all can use. Further, we found that having mediation skills gives them confidence and self-esteem, and helps them respect and value differences in people, as illustrated by the following example. Early in the program's history, a male mediator was confronted with a dispute over another student's sexual orientation. After the mediation, the student mediator reported that he had really had to consider his own homophobia. Although his religious background still prevented him from condoning homosexuality, he said he "understood gay students more."

Some of our most reliable and competent mediators are students who themselves had been involved in disputes, had been victims of racism, or had been seen as "troublemakers" by administrators and/or staff members. Students trained in mediation and those using the process see a possibility for a fair resolution. We conclude that empowering students, and trusting students to solve their own problems, provides them with a sense of justice.

Over seven years we have recruited mediators from the student population in a variety of ways. We have invited students to be mediators, have taken referrals from other students and staff members, and students themselves have applied. Despite our efforts to encourage diversity, most of those who apply continue to be European-American females. Very few males of any race apply. Further, we have found that the number of mediations involving females is far greater than those involving male students. We attribute this to male students being less willing than female students to share their thoughts and feelings. Instead of perceiving conflict resolution as a means to a just solution to a problem, male students often view use of mediation as a sign of weakness. This seems to mirror patterns in American society: Males are taught to be "strong." Showing emotion and true feelings is not the way to solve problems, but force is. Of course, the use of force can hardly lead to justice. However, the male students who *have* become mediators or who have willingly submitted to the mediation process, have gleaned the same benefits as female students. As respected male students are trained as mediators and/or use the peer mediation process, male student willingness to participate seems to be increasing.

Few African-American students have been willing to use mediation as a means to solve conflict. Although we continue to actively recruit among all groups of students, we still have difficulty enlisting students of color as peer mediators. Being a peer mediator may be perceived as a "white" thing, or perhaps black students may feel that justice never can happen anyway. If one looks at the criminal justice system in this country and the incarceration rates for young African-American males, it is not surprising that many of these students would not trust any program aspiring toward justice. Further, to be part of the mediation team or to use the process, may be perceived as "selling out" to the dominant power structure in which they have never been allowed to fully participate. Ironically, some of our best and most effective mediators in the last seven years have been male and female African-American students. As an anecdote, one of our first student mediators, an African-American student, joined the Marine Corps after high school and was asked to employ his mediation skills through an interpreter in Somalia. The former student tried to help feuding warlords reach what they felt to be a just resolution over a territorial dispute.

The Color of Justice

Two scenarios occurred in Geoff's African-American history class that may serve to illustrate how cultural differences frame students' perceptions of justice. Portland Public Schools has its own school police force. Officer X is European American but has an African-American–centered lifestyle. He has several years' experience working as a police officer in the African-American community. Geoff invited Officer X to speak to students about how they might handle themselves if they were stopped by the police. The students in this African-American history course are fifteen years old. This is important, because their immaturity surfaced as the discussion progressed. It is not uncommon for African Americans to view police as enemies or invaders. A common perception in this community is that often "justice" means 'Just Us.' This opportunity to speak to students was a chance to challenge this idea. The officer wanted students to understand that he knows how he might be viewed by African-American young people. Officer X discussed how to be polite and have a positive attitude when being stopped. He attempted to have students understand the police need to protect the community. Many of the students gave the officer a bad time. Geoff imagines that some of the raunchy responses reflected attitudes expressed at home and in peer group, rather than students' own beliefs. In any case, students were unable to hear Officer X's point of view. One student remarked, "The po-po's [police] are out to arrest and harass black kids because they will get promoted." Even though he understands the perspective from which these students responded, Geoff still found their resistance to Officer X surprising. It demonstrates that young people's attitudes regarding race, color, and justice are deeply entrenched.

The second scenario involved the only European-American female in Geoff's African-American history class. Lynn was a senior and taking the course for elective social studies credit. White students often take this course. Lynn was an excellent student. She was always prepared and asked wonderfully deep and engaging questions. The African-American females in the class gave Lynn nasty looks and cutting remarks. Some of this occurred out of Geoff's view. Lynn decided to leave the class at the end of the first semester because, as she stated, "It's just too difficult to come and endure." Lynn chose to complete the class through independent study.

She read *Race Matters* by Cornel West, and met weekly with Geoff to discuss the book. In her final paper she wrote about the value of her experience as a minority: "My experiences in Afram [African-American U.S. history] were educational beyond the realm of textbooks and homework. It was the very first time I had been in a classroom dominated by African-American females, who had the power to make me silent in class discussions. Previously, I had not known what "racial tension" was, nor had I known that racism was still a very real problem in the United States. From being in Afram, I learned what it must be like for the nonmajority 'races' in America when one is judged solely by one's skin color and stereotyped by one's appearance."

Cultural differences cause us to constantly reevaluate the mediation program and to discuss with students whether they consider the process ethnocentric in nature. We say this especially considering the Asian student population.[2] These students are rarely willing to be mediators (we have had only two in seven years), and very rarely use the process to settle disputes. There are a variety of variables that lead to their apprehension about using conflict resolution. The more recent immigrants often are embarrassed by their lack of English language proficiency. Beyond that, Asian students tell us they are not comfortable talking about their thoughts or feelings with people they don't know. Further, they say justice is something imposed by authority figures on people. We have already discussed African Americans' sense of justice and their varied perceptions of mediation as an avenue toward justice. Our students' varied perceptions cause us to continue to wrestle with the concept of justice and all the ways in which it is culturally defined. The uneven participation of students of various cultural backgrounds raises the question, If justice is culturally defined, which of the myriad cultures in our schools gets to define what we call justice? We would like to see wider participation among students from all backgrounds, but are uncertain how to achieve this.

The mediation program is successful for those students who choose to participate in it. It has made a difference in the life of the school. The success of the mediation program is due in large measure to the willingness of adult authority figures—both teachers and administrators—to accept the mediated solutions negotiated by the students. We must always remind administrators that students cannot be coerced into mediation in lieu of suspension without compromising students' sense of justice. For the adolescents to "own" the resolution, they must want to resolve their conflicts and must not be forced into mediation. Through an opportunity to participate in self-governance, mediation programs offer adolescents experience in practicing democracy in a real-world context.

---

[2]Franklin serves students who consider themselves to be Asian American as well as students whose families have recently immigrated from Asian countries. Russ teaches several classes for ESL (English as a second language) students.

References

"Conflict Resolution and Peer Mediation Training." 1994. Portland, OR: Portland State University.

Fisher, Roger, & Scott Brown. 1988. *Getting Together, Building Relationships as We Negotiate*. New York: Penguin Books.

Fisher, Roger, & William Ury. 1981. *Getting to Yes: Negotiating Agreement Without Giving In*. Boston: Houghton Mifflin.

Fitzell, Susan Gringas. 1997. *Free the Children: Conflict Education for Strong and Peaceful Minds*. Gabriola Island, BC, Canada, and Stony Creek, CT: New Society.

Kivel, Paul, & Allan Creighton, with the Oakland Men's Project. 1997. *Making the Peace: A 15 Session Violence Prevention Curriculum for Young People*. Alameda, CA: Hunter House.

"Peer Mediation Training." 1999. Salem, OR: Center for Dispute Resolution, Willamette University and American Bar Association.

Sadall, Gail, Manti Henriquez, and Meg Holmberg. 1997. *Conflict Resolution: A Secondary Curriculum*. San Francisco: The Community Board Program.

"Student Mediation Resource Guide." 1998. Nyack, NY: Creative Response to Conflict, Inc.

Special Acknowledgments to:

Classroom Law Project, Portland, Oregon: Marilyn Cover
Cleveland State University, Cleveland, Ohio: Elizabeth T. Dreyfuss
Franklin High School, Portland, Oregon: Peer Mediation Team
John Marshall High School, Rochester, New York
Martin Luther King High School, Cleveland, Ohio
National Association for Mediation in Education, Amherst, Massachusetts
Neighborhood Mediation Center, King Facility, Portland, Oregon
Resolutions Northwest, Portland, Oregon: Marguerite Aichele-Smith
Roosevelt High School, Portland, Oregon

10   *Street Justice by Street Kids*

Theresa Kauffman

Teaching at a small, urban, special-focus middle school was the most challenging assignment I had taken in my nearly twenty years of teaching. If you think about the educational system as analogous with the medical field, our school would be the emergency room of the system. Students come to our school not deformed, as some have labeled them, but rather as healthy, vibrant students who need some extra special techniques and encouragement in order to return to the regular educational system and continue successfully. Most of them are economically disadvantaged and often expressed hopelessness about the community. Gang shootings and violence were a part of their everyday experience. Just as in an emergency room, some students have more critical needs than others, and some do not make it despite all our best efforts. But they and their families sought us out because they are frustrated and desperate for someone to help them see their own brilliance.

For the students at my school, gang violence was a very real issue that impacts their quality of life. It was a common discussion in our class to debrief the drive-by shooting that had occurred the night before, and how to feel safe in their community. Some students had brothers and sisters who were actively involved in gang activity and talked about the rag on the tree across the street to mark the territory in their neighborhood. Other students struggled with parents and other family members who were using drugs. Several came from single-parent families where the children were raising themselves. One student wrote, "They don't have anyone like a role model to be like and tell all the little stuff to. They don't want to go to their mother or father because they smoke drugs or sell them."

Without even textbooks to refer to, I struggled to engage students in a curriculum that was project based, while holding high standards for the content they pursued. I remembered a quotation from Howard Zinn that said, "The small circles of our daily life might be the beginning of justice." So I began to look for ways to engage these students in the circles of their daily life to show their own genius and understand the world around them a little better in the process.

Discovery

In January, I began a unit with my seventh- and eighth-graders with a whole-class discussion of some of the common problems facing communities across the United States. I found an incredible curriculum from the Center for Civic Education called *Project Citizen*[1] and used this as a guide to suggest categories in general, such as problems in schools, problems regarding young people, problems involving community standards, problems involving basic liberties, and problems concerning the environment. We discussed concerns in each category, such as that a large number of people do not vote in elections, or that some students use language and other forms of expression that are insulting to certain groups. Our discussion included examples of students impacting policy decisions that were familiar to my students. There were several local examples of classrooms that had successfully and not so successfully made a change in the community. One local elementary classroom had successfully petitioned to have a billboard about smoking removed near the school. The next year, the same class was not as successful in their campaign with the state legislature to ban children riding in the bed of pickup trucks.

When we had thoroughly sparked the thought process about community problems, I divided the class into groups of six students. They brainstormed a list of topics that they felt were problems in our own community. The students eagerly attacked this assignment, finding many problems to discuss. I was excited about the spark they exhibited. One group listed gang violence, drug sales, alcohol near schools, crazy people, homeless people, bums, prejudice toward skaters and boarders, drive-by shootings, and old buildings that look like a ghetto. Another group suggested gang violence, homeless, jobs for homeless and ex-criminals, pollution (water, ground, air), selling alcohol and cigarettes to minors, graffiti/litter in neighborhoods, and speeding in neighborhoods. One other group listed drugs, graffiti, litter, money issues for schools, gambling, prostitutes, gang violence, and boosters (people who steal and then sell merchandise for money). The last group listed gun violence, drive-by shootings, homeless, prostitutes, and school violence. All these topics touched my students' lives in real ways. The pursuit of justice involves issues about the quality of life. My students were beginning to think about justice in the daily circles of their personal lives.

---

[1]For additional information, direct inquiries to Project Citizen, Center for Civic Education, 5146 Douglas Fir Road, Calabasas, CA 91302-1467, (818) 591-9321, **projectcitizen@civiced.org**, **http://www.civiced.org**

Information from Letters or Interviews—Documentation Form

Name(s) of research team member(s) _____

Date _____

Problem being researched _____

1. **Source of information.** (Include the name of the person providing the information. If appropriate, include the person's title and group or organization.)

   Name _____

   Title and organization _____

   Address _____

   Phone _____

2. **Request information about the problem.** After introducing yourself by letter or phone, ask for answers to the following questions.

   a. How serious is this problem in our community?

   _____

   _____

   _____

   b. How widespread is the problem in our state or nation?

   _____

   _____

   _____

   c. Why is this a problem that should be handled by government? Should anyone else also take responsibility for solving the problem? Why?

   _____

   _____

   _____

   d. Which of the following do you think is true?

   ■ There is no law or policy for dealing with the problem.   Yes ____   No ____

   ■ The law for dealing with the problem is not adequate.   Yes ____   No ____

   ■ The law for dealing with the problem is adequate, but it is not being well enforced.   Yes ____   No ____

   e. What levels of government or governmental agencies, if any, are responsible for dealing with the problem? What are they doing about the problem?

   _____

   _____

   _____

(continued next page)

FIGURE 10–1   *Project Citizen Documentation Form*

Information from Letters or Interviews—Documentation Form (continued)

f. What disagreements, if any, exist in our community about this problem?

_____

_____

_____

g. Who are the major individuals, groups, or organizations taking sides on the problem?
- Why are they interested in the problem? _____

_____

_____

_____

- What positions are they taking? _____

_____

_____

_____

- What are the advantages and disadvantages of their positions? _____

_____

_____

_____

- How can we get information on their positions? _____

_____

_____

_____

- How are they trying to influence government to adopt their solutions to the problem? _____

_____

_____

_____

h. If our class develops a policy to deal with this problem, how might we influence our government to adopt our policy?

_____

_____

_____

FIGURE 10–1   *Project Citizen Documentation Form* (continued)

Each group then talked some more about each problem and narrowed their interests to one topic from their list. This took some heated discussions in several groups. One student wrote, "Drugs are a problem in our community because they are killing other people and because it could be your brother doing the drugs." Another argued that "Both drugs and gangs affect us because they bring crime into the community." Through this process, we narrowed to four topics to investigate: gun violence, gang violence, prostitution, and graffiti/litter in our neighborhoods. Each table group spent the next few days investigating their topic, collecting information from interviews, print sources, and media sources. The task now was to see how readily available information was about their topic and present what they found to the class, so the class could make an informed decision about which single topic they would pursue together. The *Project Citizen* materials were especially helpful here because they provided data collection sheets to be filled out that guided the students' inquiries.

When each group shared what they found, we discovered that two topics were very difficult to investigate. Information was scarce and hard to find. Either the group interest waned, or the climate at the time of our inquiry was such that little information was gathered about prostitutes or the graffiti/litter problem in our community. So we were down to gun violence and gang violence. The class continued discussion of the issues for an entire class period, and decided that since gang violence included guns, they would choose gang violence in NE Portland as their topic. A majority vote of the class cinched the decision.

In Search for the Truths

The next step was to regroup. I wanted the students to view their community as a resource, and we set out to gather research about the gang problem. We identified eight sources of information to explore regarding gang problems in Portland. Each student listed a first, second, and third choice for where they would like to dig deeply for information. I was able to assign two to four students to each source. Our sources included library sources, media sources, professors and scholars, lawyers and judges, community organizations, legislative offices, government sources, and electronic network sources. Again, the Center for Civic Education materials provided a nice framework for our data gathering. The student text includes guidelines for interviewing on the phone and in person, a script to follow when interviewing, and how to request information in writing. For example, the guidelines told students to introduce themselves, their grade level, teacher, and school name. The materials went on to give specific language for explaining this project and the problem our class was studying, and asking if the student could ask a few questions, or call back at a more convenient time, or get a referral to another person the student should call.

My students jumped into this stage of the process with both feet. Our room became a swarm of activity. Each student wrote a brief research plan describing where they wanted to seek information and what they needed from me. I was providing phone books, suggesting names to contact in each area, writing phone passes for students, coordinating guest speakers students wanted to invite to our classroom, and scheduling in-person interviews during the day. We came together each day with a class meeting to hear how everyone was doing and what they might need next. It was a hectic but exciting time, and *every* student was engaged in their part.

One student, Eddie, contacted A. Halim Rahsaan from the Youth Gang Outreach program, who had been a guest last year in their class. Eddie remembered valuable information about the history of gangs that Mr. Rahsaan would be able to share with us. Mr. Rashaan, who works closely with a community group that monitors the educational process in Portland, was available to speak for a fee. So I put Eddie in touch with our PTA to ask for the funding in this project. He went to their next meeting and offered his rationale about how the money would benefit students. In the conversation, Eddie offered to have Mr. Rahsaan speak to both seventh- and eighth-grade classes, and the PTA then agreed to sponsor his visit. On March 2, Mr. Rahsaan spoke to both classes about the history of gangs in this country and Portland, Oregon. He also gave statistics about why people join, what can be done (especially about graffiti), and what is happening in other areas of our country that we should be wary about in Portland.

We wrote a thank you note for the time our guest spent with us, and as a result of Mr. Rahsaan's speech several students shaped how they continued their investigation about the problems. For example, one student listened to Mr. Rahsaan describe how the female gang problem is growing in California. She proceeded to investigate this aspect and turned in a full report individually, about what is happening in other states and why we should be concerned. Another student heard Mr. Rahsaan describe the reasons people join gangs and added another question to his interviews of our community resources to gather more opinions about why people join. This information eventually became an important component of the final presentation and the students' reasons for their solution.

The group of students gathering information from lawyers and judges had a hard time getting in touch with these very busy professionals. They did contact two judges and one granted a phone interview, while the other judge invited them to lunch. The three members of this committee, Kristina, Tasha, and Erin, were thrilled to visit with District Court Judge Roosevelt Robinson, who also introduced them to a federal judge who happened to stop by while they were lunching. They brought back statistics about gang violence and his perspective about the policy in place to deal with gang violence, as well as powerful memories of the judge who invited them to lunch.

We all collected information, statistics, and printed materials, and reported to the whole class daily with updates about what we were doing and finding. The constant mixture of independent research work and reporting to the whole class proved valuable as we began to look for solutions later in this process. The students sometimes joined groups to share their information. For example, when their phone contacts resulted in a constant phone tag game, the legislative group and the government agency group joined forces to draft written requests for information. They shared letters they drafted together, and then worked to search government websites for statistics about gang violence. This group was one of the most frustrated, because there wasn't immediate response or many times their calls were not returned. Because of the lack of response and the ensuing frustration, this particular group eventually gave up.

Becoming the Tour Guide

After a week of collecting bits and pieces, I decided I needed to check in more formally with the students. I had each student write a one-page summary of what they understood our topic to be, what they found so far, and what they thought their next steps should be to continue or complete this project. This helped me see who was on track with our purpose, what was being done outside class time that I wasn't aware of, and where they needed more assistance or direction to continue toward our goal. I found out from their responses that most just needed more time on the Internet, or typing on the computer, or another trip to the public library for more text information. Two students told me they were having trouble scheduling an interview, so I was able to intervene and facilitate that process. Another student wrote that she wasn't sure what her next steps should be, and I was able to sit down and clarify that with her. And another student wrote, "First thing for me to do is to stop forgetting the pieces at home, then to put the information on the interview sheets." This written check-in proved valuable as we juggled so many different directions to this project.

When a significant amount of information had been gathered, I invited our principal, Mary Scheetz, to brainstorm with the students what a stock-and-flow systems analysis diagram (a charting technique used in the social sciences and corporate world) might look like for the gang problem, because the students were used to looking for patterns and problem solving with this tool. Our school, the Northeast Community School, had benefited from a grant from the Waters Foundation to support curriculum integration of systems thinking. The staff used systems thinking to organize our own interactions as a staff, as well as curriculum integration. In the classroom, this took many forms. We used systems thinking strategies to look at the salmon population problems in the Columbia River Basin, but also to simply analyze influences for improving the climate in our classroom. Students had access to the STELLA® computer model to assist as we developed stock-and-flow diagrams of the particular systems we were studying at the time. The students were familiar with this process, and we used it throughout the school year in science, health, math, and social studies curricula. Ms. Scheetz and I felt this might help students organize what they were finding in some form that made sense to them. We also wanted to guide students toward some solution that made sense to them. Following the discussion and diagram process, students wrote essays about why we have a gang problem and what a solution might be. One student wrote,

> I think that people join gangs mainly because they don't get any respect anywhere else, like their parents, their friends, and other people in their life. In the gang, the other members probably respect them, and they give each other a chance to have fun. But soon, they start getting into things they shouldn't, like getting in fights, stealing, drive-bys, and other things like that.
>
> They probably get very lonely and depressed sometimes, and start taking drugs. They get high and let their anger rise inside of them, and they might take their anger out on someone else. Or, they might be tempted to commit crimes because they're offered money.
>
> But once they've realized what they've gotten themselves into, they can't get out of the gang because they are forced to stay. But even if they do manage to escape, the rest of the gang might fear that the person will report them to the police, and so the gang will kill or kidnap the person.

Another student wrote,

> I think that the gang problem is not the group of people but the actions that they participate in, and their motivation. The reason gangs are such a big problem is their violent actions. The violent behavior that they practice is the problem, not the gang itself.

I was impressed that these seventh- and eighth-graders were demonstrating critical thinking techniques that took this experience out of a classroom project and into a real-world experience. Their comments demonstrated to me their growing development of the concept of justice. Emerging from this process was their recognition that justice is a tough, complex issue. This sets the stage for preparing the brief.

Preparing the Brief

Next we presented this question to the students: Knowing what you know, what would you suggest to the policymakers to help impact the gang problem in Portland? Some students suggested schools covering topics such as child abuse and self-esteem, and most thought we needed more programs like SEI (Self Enhancement Incorporated) and the Boys and Girls Club, where students can find someone to talk to when they need it. Another student suggested that "we as a people should care about other people and act as soon as something happens." I was delighted with the sophistication in their thinking of justice as a concept beyond simply rules or what seems fair. The bottom line this class felt strongly about was making a program that can encourage kids before they get tangled in the gang. They wanted the city to provide a safe place for kids to go to when they were first approached to hang out in gangs, with someone to talk to if their own parents abused and/or sold drugs or were not available to listen. They wanted a place that told students they can be cool without being in a gang.

Just as a lawyer would prepare a brief to argue a case, we began the work of pulling our class portfolio together, and here is where we ran into complications. The hard work of collecting information was self-motivating for most of my students. But now the stream had worn down and the continuing efforts needed to polish, compile, and present the information seemed less important than the gathering process. Then came the incredible invitation.

Marilyn Cover, executive director for the Classroom Law Project in Oregon, called to see if our class would like to present their work and findings at the Legal Citizen of the Year Banquet in April. They always invite a student group to perform, and she wanted to have a middle school group this year. I discussed it with my students, and they agreed that we should take advantage of this opportunity. Here was a real-world audience to give my students' work voice in the larger community. We developed a process to apply as one of the speakers on our panel, and I encouraged all to complete their research portion in order to be eligible to present. This seemed like the perfect carrot to encourage completion of the portfolio. But still this was not enough motivation for most students to take the project to this final step. Five students completed their work in order to become members of the panel, and then we found out they were possibly presenting to the mayor of Portland in front of the banquet attendees. This was exactly the audience we were hoping for, so the class worked to polish their plan. We brainstormed a logical sequence to our presentation, and small groups of students met with our five designated speakers to prepare. The students really had the sense that those selected speakers were representing all our work and it should be our best.

Our panel formed and portions were assigned. Chauncey would introduce the panel and give some background information. Then Zenette would sort through and explain what we collected and all the sources used for our background information. Adrian was going to explain our systems thinking model and the snowball effect on the whole system. Camille was going to share what we found from other states and why Oregon should be concerned about these same issues. And finally, Kristina would summarize and suggest our idea for the city to provide this safe place for kids to go before they get tangled in a gang. Marilyn Cover and her assistant, Barbara Rost, came to our school to help coach these young people with their speeches. There were to be close to 350 people at the banquet, and my students were from a small middle school program. We wanted them to be as polished as possible. Barbara even drove the students down to the banquet room to rehearse one afternoon so the large room wouldn't throw them off. This was truly an effort that was supported and encouraged for the success of these students.

Just as an attorney is awe-struck by the majesty of the U.S. Supreme Court chamber, these young citizens were astounded by the grandeur of the Hilton grand ballroom. Entering what, to their young experience, was a fantasy world of crystal chandeliers, an ocean of tables, linen tablecloths, and a company that included dignitaries of the city, attorneys, and the mayor herself, they all paused at the doorway, absorbing the enormity of the environment. Most of us would expect to be accompanied by a parent at such an auspicious event, but there were only two students with parental support this evening: Chauncey's father and Adrian's mother accompanied them to the banquet. Kristina and Camille were late because of sitter problems Camille's mom encountered. Our most eloquent speaker and most motivated panel member had no transportation this evening, so I brought her. Chauncey wanted to meet the mayor in person and shake her hand, so he approached her table and introduced himself. One by one, the students began to go over, until she came to our table and met the full panel of students, the parents, the principal, and me. She visited informally with each individual.

One highlight of the evening was when Mayor Vera Katz came over to our table to meet each of the students who would present later. She asked Adrian what was the focus of our special-focus middle school? He paused for a moment and then said, "They are focused on the student." The hours of research, all the hours on the phone, and the struggles of building this curriculum with the students was all worthwhile with his comment. They had a voice.

The students were to be introduced by our former mayor and Governor Neil Goldschmidt. He had some information about our school program and the process the students had traveled to this point, but I brought notes just in case I got the opportunity to introduce my own students. On this evening, the politics of the moment did not allow me that opportunity.

The students each spoke clearly and eloquently about the information they had to share with the group and the mayor. The mayor had been given, as background information, some suggested questions about their work to ask the students after their presentation. However, she chose to ask personal questions. Rather than asking about the project, what they learned, and how they came to the suggested safe place for kids, she asked each student whether they had ever considered joining a gang.

I was angry with the mayor and felt her questions were demeaning and racist. This was a panel of all black students presenting to a room full of white attorneys, and the mayor chose to focus on whether they had personally been approached to join a gang. Her questions ignored the months of hard work and diligence these students engaged in to find a solution to improve their community, to seek justice. Our principal and a parent wrote a letter of complaint to the mayor's office following the banquet. A prominent member of the sponsor's board of directors resigned after this dinner because she was uncomfortable with the way the students were portrayed with this line of questioning. When I do this kind of project again, I will make sure the students put together their portfolio to display and point to their work as they talk. This would improve their relaxation when speaking and would help the audience see the academic rigor and discipline that led to the short presentation time allotted.

The justice of the moment was their voice about a solution to this problem they felt passionate about, and the policymaker seemed to miss that point. But my students handled every one of the mayor's questions with poise and grace. Camille even told Mayor Katz that while she thought about joining a gang once, the work she had done in this project showed her how dangerous that could really be. What I saw on this evening was a group of children who through their own exploration had a strong voice with a solution that they felt passionate about and the policymakers and those in power failed to hear them.

The Opinion

Just as in a Supreme Court decision, once all the facts are in, the justices render their opinion, I offer mine here. The Project Citizen curriculum work done at the Northeast Community School that year had numerous little learnings, little sparks of justice along the way, as students' understanding of the concept grew and deepened. We learned that policymakers are very busy people. We learned that good ideas in a democracy are expressed but not always acted on.

The value for my students and me came powerfully as a result of the student-led curriculum that was truly co-directed by my students and me. I learned again that to be successful, curriculum must be student-driven; the curriculum must not drive the students. Their engagement in this process was active and exciting. This curriculum allowed us to go deeper into the workings of our community and how the policymakers come to decisions. It let us capitalize on my students' brilliance, build on their strengths, and encourage the sense that they are capable. It allowed us to ask hard questions of ourselves and our community in order to understand. And they each had the sense that in some way, they had performed their duty as private citizens and voiced their opinions. I believe that justice is a process we continually strive for within a democracy. My students experienced that process and were engaged and involved in the justice of their own community.

Just as Howard Zinn pointed out, these young citizens have learned that justice is not a quick fix. Although the presentation to the mayor was disappointing because there was no action, street justice for street kids is a process that demands perseverance and diligence. It is a daily reassessment of our community awareness and individual involvement in issues that affect our quality of life. Unlike justice in a courtroom, which is event-oriented and has a conclusion, that is, a verdict, street justice for street kids is a day-to-day struggle. Although disappointed in the outcome, these students have learned the process and they can have a voice. Even though that voice may not be heard today, it is young, and with experience the voices of these kids on the street will become louder and stronger.

This was one group of 20 students in a school of 100 and a district of 55,000. But each of these kids will take this experience, this spark of justice, to each of their new classrooms, in each of their new schools. And as that spark grows, it will become a bonfire of community involvement. Through that involvement, our democracy will improve and justice will be served in the real world.

References

Fisher, Michael. 1997. *Project Citizen*. Calabasas, CA: Center for Civic Education.

Miller, Barbara & Laura Singleton. 1997. *Preparing Citizens: Linking Authentic Assessment and Instruction in Civic/Law-Related Education*. Boulder, CO: Social Science Education Consortium.

National Middle School Association. 1995. *This We Believe: Developmentally Responsive Middle Level Schools*. Columbus, OH: NMSA.

Northwest Regional Educational Laboratories. 1996. "Educating for Citizenship." *Close-Up No. 19*. Portland, OR: NWREL.

System Dynamics in Education Project. **http://sysdyn.mit.edu/**

Tolo, Kenneth. (1998.) *An Assessment of* We the People . . . Project Citizen: *Promoting Citizenship in Classrooms and Communities*. Austin: The University of Texas.

11

Treated Fairly
A Middle School Take on the Supreme Court

David Molloy

The idea of justice is a fairly lofty one for most middle schoolers. For the most part, they are just beginning to wake up to the world beyond their neighborhoods. They do know about fairness, though. It absorbs them. Fairness is a lens through which they view the conduct of their relationships with adults and peers alike. They are deeply disturbed by conduct that they perceive to be unfair, and have no shortage of opinions on how they, or a fellow student, should or should not be treated. So as their eyes begin to open to the larger world around them, and they begin to learn about injustices both historical and contemporary, they are ripe for considering the idea of justice and of "natural rights," and to think critically about how such ideas are regarded locally, nationally, and globally.

As part of our eighth-grade social studies curriculum, we teach about the Bill of Rights, the subsequent amendments, and the U.S. Supreme Court's role in interpreting and upholding them. I find this to be both a daunting and exhilarating task; exhilarating, because I love the material and I am delighted to teach it; daunting, because as I approach this unit, I feel hounded by questions regarding the content I should cover leading up to it. How can students understand these first ten amendments without a strong knowledge of the U.S. Constitution as a whole? In leading up to the Constitution, how deeply do I need to explore the ideas of federalism and the failure of the Articles of Confederation? Will any of this make sense if I don't examine the significance of Shays' Rebellion? And what about the events leading up to the American Revolution? The "Intolerable Acts" and all the various acts imposed by the British that led to this uniquely American sense of justice expressed in the Declaration of Independence, specifically in the section "Wrongs Done by the King." I want my eighth-graders to understand how our system of justice is rooted in struggle, imbedded in a debate over the nature on government itself.

But again, these are heady concerns. If I were a high school teacher, I would most likely arrive at a different set of answers. But I teach middle school. My primary challenge is to find ways to keep the kids interested and engaged, and if I want them to come away from this unit with any sense of the material at all, I need to remind myself whom I am trying to teach. So before I approach any work with middle schoolers, I force myself to reflect on some "self-evident" truths about them; namely, that they are in a fascinating developmental stage of their lives and that they are:

Full of energy (not to mention hormones)

In the process of reexamining and redefining their world

Testing the boundaries

Preoccupied with their social lives

Moving from concrete to abstract thought

In need of a participatory, interactive, and engaging curriculum

Concerned about fairness

Once I have reminded myself that I am not out to transform them into historians and legal scholars, but rather to interest them in the material and have them see some of the broader brushstrokes, we can move forward. I am not suggesting that background material is unimportant. I prefer to do a rather thorough job teaching the events leading to the Revolutionary War. An examination of the British and the colonists' response lends itself nicely to lessons on cause and effect that can effectively convey how the American sense of justice derived from wrongs done by a higher authority. I actually have teams of students write a Declaration of Teenage Independence. Students have to write it in the three parts, based on the Declaration of Independence, which forces them to confront issues of authority, responsibility, the nature of government, injustice, and independence. But as I have tried to convey, there is no best way to get at this material and it is not necessary to unravel the endless layers of history to successfully conduct mock Supreme Court hearings at the middle school level. You should, however, aim toward a sense of justice that you and your students agree on. Once you have done so, you can move on to the trials.

Criminal Trials

Mock criminal trials are a great way to teach about courtroom procedure. They are also an interesting way to explore social issues. I have conducted mock criminal trials to examine the issue of students' rights through a "search and seizure" case involving items confiscated from a locker. I have also done criminal trials to explore issues that have nothing to do with the U.S. law or systems of justice whatsoever. For example, while doing a unit on Africa with my seventh-grade class, we did a mock trial to explore the issue of poaching. In preparing to defend, convict, or judge some alleged poachers, the students confronted an array of cultural, economic, and ecological issues. The pretrial activity then became the vehicle for genuine inquiry.

The major challenge in conducting a criminal trial, as opposed to a U.S. Supreme Court hearing, is that since the facts are in dispute, the students tend to introduce unanticipated variables in the name of evidence ("they weren't even *real* rhinos") that can make a criminal trial difficult to manage. Witnesses' roles, as well as the evidence in question, must be tightly scripted, or the proceedings can unfold in some fairly absurd ways that may not have much to do with the actual issues being raised by the case. But students typically realize this and decide that it is more fun and interesting to debate the issues during the trial than it is to get a hypothetical conviction of their peers.

I enjoy doing mock Supreme Court hearings because they are solely about constitutional matters, which get at the very core of our concept of justice as laid out in the Bill of Rights. The facts of the case are not being disputed. The questions tend to be simple, yet highly conceptual. Whether the issue at hand is gun control, freedom of speech, or the limits of governmental power, the students understand that the outcome of the trial entirely depends on their performance, which is entirely hinged on their ability to articulate how the Constitution supports their arguments. I have also learned through trying to teach about the Constitution that there are countless ways of going about this. Each time I teach it, it happens a bit differently. But I will share some of the ways that I have tried to unpack this fairly cumbersome, yet lively and interesting topic.

I begin our study with a simple, ten-frame comic strip that I distribute to the class. The first frame shows a woman (Mrs. Cook) reporting a prank call, and the comic strip ends with a young boy named Gerald Gault receiving a six-year sentence to a "state training facility." In between are eight frames that highlight the procedures of the *Gault* case, from his apprehension—where he says to the police officer, "My parents won't know where I am. Where are you taking me?"—through two hearings, to his sentencing. The dialogue is simple, but it shows the *Gault* case as raising questions about the proceedings.

"Judge, shouldn't someone be keeping a record of this trial?" asks Gerald's mother at the first hearing. At the second hearing, Gerald's father asks, "Judge, why not bring Mrs. Cook here so she can tell if it was Gerry?" The judge refuses. He sentences Gerald until his twenty-first birthday.

After students have read the comic strip, I ask them to list some of the things that happened during the process that they thought were unfair or unjust. The typical responses cover the basics of the case:

"When Gerry was taken in, nobody told his parents where he was."

"He wasn't read his rights."

"The neighbor lady's complaint isn't enough to arrest him."

"They didn't keep track of what people said at the first hearing."

"The neighbor woman didn't have to be a witness at the trial."

"Six years is way too much for a prank call!"

I like to seize on "He wasn't read his rights." This one invariably comes up each time I present the lesson. By eighth grade, these kids have seen their share of television arrests and know the procedure. Sometimes a student will mention that Gerald had the "right to a fair trial," but for the most part, they are not quite sure what legal rights he, or any other juvenile for that matter, has in a situation like this. But the students, whether they know the rights of juveniles or not, conclude that this treatment was definitely unfair or unjust. Somehow, whether through television or through their own personal experiences, the students have connected these "rights" to our systems of justice and our concept of justice. I tell them that the Supreme Court of the United States agreed with them, that Gerald Gault's case was indeed a real one, and that in 1967 the highest court in our country concluded from this case that juveniles who are accused of crimes that could send them to an institution have the following rights:

1. Right to notice of charges
2. Right to counsel
3. Right to confrontation and cross-examination
4. Privilege against self-incrimination

Through class discussion, we unpack the meaning of these rights and I ask the class to help me generate a list of questions that we would like to answer about this court that ruled in favor of Gerald Gault. Their questions are usually obvious but good ones:

"What does the U.S. Supreme Court really do?"

"How many people are on the Supreme Court?"

"How does someone get to be on the Supreme Court?"

"How long do they stay on the Court?"

"How do cases reach the Supreme Court?"

"What are some other famous Supreme Court cases?"

I also tell the class that we are going to get at these questions and learn about the Bill of Rights, from the inside out, by conducting some mock hearings. I have yet to hear a complaint when I announce this. I inform them that each student will have the opportunity to be an attorney and to argue a case before the Supreme Court, as well as take their turn as a Supreme Court justice and to be a part of a landmark ruling.

The Bill of Rights

For the first couple of times teaching this unit, I had struggled with how to present the students the Bill of Rights before we began the trials. Obviously, I want them to know the Bill of Rights, not only because of its importance to our system and concepts of justice, but also for a very practical reason: Students will need to articulate the meaning of the rights during the hearings. But I am typically averse to assigning rote memorization to middle school students. I have rarely found it an effective method of instruction. Furthermore, most eighth-graders understandably struggle with the language of the amendments. Although most texts of the amendments have an accompanying translation, they rarely make the connection to real circumstances and events. Then a colleague shared an idea. She had woven the study of the Bill of Rights into her current event assignments. In short, students are assigned to locate two print articles related to each of the first ten amendments (except the third, because the quartering of soldiers in private homes is rarely an issue in the courts). For each of the articles, the students have to write a brief explanation of how a citizen's constitutional rights are either being upheld or denied.

I was pleasantly surprised at the success of the assignment. It asks that students not only grapple with the language and meaning of the Bill of Rights, but also often forced them to confront their own opinions on the issues of gun control, abortion rights, and the death penalty. In relating an article on a death penalty case in Florida, Sara thoughtfully questioned, "Doesn't the Eighth Amendment protect people from 'cruel and unusual' punishment? If several attempts to kill him in the electric chair and making his face catch fire is not 'cruel and unusual,' then I don't know what is." And sarcastically she added, "Why don't they just burn him at the stake?" By looking at the bungling of this execution, Sara appropriately questioned whether this is fair or just treatment of the death row inmate.

Conducting the Hearings

I have found a few different ways to conduct mock hearings. Typically I like to use an actual case, such as the landmark *Gideon v. Wainwright* or the *New York Times v. the U.S. Government* (the famous Pentagon Papers) case. I have also taken real cases and have fictionalized them to limit the possibility that student "justices" will learn the outcome of the actual case before they formulate their own opinions and make their own decisions on it. Normally, however, middle school students will not go to such lengths in researching their cases.

Here are several questions pertaining to the organization and structure of the hearings that I need to deal with before I begin:

How do I set up my classroom for a hearing?

How do I establish the legal team?

How much time do the legal teams need to prepare?

What information/materials do I provide the legal teams?

How many students sit on the Court during each hearing?

What is the procedure for conducting the actual hearing?

What instruction do the students need regarding their role as Justices?

How do I evaluate students during this unit?

How Do I Set Up My Classroom for a Hearing?

I think that the atmosphere of the room during the trial is important. I suggest that one day toward the beginning of the unit you set up your classroom to look like a courtroom. When the students walk into the "courtroom," it gets them excited and motivated to take part in the activities to come.

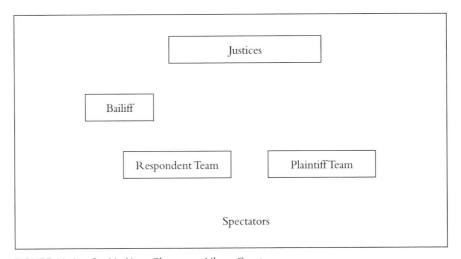

FIGURE 11–1   *Set Up Your Classroom Like a Courtroom*

How Do I Establish the Legal Team?

I try to balance the legal teams just as I do with any other group work. I try to factor in personality types, academic strengths, and verbal abilities, to balance the groups as best I can. Three or four students per team seems to work well. Since I have thirty-two students in my classes, I need to have four cases being prepared simultaneously. That makes eight groups: four plaintiff and four respondent teams.

How Much Time Do the Legal Teams Need to Prepare for the Hearing?

How much time you need to prepare depends on how productive the in-class work sessions are, but three hours of in-class work time over the course of the week should be sufficient.

What Information/Materials Do the Legal Teams Need in Preparation for the Hearing?

What information/materials are needed is one of the most important and time-consuming considerations of all. It also obviously depends on what cases you would like to have your class look at. Most states have a law-related education program that can be an invaluable resource for pulling together information for mock hearings. Once I have decided which cases I would like to focus on, I like to find or create some type of brief for the legal teams. Because the facts of the case are not being disputed in U.S. Supreme Court hearings, a straightforward summary of the case should be given to each team. Here is an example of the brief that each side will receive for the case of *Gideon v. Wainwright*.

> On June 3, 1961, Clarence Earl Gideon was arrested for breaking and entering the Bay Harbor Pool Room in Panama City, Florida. He was 51 years old. He had a history of arrests for burglary and gambling and had served time in several prisons before this arrest.
>
> Gideon went before Judge Robert L. McCrary and a jury of six people in the Bay County Court. When asked if he was ready to go to trial, Gideon responded, "I am not ready, Your Honor."
>
> "Why aren't you ready?" McCrary asked.
>
> "I have no counsel."
>
> "Why do you not have counsel? Did you not know that your case was set for today?"
>
> "Yes, sir, I knew it was set for today"
>
> "Why, then, did you not secure counsel and be prepared to go to trial?"
>
> Gideon answered but his comments were inaudible. When the judge pressed him to speak clearly, Gideon indicated that he wanted to have the court provide counsel for him.

McCrary replied, "Mr. Gideon, I am sorry, but I cannot appoint counsel to represent you in this case. Under the laws of the State of Florida, the only time the court can appoint counsel to represent a defendant is when that person is charged with a capital offense (one punishable by death). I am sorry, but I have to deny your request. . . ."

Gideon was tried that very day. He had little success. He acted as his own lawyer and even called eight witnesses. His lack of experience in questioning was apparent, and little evidence in his favor was introduced. The questioning of the state prosecutor was much more effective. He had a key witness named Henry Cook who testified that he had seen Gideon coming out of the pool hall before dawn on the morning of the break-in. This evidence made it seem that Gideon was guilty. Although Gideon maintained his innocence in his closing statements, the jury convicted him of the charges, and Judge McCrary later sentenced him to the maximum sentence of five years in the state penitentiary.

While in prison, Gideon filed a writ of habeas corpus (a claim that he was being imprisoned illegally) with Louie L. Wainwright, who worked for the Florida Division of Corrections. The Florida Supreme Court refused his request. Gideon appealed to the U.S. Supreme Court, which agreed to hear his arguments. Gideon requested that the U.S. Supreme Court appoint a lawyer to represent him, which it did.

Now it is time for the legal teams to get to work. I give them a "prep sheet" with the following questions.

1. What is the case about?

2. What are the facts?

3. What is the issue? What does the court need to decide?

4. What are the best arguments for our side of the case?

5. What might be the arguments of the other side? How will we refute them?

6. What will be the harm if the other side wins?

At this point they have to dig into the language of the constitutional amendments to see how they can use them to win the case. In the beginning, the students can feel a bit overwhelmed. In the *Gideon* case, the respondent team might feel that the deck is stacked against them. They might not know where to begin. As I circulate around the room, checking in with the various groups, I will throw out ideas. To this group, I might say, "What about states' rights? Does Florida or any other state want the Feds telling them how to run their courtrooms? What amendments speak to that? Why doesn't one of you check out *Betts v. Brady,* 1942?" Once they begin to see how the language of the amendments might work in their favor, they can start putting their arguments together.

How Many Students Sit on the Court During Each Hearing?

You need an odd number to sit on the court, so that you can have a majority and dissenting group. If we have four hearings to do and 32 students, I will sit 9 on the bench, 4 for each hearing. A few lucky souls will get to go more than once. The court itself selects its own chief justice.

What Is the Procedure for Conducting the Actual Hearing?

Once the room is set up, I have the justices go out in the hallway and wait for the bailiff to bring them in. The bailiff then reads,

> The Honorable, the Chief Justice and the Associate Justices of the Supreme Court of the United States. (Justices enter room and take seats.) Oyez, oyez, oyez. All persons having business before the Honorable Court, the Supreme Court of the United States, are admonished to draw near and give their attention, for the court is now sitting. God save the United States and this Honorable Court.

The justices file into the room and take their seats. After the chief justice introduces the name of the case, the plaintiff and the respondent teams introduce themselves. Once these formalities are taken care of, the plaintiff team presents its side of the case. One of the attorneys briefly introduces or outlines the legal arguments that the team is going to present. Another member of the plaintiff team reads the brief of the case. I instruct the chief justice to ask the respondent team if they accept the presentation of the brief. Because the facts are not in dispute, there is rarely any discussion at this point. The plaintiff team presents their arguments. At any time during the presentation of either team, the justices can ask questions. I strongly encourage them to do so. The respondent team presents second, after which each team makes closing arguments, with an emphasis on refuting the opposition's case.

What Instruction Do the Students Need Regarding Their Role as Justices?

I provide a handout, which we discuss as a class, regarding the role of the justices. Students are instructed to take notes on the handout during the hearing, but not to let the note taking prohibit them from asking questions during the hearing. Their job is to make the attorneys really think about their arguments. The handout has room between questions so the students can jot down notes.

Case: _____

1. Facts of the case:

2. Legal issues raised by the case:

3. Arguments offered by the plaintiff:

4. Arguments offered by the respondent:

5. Tentative decision:

After both sides have presented their case, the justices then "retire" to the hallway or another room if it is available, where they are instructed to discuss the case. The chief justice is instructed to be sure everyone has had the opportunity to share his or her thoughts and opinions. Sometimes it is interesting to have these discussions heard in front of the class, but it is important that only the justices take part in the discussion. After each justice has had an opportunity to share, the chief justice asks for any further comment or question. These discussions must reach their natural conclusion before a vote is taken. Once the court has reached a decision, the justices reenter the classroom. The bailiff ushers them in and establishes order.

The follow-up homework for justices is to write their opinions, both majority and dissenting sides. All justices are assigned to do this unless it is their second time on the Court.

Format for Writing a Supreme Court Opinion

Directions to students: Use your notes that you took during the hearing for writing your opinion.

1. Statement of the case (one paragraph). What is the issue that needs to be decided?

2. State the facts that are relevant to the case.

3. Briefly state the theories that were offered by each side. Apply each theory to the Constitution itself. What are the constitutional ideas or principles that relate to this case?

4. State your decision, and give thoughtful reasons for your decision.

How Do I Evaluate Students During This Unit?

Once the hearings have been conducted, I have the students write a self-reflection piece. I ask them to reflect on the unit, specifically on major ideas about the Constitution, the Supreme Court, and the amendments they learned during this study. I also ask them to write about how well their group performed, as well as how they functioned within their groups.

Although I have not done so in the past, this year I intend to evaluate their oral arguments during the hearings. The two areas worth looking at will be relevance of their arguments to the issues, as well as the clarity of their arguments.

Each student must also submit a final writeup based on their "prep sheet" of the case they argued, as well as a final copy of their "opinion" as a justice.

Good Ideas versus Bad Ideas

One of the most enjoyable and rewarding aspects of doing mock hearings is seeing the level of participation. It is also really fun to see eighth-graders really wrestling with some sophisticated concepts. In his reflection paper, Lee wrote, "Now I get it why everyone freaks when a justice retires and they have to appoint a new one. If they are going to be in there for life, you don't want someone with weird ideas that is going to try to bring back Jim Crow or overturn *Roe v. Wade*." I am often amazed at the connections the students make.

On a higher level, this kind of activity teaches kids about themselves. When they put the complex pieces of their cases together and present them in a convincing and articulate manner, they often realize their capability to understand a part of life that goes well beyond the boundaries of their neighborhoods. This helps them feel a bit more prepared to enter this world that early adolescence is beginning to show them. Although preparing for and organizing mock trials can seem a bit daunting, they are well worth the effort, because the idea of justice comes alive in ways that book work can never accomplish. The students really enjoy taking part because they realize that they can impact the outcome of the unit. But most of all, students come to realize that the pursuit of justice is hard work, and that if we want to be treated fairly, if we want justice, not just in our personal lives but in our communities and in our society, we have to be able to articulate and sell our good ideas better than others can articulate their bad ones.

References

Aaseng, Nathan. 1994. *You Are the Supreme Court Justice*. Minneapolis: Oliver Press.

Aitkins, Maggie. 1992. *Should We Have Gun Control?* Minneapolis: Lerner.

Center for Civic Education. 1993. *With Liberty and Justice for All: The Story of the Bill of Rights*. Calabasas, CA: CCE.

Constitutional Rights Foundation. 1991. *We, the People*. Chicago: CRS.

Hakim, Joy. 1993. *The New Nation*. 1993. New York: Oxford University Press.

Lengle, James G., & Gerald A. Danzer. 1985. *Law in American History*. Glenview, IL: Scott, Foresman.

McCuen, Gary E., & R. A. Baumgart. 1985. *Reviving the Death Penalty; Ideas in Conflict Series*. Hudson, WI: Gary McCuen Publications.

Reikes–Ackerly, James. 1980. *Juvenile Problems and Law in Action* (2nd ed.) San Francisco: West.

Reikes, Jenkins, & Armentha Russell. 1990. *Juvenile Responsibility and the Law*. (3rd ed.). Law in Action Series. San Francisco: West.

12   *Market Failure and Economic Justice*

Paul Copley

Author's Note

Economics is sometimes called the dismal science. Many middle and high school teachers and students share this view. Although it is true that it takes work to learn the basic ideas that form the "structure" or "model" of our social activity when we engage in the transactions economists call the "distribution of goods and services," this distribution system ultimately shapes the quality of our daily life in the short and long term. Therefore I ask that readers cut me a little slack, while I sketch an outline of the content I include in my advanced placement economics class. I believe this content can be accessible to a wide range of students.

I hope that by using cases drawn from everyone's experience—freeway gridlock, questions about how to pay for parks or whether we should regulate the freedom of landlords who wish to convert apartments (open to rent-paying tenants) into condominiums (open to a much smaller proportion of those looking for a place to live)—students will be willing to grapple with issues of economic justice. Ultimately, these are policy questions, and our answers shape our communities and neighborhoods.

I know that it is not easy to make these issues and questions accessible to students. To begin with, teachers must have sufficient background in economic theory and few social studies teachers begin their careers with such background. I assume that many readers of this book may not have the background to teach through an economic lens. To alleviate this common concern, I have included a bit more economic theory than I would if I were addressing an audience of economics majors.

I t has become clear to me, over my thirty-two years of teaching, that the most fulfilling aspect of the work is experiencing the link between student learning and my own learning. We ultimately teach in much the same way we ourselves go about learning. I avoided economics as a discipline for many years, preferring a mode of inquiry that found my teaching files loaded with accounts of historic and contemporary injustice. Over time I realized that the roots of the injustice contained in most of these accounts were economic at their base, blind pecuniary greed, the power of capital, and the pursuit of wealth without work. For many years my classroom reflected a similar inquiry into the struggle of labor versus capital, the "haves versus the have-nots," and the impact of money on the land. I was satisfied to witness the same incredulity, predictable anger, and dismay with the side effects of commercial power in my students that I myself felt. I had infused economics as a social science, my classroom was inviting critical thinking and writing, but I found my role as a teacher gradually evolving. I began to add to my own reading an exploration of economic models, economics as a discipline, even business economics, in order to develop my own skills in evaluating the awesome forces of the market economy. I wanted to develop for myself what C. W. Mills called the "sociological imagination," or the capacity to understand context, to be able to apply theory to practice, to transcend the tendency to be overwhelmed by the principles behind monetary/fiscal policy, banking, productivity, the cost structure of the firm and the fundamentals of international trade. I added to my preference for Neo-Marxist writing the study of economists such as Robert Heilbroner, Thorstein Veblen, and Lester Thurow, as a way to grasp market theory through a critical lens.

That interest led twelve years ago to an invitation by the College Board to write an advanced placement course, one that I have taught since, as well as serving as a test designer and reader in economics. I also teach economics integrated into my modern American history program. Both courses mix micro- and macroeconomic principles with an inquiry into economics as a force in our material lives, as a force in shaping our nation's history, and as the following unit demonstrates, as a force in our very concept of justice.

The AP class, a senior elective, usually open to thirty-five to forty-five students on teacher recommendation, includes students from our own suburban high school, and a few from neighboring district high schools. The class favors a seminar approach. I model and directly teach theory, providing context at the beginning of each unit, in much the same way as I do in this chapter. The class moves rapidly to practice, with students responding to questions and problems, scenarios, and case studies on which to apply the theory. Students work in teams, coming to tacit agreement (rarely consensus), and often go to the board to draw, illustrate, and diagram the fruits of their collective wisdom. I coach, encourage, question, evaluate, and reteach. The tone is informal, with students scattered around the room and at the board, usually under some time pressure. The atmosphere is informal but intense. My role is to measure the quality of my own teaching of theory, while respecting authentic student effort and balancing that respect with the necessity to clarify, and ultimately evaluate, the substance of student efforts.

This unit—taught after three months of study into market principles, opportunity cost, production possibilities, supply and demand, elasticities, market rationing, and the structure of competitive and monopoly firms—explores three propositions about market failure:

1. Markets fail when some actor in the economy lacks the information necessary to make a rational self-interested choice. Transactions between buyers and sellers reflect ignorance, luck, or accident, not informed decisions.

2. Markets fail because a large area of production called *public goods* escapes the ministrations of the market entirely. Public goods are not effectively divided up by price nor distributed according to individual consumer utilities.

3. Sometimes the output of private goods and services has negative side effects on persons other than those who are directly involved in buying, producing, or selling the goods in question. Economists call these effects *externalities;* specifically, *negative externalities.*

Also, in some cases individuals realize benefits or positive externalities that have accrued without any personal cost.

I choose these three areas of failure to use the language and logic of the market to ask why we have a bias against social intervention and question the wisdom of current global trends toward privatization. Often students refuse to perceive any concept of economic justice that contradicts the logic of a completely free market, along with a sharp disregard for legitimate government intervention. I'm not sure why. Perhaps the cause is the worldwide decline of any ideological challenge to capitalism and the one-dimensional nature of global economic discourse. Or the glorification of personal accumulation pushed at home, or in the media, mixing with students' own vulnerable narcissism and their dreams of "making it." Some students will claim "money talks" when it comes to land development. They say, "It's just too bad; they deserve to live in a box," when struggling with homelessness or a housing shortage. Other students, who consider such callousness shallow, exhort, "We must step in to help those in need," without much logic beyond a genuine display of social conscience. This unit is designed to give students with all degrees of sensitivity the tools to take on economic ethics within the logic, language, and limits of our market economy.

The foundation of the unit is student exploration into about eleven case studies I created to engender critical reflection into what is just or unjust concerning the application of free market principles. Before we discuss the formal cases, I ask the class to suggest certain benefits that should be enjoyed by all citizens. I don't expect much agreement, but after two months in the textbook, I hope for some thinking that challenges strict free market sociology. For example, one student last year claimed that such benefits should include "the right of everyone to be free from hunger, sickness, and cold." It sounded like Franklin Delano Roosevelt's 1936 inaugural address to the nation, and it got us started on a discussion of fundamental economic rights. Another student, representing a classical free market philosophy, countered, "No one should be guaranteed anything, otherwise they won't work and our whole system will collapse." This was followed by substantial agreement.

I steered the class toward specificity, choosing housing as an example. Careful to avoid any prejudgment of student bias, I introduced the possibility that the free market fails when it rations housing only by income. We went on to discuss benefits such as freedom from discrimination, clean air, water, peace, and quiet. With no specific interest in consensus, I wrote each benefit boldly on the bulletin board for all to contemplate for the next week.

The class focused on benefits that clearly everyone does not enjoy. To prepare the class further, I turned to a review of Adam Smith's "invisible hand" and the possibility that the market mechanism, in our current setting, might require outside help.

I wanted them to know that before Adam Smith, economics did not exist as a separate discipline. The study of people's material life, trading, producing, and investing was confined to "moral philosophy." As this was Smith's training, it is little wonder that Smith was himself concerned about justice. In his 1776 *Wealth of Nations*, Adam Smith developed a model of market competition in which a self-interested seller, producer, worker, or consumer can maximize their own interests only when their self-interested actions accrue to someone else's net worth. Smith believed that an *invisible hand* leads individuals to see their own interests aligned with the interests of others. Under perfect conditions the principle of reciprocity implicit in this invisible hand leads society to achieve the optimum use of scarce resources because the value of those resources is determined by the public. To Smith, this was the highest form of economic justice because what a society produced, and how, would be determined by the free expression of the public.

Market Failure

Many critics contend that the market has a mercenary attitude toward allocating or rationing goods and services. They claim the market stresses efficiency over fairness and has little regard for any measurement of equality. Smith was aware that individuals will manipulate political power to advantage themselves at the expense of others. In many places today, modern capitalism is driven by a "visible hand" that uses market theory to defend inequalities in the distribution of economic resources, but this unit asks students to focus on how the supposed self-regulating "free market" often fails without any specific or intentional manipulation of power. The market fails because, in certain cases under specific circumstances and with certain goods, it simply does not deliver on its promise. It doesn't allocate resources efficiently. It fails to provide incentives that deliver what society wants. It rewards some while at the same time specifically harming others, or it gives benefits to some while costing them absolutely nothing. For economists, market failure occurs because the market unwittingly leads to injustice when relationships between participants lack the kind of reciprocity that Smith intended. In this unit there are no evil people, only free, self-interested individuals; however, these individuals are sometimes led to profit by harming others, or they may benefit without paying any of the costs.

After the review of Smith's philosophy, the class examines some scenarios designed to clarify the three areas of market failure. For example, few of us are immune to the irritation of getting caught in traffic congestion. Ironically, none of us consciously intend to contribute to that congestion, nor are we really "caught." We just get stuck in gridlock, and our self-interest is compromised. In 1968, Garrett Hardin wrote an influential article for *Science* magazine, entitled "The Tragedy of the Commons," which illustrated an important principle related to the failure of free markets. Hardin's subject was overpopulation and the need for social intervention. Hardin writes of a pastureland, an eighteenth-century "commons"—a piece of land open for all to explore their self-interest. Each herder, maximizing privately, overgrazes the commons; the net result is long-run famine and death. The result, Hardin explains, is ruin for all. On a freeway, similar behavior results in gridlock. Each driver is pursuing his or her own interest, but contrary to Smith's theory, this produces the opposite of social harmony: stress, rage, or worse, extended exposure to talk radio (its own kind of intellectual famine and death). This happens because like the commons, the freeway is free to all, a public good. Self-interested behavior does not work because public goods have not passed through a market-valuing mechanism. It is a "*free way*." Each participant sees a much more pronounced personal benefit. At the same time, they do not perceive themselves as personally contributing to the collective negative. They see only who is in front of them, not whom they are in front of.

What options are available to avert this congestion with its attendant social ills? Appeals to social conscience? "I will refrain from taking the freeway because I am contributing to gridlock." Few of us are like that. Should we privatize the freeway—pay a toll at each on-ramp? That could work: Each person would at least know that those in front of them have paid for the privilege. Should the freeway stay, but public access be rationed? You drive on odd-numbered days, I drive on even-numbered days? Hardin calls this "mutual coercion, mutually agreed upon." Should the state tax everyone to build more lanes? No individual has done anything wrong or unethical; public goods just don't respond well to such free-market, maximizing behavior.

When it comes to privatizing, city streets offer an even greater technical problem. How do you gather user fees or tolls on surface roads? They cannot be allocated through a price-rationing system. They belong to a class of goods, such as national defense, for which one person's consumption does not rival the consumption of another. For example, a lighthouse or a weather service is as effective for 100 boats as it is for one. These goods are available to all regardless of who pays for them and who does not. In these cases, the invisible hand doesn't work because a person will not, or cannot, buy just the amount he or she wants. Everyone can enjoy the weather service, the lighthouse, and the national defense that someone else pays for. It would be different if boat owners purchased the use of a lighthouse. They would be concerned with others' "free riding" or using their service at no personal cost. Similarly, a private park in the city would have difficulty restricting benefits only to those who owned it. "Free riders" could enjoy its beauty, residents of adjacent buildings its view.

Across the nation, some municipalities have experimented with radical privatization of public goods. Some are selling fire protection: firefighters answer calls to only those dwellings whose owners have purchased fire protection. If rationed out, you might find the city fire department watering the homes of neighbors while yours burns to the ground. Thousands now live in "gated communities" with guards and other security systems. Some of these communities have collectively petitioned officials for a reduction in taxes. They argue that a reduction is just compensation because they are buying safety in the private market. Do these experiments offend your sense of justice? Is everyone fiscally responsible for safe streets, or is safety a good that is divisible, allocated through the market? Through these and similar case studies, students explore these questions of economic justice:

1. What is a legitimate public good?

2. Why does the market fail to allocate some goods and services equitably?

3. What privatization schemes seem just, which do not?

4. What is "free riding," and why is it a market failure?

5. How am I as a student developing a framework to judge market failure?

Externalities

Society-wide costs and benefits "outside" the market are called *externalities*. When it comes to economic justice, environmental issues such as air and water pollution have illustrated that the market is not always effective in accounting for all the costs. Those that benefit from industrial output (workers, stockholders, suppliers, and consumers) are passing on some environmental cost to individuals outside the transaction. These costs are called *negative externalities*. Examples such as polluted groundwater, infected livestock, innocent people with emphysema, foul-smelling air, and acid rain are chronicled in most economics texts. Negative externalities are the source of countless case law litigations. Consider a loud bar, airplane noise, or hideous advertising signs. Some environmental externalities can be measured—the number of livestock harmed, or the level of mercury found in a stream—but others are more difficult to measure. How high into the sky do property rights exist? Although some may not be negatively affected by "hideous advertising" along the roadway, are enough people negatively affected to suggest that the social costs exceed the private cost paid for the advertising?

To these negative externalities are added *positive externalities*. Consider the private cost of a flu shot. Could a strong case be made that social benefits are actually greater than the private benefit? Has not society been spared potential infection because of one person's innoculation? Should others, because of these benefits, pick up some of the individual private cost? In a sense, society is getting a "free ride" on someone's private decision. I wrote some cases of positive externalities explicitly to explore this free ride, as another way to measure a degree of economic justice.

The final step prior to undertaking the case studies is to introduce students to ways that government intervenes to repair market failure. The three standard remedies—regulation, taxation, and subsidy—can be usefully categorized so students are able to weigh the appropriate choice remedy for each case of market failure presented in class. Economist Charles Schultze, in a 1977 *Harper's* essay entitled "The Public Use of the Private Interest," compared the wisdom of using "output-oriented" interventions, with "process-oriented" interventions. For Schultze, any government response that replaces the market incentive structure in order to achieve a specific result is output-oriented. Government regulation that tells industry the acceptable level of specific chemical emissions into the water is an example of output intervention. The government decides the output level of acceptable emissions, and business complies or is taken to court for violating the law.

Process-oriented interventions, championed by the deregulators of the late 1970s and 1980s, favor using market-based incentives, such as the drive of business to cut costs in order to compete, to eliminate the market failure. Instead of ordering industry to comply with emission levels, firms would purchase pollution rights from the government, a cost it is assumed they would want to cut. The choice is up to business.

Each case study was inspired by journals, articles, or news stories. I didn't go out of the way to look for market failure; examples are everywhere. Textbooks contain many fine cases as well, particularly those related to environmental problems. The facts in the cases are purely my invention. I chose issues to provoke students to reflect on whether or not they believe the market has failed. I want to invite students to use their own sense of justice as they reflect on and discuss the following:

1. Has the market failed? Students defend their position, taking a stand (often moving to one side of the classroom or the other to show their position). Students write a response and keep a journal to see if their thinking is internally consistent.

2. Does an externality exist? Do they see free riding? Students apply theory to defend their position and use market diagrams when useful.[*]

3. What mode of government intervention is called for and why? Would the cost and/or consequence of intervention exceed the benefits to society?

---

[*] Some students may have worked through market supply–demand diagrams, elasticities, ceiling/floor price intervention, and positive and negative externalities shown in diagrams. These cases invite that kind of market analysis. I will endeavor to work through some examples in the cases themselves. I have taught this unit recently requiring diagrams, but I have also taught the material without expecting students to draw any diagrams at all.

Two Sample Case Studies

Sample Case 1 Nitny vs. The Sheetmetal Sisters

Poor Helen and Freeda Sheetmetal. They are widowed sisters in their early eighties. They currently are in their fourteenth year of residence in a comfortable but unpretentious apartment in northwest Portland. Their monthly income is fixed at $530 for Helen and $830 for Freeda. Neither worked, and on the death of their husbands, they inherited the social security checks that account for all their monthly income. They have no other assets save personal belongings. Their rent is $600 per month. It has gone up only 10 percent in three years.

Fred Nitny, who has owned the building for eight years has joined with three other builders on the block to convert each apartment building into condominium residencies. Nitny has waited for all leases to expire. The conversion will be costly: $45,000 per unit. His units will be sold only after each of the forty-five current tenants has 90 days to finance the cost of their former apartment, soon to be an upgraded condo. Helen and Freeda are given the 90 days to finance the $130,000 condo price. Included in the purchase price is Nitny's willingness to find alternative housing during the renovation at the rental price.

Alas, with no assets Helen and Freeda cannot qualify for any private loan. In two weeks, they will have to pack up. The sisters are encouraged to join with 175 other elderly people who also are being "forced out." This community action group of senior citizens appeals to city authorities in an attempt to stop Nitny and the other builders from decreasing the supply of affordable rental housing units.

Following the evening's homework, which includes reading, reflecting, and writing a rough position in preparation for discussion, the class divides. Students move to one side of the room or the other depending on whether or not they see a market failure. Student ambivalence is evidenced immediately in Kate's response: "I see market failure, but how can we fault Nitny? It's his property. They both have rights—the ladies need a decent place to live, and Nitny has the right to make a profit."

Abby steps in: "I agree. It's not his fault, but he should be the first to step forward." Then Ray responds, "I agree the old ladies are out of the market, but it is because of their low income, not because Nitny has done anything wrong." All three early respondents want to form a compromise position, which is OK with me. They draw much of the class their way.

After discussing further case details, and the responsibility of the city as a housing safety net for the sisters, David divides the class by asserting, "The ladies do not deserve any assistance. They can find some other place to live." Paula retorts, "Right, David, they can find a box on the street. That's the problem with you, you care more about money than people's welfare!" So far this is exchange of rhetoric only, then David adds in a superior confrontative tone, "Where are the externalities, Paula?

The Sheetmetals are not innocent bystanders. They are low-end buyers in a housing market. People get what they can afford. No way should the city help, otherwise we will have bums moving in to take advantage."

John, who has been drawing diagrams between conversations with David, pops up to the back chalkboard and draws a classic rent control market diagram like the one depicted in Figure 12–1.

(With rents set below market equilibrium, the textbook result is a Q_s to Q_d shortage, as suppliers of housing are rationed out by the low price, whereas there is an increase of renters drawn in by the lower-than-market rents.)

David moves in to help John explain the diagram. David argues that "The sisters get a free ride, while others in the housing market can't find units." Abby responds, "David, that is not the 'free ride' Mr. Copley explained, because the sisters are paying their way the best they can. The government should not help them by freezing rents. That could be why Nitny is getting out, but the government should subsidize their incomes." At this point in the discussion, I interject, reteaching the distinction between process and output intervention. I ask the class to link Abby's

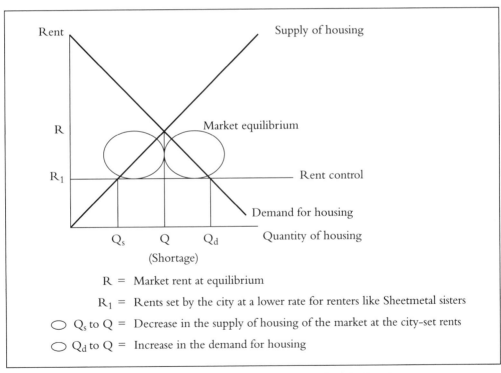

FIGURE 12–1 *John's Work Showing a Ceiling Price (Rent Control) at the Board*

solution to the process mode, and invite students to the board to illustrate the difference. Ahn and Mark sheepishly go to the board too, and the class works together, with a little help from me, to make the distinction shown in Figure 12–2.

Abby's augmenting the sisters' housing income is *process intervention* on the demand side. It increases the sisters' income, rationing them back in; but the downside is that it confirms the higher rents (R to R_1 in the diagram). *Output intervention* would either be to establish ceiling rents, as John had illustrated, restricting conversion altogether or to produce increased supply by the construction or purchase of city housing units. The price would be lower, but the city would be in the housing business, responsible for maintenance, and so forth.

David is still not satisfied with either move: "I still don't see the justification." Paula heads to the board and explains to David that it is Nitny and his colleagues that are, as she puts it, "messing up the rental market." Paula draws the decreased supply of units caused by the conversion, to show how the sisters are rationed out of the housing market.

This is the first of eleven cases the class will analyze. I start with this because it is not clear that government intervention is needed. David is right; no direct negative externalities exist, and in many years I have moved on to the next case. But last year student May Lim, in a thoughtfully prepared prewrite, took the class in a unique direction. Agreeing with David that no negative externalities existed to justify help for the sisters and that housing is not a public good by nature, she also

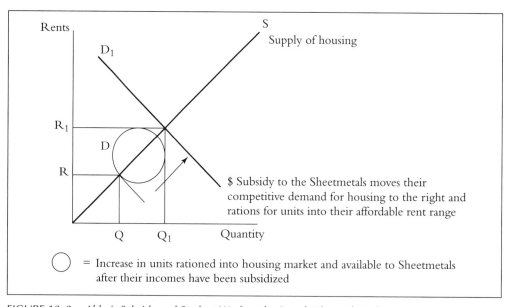

FIGURE 12–2   *Abby's Subsidy and Student Work at the Board (Ahn and Mark)*

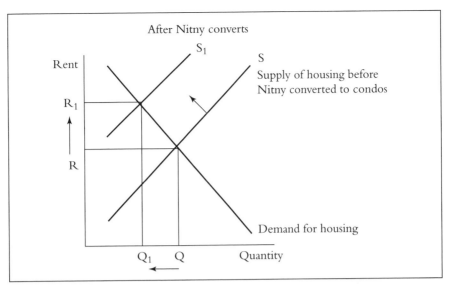

FIGURE 12–3   *Paula's Claim That it is Nitny Who Has Changed the Housing Market*

agreed with Paula that Nitny was changing the market and that some government response was called for. May Lim wrote,

> Fred's improvements to the apartments should raise community property values, thereby giving the neighborhood positive externalities, while the sisters and other low-income residents, unable to buy the condos, pay an indirect cost of this rise in value as they are rationed out on the street.
>
> The city should enter the market to ease the burden by subsidizing the elderly. This is rationalized by the higher property values (the positive boost in value enjoyed by those not immediately involved in the market), and the increased revenue to the city and county that follows. The city should subsidize the displaced residents with no-interest loans that would allow them to purchase their apartment/now condo. The city would be co-owner and would inherit the unit upon the passing of the subsidized person(s). The builders (Nitny) would be obligated to buy back the condo from the city at market price.

Everyone benefits, and the true costs more closely reflect the social benefits. May's prewrite for the discussion, subsequently integrated into her paper on this unit, creates a hybrid of output and process solutions. The government's co-authored loan is short-term, a transition cost for the sisters. I printed copies of May's thinking and passed them out. A number of students inquired how she came up with this approach. She answered, "I knew the Sheetmetals were victims, but I couldn't blame Nitny, so I thought that those needing to pay were those who benefited the most—

all the landlords collectively through increased property values and the city in general with increased taxing capacity."

Even David agreed with her compromise, and I personally enjoyed witnessing the fruits of a serious, though not perfect, attempt to apply theory to a real problem. May had led the class to see that justice is served when substantial agreement can be reached, justifying the principle of collective acts on behalf of individual victims.

Sample Case 2 RMF Development v. The County Planning Commission

In this land development case, students explored both positive and negative externalities, as they defended and attacked output-oriented regulations such as the Portland Area Urban Growth Boundary (UGB). Before this case, I taught a diagram to describe negative externalities in a case of air pollution, and students read portions of David Orr's *Earth in Mind* (Island Press, 1994), to study the link between economics and the environment. Orr explores the consequence of failing to link market price and value to the "true cost" of producing. In a way (as Hardin explored decades earlier in his "Tragedy of the Commons"), externalities are an attempt to instruct us about the real cost (the cost to the earth's resources) of an economic undertaking. I always wonder going into this case how successfully my AP students will apply these concepts. This last year, I was not disappointed.

> The Urban Growth Boundary is a plan to control growth in the Greater Portland Area. RMS Development has presented a plan that contests the planners' attempt to contain growth to certain areas of the region. The UGB is based on the premise that existing urban areas should be developed before population "leapfrogs" onto existing farmland and open space. RMS contends that the plan ignores the wishes of citizens who are willing to pay top market dollar for living space free from the noise and congestion of the city.
>
> RMS has purchased 2,000 acres in the foothills around North Plains, about 20 miles from downtown Portland. They plan a phase-in of roads, utilities, small commercial shops, and 800 upscale homes on half-acre parcels and two golf courses with what they say is a minimum of environmental impact. They have presold 75 percent of the homes, pending an amendment to UGB restrictions. RMS has substantial support for their plan from certain independent environmental groups that monitor development plans. They have praised RMS for the corporation's sensitivity to local vegetation, water, and wildlife. RMS further states that its plan will take pressure off congestion in suburban counties directly outside Portland.
>
> Spokesmen for the UGB argue that RMS directly violates the premise behind regional planning. The proposed RMS Development would produce increased traffic on local roads, and on main highways. It would impact infrastructure of the area, increase the need for schools, parks, and despite its environmental sensitivity, the development would result in the loss of hiking trails, natural habitats, and farmland. They argue that reversing this kind of project, advocating for controlled

growth where infrastructure already exists, is part of the UGB charter and RMS must be prevented until approved areas are fully developed.

The class begins as students choose opposite sides of the room based on their agreement with either the goals of UGB or RMS. Surprisingly, only Brandon and four other students support the development. Brandon begins the discussion: "RMS has shown it has responded to demand, and I think the UGB is wrong in that it is restricting personal freedom." His response is countered by the majority of the class. Six or seven hands are raised with John suggesting that "RMS affects the whole state because it is reducing necessary farmland."

Ray agrees: "So much is made from selling farmland and open space. We should use the money to preserve green spaces like Forest Park."

Abby, always interested in reasonable compromise, considers a classic process alternative to the UGB output approach: "Doesn't it make sense to subsidize the price of land in the city, making it more desirable and cheaper to develop than farmland? That way people will want to live closer in."

Ahn agrees with Abby and begins to take the class in a direction similar to May's application of externality theory in the housing case: "If true market price reflected all the costs, then would RMS be able to sell the lots to individual buyers so easily?"

Jessica Black grabs a piece of chalk, and with serious intent, explains to the class the negative externality diagram's application to this case. She calls on both David Orr and Garrett Hardin's arguments that the class learned in the first month. Jessica says, "The UGB exists to protect 'The commons.' A market economy could not exist if all resources were ravaged. There have to be limits. RMS development, despite claiming that they and their home-owning clients are environmentally conscious, have simply skirted the issue. There is no way that the prices of lots reflect current and future costs. The county, and the city, will have to pay for infrastructure, sewer, water, roads, and schools, and then the commercial building will follow the thousands of residences. Within a few years, another upscale city will exist. No matter how the golf course is designed, animal habitats will suffer, future hiking trails will be extinguished, and current forest and farmland lost forever. David Orr showed us that existing food prices do not reflect all the cost of soil erosion, damage by pesticides, and all the costs that are so difficult to monetarize because we do not know how to price the loss of the biosphere." Jessica had read this case the prior evening at home and was more than prepared to diagram on the board the nature of the true cost of RMS's development. Together, other students and I helped Jessica to refine some of the axis points in her diagram (Figure 12–4) to reflect the true cost of housing. Jessica's work demonstrates a level of price per lot to reflect RMS's costs, plus the externalities that she had argued convincingly.

Jessica's solution created a price per lot that better reflects the real cost to the environment and to the community. Depending on the elasticity of lot buyers, this true cost (or social cost) would result in a decreased quantity of lots that would clear the market. Compared to the divergence of classroom opinion on the

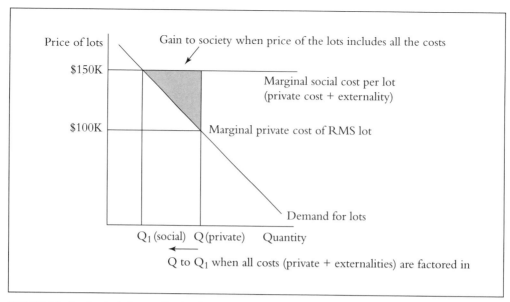

FIGURE 12–4   *Jessica's Externality Analysis in Diagram*

Sheetmetal case, the class majority saw justice in a process method that would challenge not the intent of the UGB, but its output-oriented, market-replacing regulatory methods.

Students' Vision of Economic Justice in a Market Economy

As these cases illustrate, a market economy that expects and rewards maximizing behavior simultaneously develops socializing rules. Students' eye on justice is really looking at limits. They say justice requires limits on the free exercise of self-interest, and on social intervention to modify and inform market participants. Once students learn some rules about market failure, they can begin to construct for themselves a vision of economic justice based on empirical evidence. This vision of justice is based on the realization that there are consequences to maximizing behavior and responsibilities that transcend individual utility. Furthermore, as Jessica's and May's responses show, students recognize that there are some areas in which collective action is simply more efficient than the market in allocating goods and services.

In supporting the value of social benefits—benefits shared by all—students in my economics class rejected the kind of narrow self-interest ideology that exploits adolescent narcissism and is so often promoted in modern media. Social harmony, if not social justice, is for most high school students an abstraction. Like our case law, justice is based on balancing individual freedom with social consequences. Like case law, economics recognizes a certain logic in the market's failure to perform in certain circumstances. Out of that logic, economists have developed certain guidelines. Applying these limiting principles helps adolescents to "see for justice" and develop a confidence in their ability to apply school knowledge in the situations of real conflict in their communities.

References

Buchholz, Todd. 1989. *New Ideas from Dead Economists*. New York: Penguin, 10–41.

Heilbroner, Robert, & Lester Thurow. 1998. *Economics Explained*. New York: Simon & Schuster, 26–32.

McEachern, Robert. 1997. *Economics: A Contemporary Introduction*. Cincinnati, OH: Southwestern College Publishing.

Schultze, Charles. 1977 (May). "Public Use of The Private Interest." *Harper's*: 43–62.

Hardin, Garrett. 1968, rpt. 1995. "The Tragedy of The Commons." In *The Immigration Dilemma: Avoiding the Tragedy of the Commons*. Washington, DC: Federation for American Immigration Reform, 13–31.

You can receive copies of the next eight cases by writing Paul Copley, Sunset High School, 13840 Cornell Rd., Portland, Oregon 97005:

Case 3, The *Frost* case explores the positive externalities of public education.

Case 4, *Peekaboo v. Cheak,* an adult bookstore moves in across the street from the school. Do negative externalities exist?

Case 5, *Sexual discrimination* case: Do negative externalities exist in the labor market?

Case 6, The *Landendown* case, evaluating public goods and positive externalities in "gated communities."

Case 7, *Last Horizons v. The Board of Health:* Does the regulation of nursing homes create special reasons for state oversight?

Case 8, *Builder Bob v. The County Bureaucrats:* What about codes protecting current and future home owners?

Case 9, *Riverplace v. United Airlines:* How high in the air do property rights exist? What about noise pollution?

Case 10, *Big John v. The Shabbyville 5:* The case of a "company town" plus three other cases.

My appreciation to Sunset High School colleague John Farra for his skillful counsel and advice on this project.

13 Our Needs and Their Destruction— Oil Drilling in Nigeria

Engaging in the Struggle for Social Justice

Sandra Childs and Amanda Weber-Welch

The Facts

No roads. No clean running water. No electricity. No schools or hospitals or jobs or usable farmland. Welcome to the Niger Delta. The land of plenty for Shell and Chevron, Mobil, Texaco, and Arco. However, the people of this region that produces 90 percent of Nigeria's earnings ($10 billion annually) can't even afford to buy the oil it produces. With average salaries at $320 a year, the people can't afford much of anything. But have no fear. The delta does have lots of oil for you and me to buy. Lots of oil for companies to profit from. Lots of oil for the Nigerian government officials to get rich from. And lots of gas flares, acid rain, spills, leaks, soot, respiratory problems, and repression. Between 1976 and 1991, there were 3,000 separate oil spills, averaging 700 barrels a day. Many of those spills are still leaking. Cleanup cannot reverse the damage to the land and water and people.

From 1958 to 1998 Shell Oil Company made over $30 billion in oil from Ogoniland in the Niger Delta. The military dictatorship of Nigeria profited from their arrangements with the oil companies but did little to "give back" to the region. Instead, the government and the oil companies cooperated to silence, torture, and kill the native peoples of the delta who stood up and spoke up to protest the exploitation and destruction of the land. This past year Nigeria finally had "free elections," but many elections in the delta were canceled due to "unrest." The new government promises to be free from corruption and greed. So far no change has been felt in the delta.

The Teacher's Dilemma

Now, how do you teach this story without plummeting yourself and your students into depression? How do you turn the situation in the delta from a lesson about so-cial *in*justice to a lesson about social justice? We must do more than let the students know about the organized resistance of Delta peoples since 1971 or the organized boycotts of MOSOP (Movement for the Survival of the Ogoni People) or the sit-ins, and takeovers, and sabotage efforts of the delta youth that shut down two-thirds of the oil production through acts of resistance. These facts are not enough. Because with these facts come more stories of repression. More stories of torture and death.

The Teachers and the Students

As high school global studies teachers, we faced this dilemma. Amanda Weber-Welch teaches at Gresham High School, a large suburban school outside of Port-land, Oregon. Sandra Childs teaches at Franklin High School, a working-class city high school in Portland. Our students were already immersed in the long history of colonialism and oppression prior to this unit on Nigeria. At both schools our stu-dents had studied colonialism and engaged in several activities that helped them to better understand its historical and contemporary effects. In addition, at Franklin they had looked at the United Nations Declaration of Human Rights; and at Gre-sham, they had also read Nigerian author Chinua Achebe's definitive novel, *Things Fall Apart,* a story exploring the impact of colonial entrance on native tribal systems. Both groups saw the current situation in Nigeria as rooted in a long history of op-pression and resistance.

We decided to work together to create this new unit of study and to use it at our respective high schools. Sandra had been collecting news articles and informa-tion off the Internet for the past several years, because Nigeria had become embroiled in various human rights scandals in the early 1990s. Amanda and her teaching part-ner were eager to find a modern issue in which to further explore colonialism's im-pact. Since we had previously team-taught and shared curriculum over the years, it was not difficult to collaborate. As teachers committed to relevant, engaging cur-riculum, we had extensive experience creating our own lessons and activities. Be-cause this is what good teachers do. However, tackling something this elaborate and complex was somewhat daunting. Especially as two committed teachers, we might never find the time. This is where developing a true teaching community can really pay off. Despite the busy teaching schedules of educators, we both have remained committed to sharing with and being inspired by a group of educators in the Port-land metro area. Our involvement in this group has led to some terrific curriculum exchange and development, as well as creating a network of support that goes beyond the staff at one's own school.[1] Because we had used many excellent role-plays written by Bill Bigelow and other teachers in our group, we felt it was both possible and our obligation to write a role-play of our own. The oil fires in the delta during the autumn of 1998 made the need for a role-play urgent.

Putting the Role-Play Together

Our students had background on colonialism to give them a basis for this role-play, but we needed to provide some factual information specific to the current crisis in Nigeria. Now it was time to rummage through Sandra's stack of old news clippings and to search the Net in order to put together a fact sheet and to begin constructing possible roles (see References at end of chapter for sources). As we skimmed the clippings, we wrote down key points and then placed them in chronological order. Yes, it was tedious, but it was exciting to see this useless file folder becoming an activity that students could connect with.

One of the most useful resources, both for helping us frame the role-play and develop the roles, was the PBS special and its companion website *Globalization and Human Rights,* presented by Charlene Hunter-Gault, exploring the disconnection between economic policy and human rights. The documentary opens at the 1998 World Economic Forum held in Switzerland that invited international labor organizers and human rights activists to join government trade officials and corporate spokespeople and economic analysts to participate in a discussion of globalization and international trade policy.

Beyond the Traditional Classroom

At the start of the role-play, we gave students the fact sheet we had compiled covering relevant background about Nigeria and its history of oil. (See Appendix A to this chapter). They also watched parts of the PBS video. It allowed students to see that conference that they were going to participate in was an actual event. It was also important for students to realize the conference in Switzerland didn't result in any change in government economic policy that would consider human rights, labor, or environmental issues when setting trade policy. This is not surprising. No doubt the human rights and labor organizers invited to attend did not expect dramatic change.

---

[1]See Childs, 1999 for a description of Portland Area Rethinking Schools' Globalization Workgroup.

No doubt they realized their invitations were simply token nods in order to silence the protest. However, such activists must also take heart in the fact that they were finally recognized as a nuisance/voice significant enough to appease in some way. This is a step, a tiny step—one we wanted our kids to experience at firsthand. So they did. To simply teach the narrative, to tell them the story, would be just one more example of how horrible and unfair the world is. But to give them a chance to engage in a dialogue and become the players changes everything. Not only did they experience the triumph of a conversation that considered human rights and trade at the same time, they also experienced the frustration. This is because we didn't just tell kids the story, we made them act it out.

The Role-Play

Ogoni leaders sit solemnly on the floor, looking defiantly at their oppressors, the Nigerian governmental officials. They know this is their opportunity to state their case in relative safety and they are not about to lose this chance. In an atmosphere of tension, the dialogue begins. Alexis Young becomes Alexis Nopetrol as she tells the forum how she became a human rights activist. She speaks out against the atrocities in Nigeria. Ogoni leaders nod in response, as the U.S. trade secretary shifts uncomfortably in her seat. Seeing that this situation is volatile, the Nigerian governmental officials try a diplomatic tactic and speak of changes on the horizon. Representatives of the oil companies sigh in relief, although environmentalists quickly point out that the spills they claim to have already cleaned up are currently killing people.

Am I describing the real conference or our kids' role-plays? Hard to tell, because for our students it becomes real. Using the 1998 World Economic Forum as a guide, the students participated in the World Economic Forum hearing on Nigeria oil and human rights, acting as Nigerian government officials, U.S. trade secretaries, human rights activists, oil company representatives, environmental activists, and MOSOP— tribal—activists (see Appendix C to this chapter). The students were asked to consider whether economic policy should be linked to human rights issues and to consider the particular situation in the Delta. They were asked to come up with, discuss and vote on resolutions that would deal with issues of human rights, trade, business practices, responsibilities, and environmental regulations.

Members of each group read their role and wrote internal monologues in the voice of their character, embellishing to personalize the role. The best of these were shared with the entire class. Then students began to prepare a statement of concerns and response to specific questions (see World Economic Forum instructions, in Appendix B to this chapter). Once they had prepared the preliminary work, traveling negotiators from each group tried to work out deals with other participants. They went back to their own group and formulated resolutions dealing with human rights, the environment, and trade. Now the forum was ready to begin. One group presented their resolution and the proposal went up for amendment and debate. We continued resolving, amending, debating, and voting for two class periods.

It went anything but smoothly. In both our classrooms, this role-play was one of the most contentious and unruly this year. This was reflected in the students' post conference reflections (see Appendix D to this chapter). For example, Amy Lemon, a Franklin High School student who acted as an Ogoni tribal woman and MOSOP activist, stated:

> Those $#*@! were foolishly stubborn; they refused to listen to the numbers arguments, facts, and statistics that were presented. They were unreasonable and arrogant, apathetic and unconcerned for the horrendous damage they are causing the people and the earth. Anger and frustration overtook many of my fellow MOSOP activists, and the environmental and human rights activists were livid as well. . . .

At Gresham High School, MOSOP activists, frustrated at the denials of the Nigerian governmental officials, walked out. Gabriel Guard, playing a member of MOSOP, muttered, "This is our land, and our people are dying. How can we work with you when you refuse to care about anything but your own money?"

Given the roles, there was no way that all the parties were going to agree. But that wasn't the point. In a role-play, we often have two goals: (1) students learn to identify with a different point of view than their own, and (2) students learn to listen to a point of view other than their own. Often what happens is that kids get off on arguing and forget to listen. This role-play was no exception. In our roles as forum moderators, we reminded the participants that the forum was being "televised" and that their behavior would reflect on the parties they represented. We had hoped this would help students maintain composure and work on their respectful listening skills. However, once again, the students became so identified with their characters that they felt their pain. Instead of a calm, academic discussion, the result was a passionate struggle. No one doubted that these kids were engaged. In this way they certainly understood that any move toward social justice is fraught with dissent, struggle, and frustration. Some kids were frustrated at the evasive and unresponsive remarks of the Nigerian government; others were frustrated at the U.S. trade secretary's obvious lack of morality; others were frustrated at human rights activists' unwillingness to compromise or the MOSOP's righteous attitude. And of course that is the point. Social justice is struggle. Making change is hard. It takes practice and patience and lots of work.

Both classes did come up with three resolutions looking at questions of the environment, labor and human rights, and consumer boycotts. At Gresham, proposals included (1) requirements to clean up previous oil spills and to take precautions to ensure that these spills were minimized in the future, (2) to improve the quality of life for the people of the Niger Delta, and (3) to allow human rights groups to independently observe actions of the Nigerian government and the oil companies and to suspend trade if human rights were violated. However, the polarized views of the participants prevented passage of the Gresham resolutions.

At Franklin, three resolutions were adopted. Franklin students agreed that (1) all workers will have the right to organize and strike by approval of an international labor rights committee. If a country or company violates that right, a penalty may be imposed after a hearing by an international tribunal. (2) The Nigerian government will give oil companies (an additional) 10 percent tax break. The oil companies will use 5 percent for environmental clean up in the region. (3) Within a year, if spills not caused by sabotage are not cleaned up by oil companies or the Nigerian government, and if human rights have not improved, an international tribunal will convene to entertain a boycott. Although the ideas sounded good, there were no teeth to the resolutions. In fact, Franklin High student Chris Brummer, a human rights activist in the role-play, commented, "The resolutions that were drafted and passed in the simulated forum will have little benefit to those most in need." How would the impoverished workers bring a case before an international tribunal? Just how much is 5 percent of 10 percent? And how many years would it take to determine if a spill was caused by sabotage or not? Although the students genuinely tried to focus on solutions, the only resolutions that could pass were ones vague enough to have no real impact. In this way, students experienced the real difficulties of policymaking. In the process, they made use of information about issues in the delta and they learned that the struggle for social justice, is, in fact, a struggle of many competing interests.

So What Just Happened?

More important than the role-play itself is often the debrief about the role-play, where we get to dissect the resolutions (and their ineffectiveness) and the process. How did people respond to each other? What would have been a more effective means of communicating? What can be done now? After the role-play, students were required to write a reflection both as the character they played and as a student. We asked them specific questions about both the process and the content of the forum. Students had to predict what the long-term consequences of their forum might be, had it been real. They also had to express their own final conclusions about the responsibility of governments and business regarding human rights and the environment. In addition, Franklin students had to analyze some key quotes from the film *Globalization and Human Rights*. Most importantly, students had to plan future strategies to influence international policy. In other words, no human rights policy was inserted into trade policy in real life—so what do the people of the delta, the environmentalists, the labor organizers, the human rights activists do now?

Written reflection in hand, the students then had a chance to review the experience with each other. It was essential to have the students talk about what happened and why. Civil discussion, working things out together, takes practice. Lots of it. Every role-play (whether it "works" or not) is another opportunity for students to practice this skill. When its over they must figure out what they did well, what they could improve on, so that in the next role-play or the next real conflict they have, they can step back and think about what makes effective dialogue.

After this students began to talk about the issues, but this time, as themselves. The class began to consider which groups make these decisions in real life. After the role-play, the dynamics were clear—if Nigerian government officials, U.S. trade representatives, and oil company representatives were formulating policy toward the Niger Delta, environmental, labor, and human rights policy were not considered. As Chad Van Horn, another Franklin student, so bluntly stated, "The oil companies and governmental officials have the loudest voices since they have the fattest wallets." Amy Lemon of Franklin High described it this way, "It was essentially a very large cocktail party where world economic leaders kissed up to each other and human rights and environmental activists were merely tolerated rather than courted."

Time To Act

Therefore, labor, human rights, indigenous, and environmental activists need to find other ways to change corporate and governmental policies. For this change to be effective, these groups need to recognize their common interests. Amy Lemon concluded her reflection by saying:

> I have a favorite analogy that works with this situation. As of now, we are but small drops of water scattered about, and we can change only small things. But group us all together, and even the tiniest stream can wear away the rock and change something. That is what we must do; group together and fight together.

The kids learned about what these activist groups are doing. For this role-play to be effective in teaching social justice, students must not only understand the dynamics between those in power and those striving for change, they must also act. Adrienne Armstrong explains,

> Knowing is only half the battle. More comes into play when trying to change a system after it has already been established. In order to change something we must take action and be proactive, not just educate ourselves. History is important but action is what makes changes.

Where Do We Go from Here?

What is social justice, after all? What can the lessons we designed around the Nigerian oil issue help kids understand about justice? One thing we hoped kids would learn was that social justice is a struggle, a long, ongoing struggle that takes time, perseverance, patience, and collective action. We have no doubt that our lessons helped students understand the struggle, the frustration, the need for patience. However, of central importance is whether our lesson helped kids commit to the struggle, hold the frustration, strive for the patience.

In looking at the work our students did this year, we realize that they did learn how change is achieved. Not always, but often, we kept the emphasis on social justice movements rather than on social injustice and human rights abuse. In this unit we ended with a speaker, Josey Kpobe-Tee, a Portlander from Nigeria and a member of Amnesty International. She was able to talk about the resistance. In many ways she echoed the issues discussed in the students' economic summit. But that was not the end.

Indeed, some kids did keep going. Chris Brummer of Franklin High School is trying to start a school chapter of Amnesty International. Emily Wood, Gabriel Guard, Mandy Leasure, and many others from Gresham High School are active members of a school group called Youth for Change. They helped to organize a citywide, student-led conference looking at globalization. Alexis Young, Amy Lemon, and others of Franklin created some websites. Many students from both schools wrote letters to Shell and the U.S. Trade Secretary's office, became involved in web-based corporate watchdog groups and a variety of social justice organizations, participated in boycotts, wrote poetry they read to the larger community, and published further research for other classes. The opportunity to engage in these other activities is essential. Students were immersed in the struggle for change, allowing them to fight, in spite of the frustrations, allowing them to "keep keeping on." Taking action allows students to move from a position of powerlessness and despair to one of possibility.

See, for any lesson on social justice to be truly effective, it must move outside the single classroom. The role-play and semester projects allowed this to happen. But not just for the kids. As teachers, to be effective in teaching social justice we must also move outside our isolating classrooms and give ourselves the opportunity to collaborate and create. This role-play would not have happened if the two of us had not sat down together to do it. The task was too immense, our schedules too full, our spirits too exhausted. But our ongoing commitment to Portland Area Rethinking Schools Globalization Work Group inspired us to create this unit. Others in the group had created activities equally powerful, and we wanted to give back.[2]

---

[2]See Appendix E to this chapter for materials and instructions for this role-play.

Thus this role-play is an embodiment of the key to social justice—working together for the long haul.

References

Childs, S. J. 1999 (Fall). "Moving Beyond Tired." *Rethinking Schools,* 14(1): 8.

Childs, S. J. 1999 (Fall). "Networking, Organizing, and Resisting." *Rethinking Schools,* 14(1): 9.

Cohen, Roger. 1998 (September 20). "High Claims in Spill Betray Depth of Nigeria's Poverty." *The New York Times.*

Cohen, Roger. 1998 (August 23). "Nigeria's Painful Paradox of Self-Imposed Poverty." *New York Times.*

Corporation for Public Broadcasting. 1999 (December 12). "Globalization & Human Rights." **http://www.pbs.org/globalization**

Corpwatch. 1999 (April 3). "Shell in Nigeria." *The Assault on Human Rights.* **http://www.corpwatch.org/trac/feature/humanrts/cases/nb-shell-shock1/html**

Drogin, Bob. 1995 (October 14). "Beneath Nigeria's Oil Glut Lie Barren Lives and Fear." *Los Angeles Times.*

Fleshman, Michael. 1999 (April 3). "Mobil in Nigeria. Partner in Oppression." Corpwatch. **http://www.corpwatch.org/trac/feature/humanrts/cases/nb-mobil.html**

Goodman, Amy, & Jeremy Scahill. 1999 (March 15). "Killing for Oil in Nigeria." *The Nation.*

Goodman, Amy, & Jeremy Scahill. 1998 (November 16). "Nigeria: Drilling and Killing." *The Nation.*

Gordimer, Nadine. 1999 (May 25). "In Nigeria, the Price for Oil is Blood." *New York Times:* A1.

Long, James, Carlos Petroni, & Edith Akaele. 1999 (February). "Nigeria: Transition to Where?" *San Francisco Frontlines:* 15–16.

Long, James. 1999 (February). "The British Crafting of Nigeria." *San Francisco Frontlines.*

McAuley, Tony. 1998 (October). "Nigeria: Human Rights Activists Consider Suit Against Chevron." Corpwatch. **http://www.corpwatch.org/corner/worldnews/other/230.html**

Morgan, Barry. 1999 (September 24). "Turmoil in the Niger Delta." *Upstream* 4(38): 16–18.

Onishi, Norimitsu. 1998 (November 22). "Nigeria Combustible as South's Oil Enriches North." *New York Times.*

Pacifica Radio. 1999 (May 3). "Voices from the Nigerian Resistance." *Democracy Now!* **http://www.pacfica.org/programs/nigeria/**

Peart, Karen. 1996 (February 23). "Nigeria: Waiting to Explode." *Scholastic Update.*

Royal Dutch Shell Corporation. 1999 (May 3). "The Environment." **http://www.shell.lnigeria.com/shell/environ_rhs.asp**

Royal Dutch Shell Corporation. 1999 (December 12). "Human Rights." **http://www.shellnigeria.com/shell/hr_rhs.asp**

Royal Dutch Shell Corporation. 1999 (May 3). "The Ogoni Issue." **http://www.shell.lnigeria.com/shell/ogoni_rhs.asp**

Sierra Club. (May 4). "Boycott Shell Oil, Embargo Nigeria." **http://www.sierraclub.org/human-rights/boycott.html**

APPENDIX A:
NIGERIA FACT SHEET

Political Background in Nigeria:

- Nigeria today is home to more than 250 ethnic groups.

- By 1800, southern Nigerian native culture had been destroyed by the trans-Atlantic slave trade and the influx of Christian missionaries; the northern regions, in contrast, influenced by slow political and economic change and Islamic presence, maintained much more stability.

- In 1885, Nigeria was carved out and claimed by the British at the Berlin Conference.

- In the early 1900s, Frederick Lugard, Britain's colonial administrator for Nigeria, followed a policy of "indirect rule" where conquered leaders in the Muslim North were given authority over those in the Christian South.

- Nigeria was given its "independence" on October 1, 1960, when the British Parliament appointed Governor General Azikiwe, a ceremonial leader representing the British monarch.

- The first elections, in 1964, were marked by boycotts and violence.

- In 1966 the first military coup took place. Nigeria's history since this time has been a series of military coups and dictatorships. Among these include the Ibo uprising of the 1967 Biafran Independence Movement, resulting in three years of war and up to 1 million dead.

Editor's Note: In any role-play that focuses on a current or recent event, it is essential for teachers to check names, titles, events, and outcomes. For example, there is a new president of Nigeria as this book goes to press. In volatile situations, power changes hands rapidly and teachers must update their information regularly to remain accurate.

- From 1985 to 1993 General Babangida (North) ruled Nigeria with an iron fist (restriction of civil and political rights, violence, and human rights violations).

- The 1993 election of a Muslim Baptist, Chief Moshood Abiola (South), was annulled by the military government. General Abacha took over.

- From 1993 to 1998 Abacha responded to rising protests with greater human rights violations: dissolved unions, arrested and killed protesters, evicted the U.S. press, dissolved the legislature, and engaged in raids and attacks on civilians.

- On June 8, 1998, General Abacha died of a heart attack; General Abdulsalam Abubakar took power, promising reforms and elections, and released some political prisoners.

- On July 7, 1998, President-elect Abiola died of an apparent heart attack while in prison.

- In February 1999 General Olusegun Obasanjo was elected President. Obasanjo headed Nigeria's government from 1976 to 1979, following the assassination of the former head of state. He also spent three years in prison for opposing Abacha. He pledged changes for Nigeria. None have been felt in the Nigerian Delta, whose residents could not participate in elections due to "unrest."

Oil Background for Nigeria:

- In 1908 the search for oil began. Shell joined the search for oil in 1937.

- In 1956 the first commercial discovery of oil in the Niger Delta was made. In 1958 exportation of Nigerian oil began—the prospects of economic expansion furthered political rivalries right before 1960 independence.

- From 1958 to 1998 Shell Oil Company took $30 billion in oil from Ogoniland.

- Chevron, Mobil, Texaco, and Arco are also drilling in the region.

- After 1970, in response to continued environmental devastation and oppression, a resistance movement began. There have been ongoing peaceful protests against Shell and other oil companies, since that time.

- These protests have been met with brutality by the Nigerian government: threats, imprisonment, death. In some cases, the oil companies have financially supported military action.

- In 1995 Ken Saro Wiwa, author, environmental activist, and leader of the Movement for the Survival of the Ogoni People (MOSOP), was imprisoned, falsely charged with murder and executed by the Nigerian government for his role in protests against foreign oil investment in Ogoniland.

- Before Saro Wiwa's execution, international human rights groups pleaded for international intervention and response. There was condemnation of the Nigerian government's actions, but no sanctions were imposed. Oil companies continued to do business in the region.

- The delta produces 90 percent of Nigeria's earnings, amounting to $10 billion annually, but lacks roads, clean running water, schools, hospitals, jobs, and usable farmland. The Nigerian government takes 70 percent of the revenue from this resource; the remainder of the money is oil company profit.

- American investments total $7 billion.

- Half of Nigeria's oil is either used directly by U.S. companies and consumers or refined in the United States and exported. It is the fifth largest source of U.S. imported fuel.

- The Nigerian Delta is one of the poorest regions in the world—annual salaries hover at $320, and most Nigerians can't afford and do not have access to oil, the most abundant resource in their country.

- In 1990, the Nigerian government removed hundreds of people from their homes in the Niger Delta in order to allow construction of Mobil Oil's facility and headquarters.

- In January 1998, Mobil Oil had an underwater pipeline snap 3.5 miles offshore; 40,000 barrels of oil were spilled. The oil company claimed only "slight" environmental damage, but Mobil announced it would compensate anyone suffering economic injury as a result of the spill. Thousands of Nigerians living along the coast have made claims against Mobil due to destruction of their fishing nets and livelihood; Mobil now says that most of these claims are false.

- Between 1976 and 1991 there have been 3,000 separate oil spills, averaging 700 barrels each in the Niger Delta; some spills are still leaking into water supplies. Cleanup cannot reverse the irreparable damage to the land.

- Other environmental problems include gas flares near villages, resulting in air, noise, water pollution, acid rain, respiratory problems, and soot everywhere.

- In 1993, Shell Oil temporarily stopped its operations in Nigeria due to sabotage and increased oil spills, but later returned, promising reform and development in the impoverished region. Communities claim few changes have occurred.

- In 1998, there was an increase in sabotage, resistance, and rebellion against the continued presence of oil companies. A third of oil production has been stopped by acts of resistance.

- Human rights groups question the alliance between the foreign oil companies and the Nigerian military, known for its repression of civilians.

- In May 1998, community activists from the delta occupied one of Chevron's offshore drilling facilities to advertise their plight and to get the international community to listen. Their demands: clean water, electricity, environmental cleanup, employment. Instead of negotiating, Chevron transported Nigerian soldiers to the facility, who shot at protesters, killing two and injuring at least thirty. Eleven activists were jailed and tortured.

- Severe oil shortages in oil-rich Nigeria led to a thriving black market for the fuel, resulting in thieves siphoning oil. In October 1998 an unclosed valve created a flammable pool of oil; over 700 villagers died when this lake caught on fire. Government officials knew of the leak hours before it sent in cleanup crews; by then it was too late.

APPENDIX B:
STUDENT INSTRUCTIONS

World Economic Forum: Subcommittee Hearing on the Niger Delta

You have been invited to participate in a World Economic Forum that hopes to develop an International Compact (Agreement) on World Trade. The central question that will be raised is whether or not economic policy should be linked to human rights issues. In other words, how should business respond to human rights abuses in the countries/regions where they do business?

This hearing will specifically focus on the practices and policies of oil companies in the Niger Delta. Participants in this hearing include human rights observers, environmental activists, tribal advocates (MOSOP), Nigerian government officials, U.S. economic advisers, and international oil companies. Your job is to develop an action plan resolving this issue. In preparation for the hearing, you will need to understand your role and all political/oil background facts and how they relate to your role. Based on this background, answer the guiding questions and consider with which other groups you may be able to align. Remember, however, that you have interests that you represent; don't compromise your position too much. Rules of etiquette apply in this hearing (this is being televised!)

1. Read the background information and your role.

2. On your own, write an internal monologue (from your character's point of view). Include the following: name, age, nationality, occupation, family, daily life activities, living conditions, hopes and fears in life, goals for this conference. *Note:* Much of this information is not available in the text. You will need to develop your persona. As long as your story does not contradict or seem out of place with the role, you are fine.

3. Individually take notes on the following questions, and then discuss them in your group. Appoint a recorder to take notes on each question.

a. List the ways your character believes the presence of the oil companies have helped and hurt the region.

b. What responsibilities do international businesses have to care for the environment?

c. Should international companies do business in countries where human rights abuses occur? Why or why not? What is the responsibility of businesses already in countries where human rights abuses are occurring?

d. Do international businesses have a responsibility to help develop and provide for the people in the regions where they get their resources?

e. Should nations boycott goods from businesses or nations where human rights abuses occur and where environmental damage is unchecked?

4. After discussing the questions, draft a resolution dealing with each issue in the preceding questions. Be sure you reach consensus in your group. Be sure each resolution deals with a specific issue.

Be It Resolved:

Be It Resolved:

Be It Resolved:

Be It Resolved:

APPENDIX C: THE ROLES

Environmental Activist

> Our rivers, rivulets and creeks are all covered with crude oil. We no longer breathe the natural oxygen, rather we inhale lethal and ghastly gases. Our water can no longer be drunk unless one wants to test the effect of crude oil on the body. We no longer use vegetables, they are all polluted.
>
> Dere Youths Association (1970)

You have long held environmental issues as central to the lives of human beings all over the world. You grew up in Saudi Arabia and have seen firsthand that caution must be used when drilling for oil. Industrialized nations have long taken advantage of the wealth in other countries to strengthen their own economy and in the process have destroyed the earth. You are very concerned about the environmental devastation that results from oil company practices around the world, especially Nigeria. Land once farmed by villagers is now owned and controlled by international oil companies who consciously destroy the environment to make more money. Villagers, in the meantime, have little say in decisions impacting this land. On- and offshore oil spills and flash fires have ruined the Niger Delta, one of the most oil-rich and resource-poor areas in the world. The spills have led to extensive air, water, and soil pollution and any potential for an agrarian and fishing economy is lost. The machinery creates constant racket, as do the flash fires, making the area uninhabitable.

Between 1976 and 1991, 3000 oil spills, averaging at least 700 barrels each, have created permanent damage to the environment. Oil spills do not just disappear; even after a period of time, the soil and water supply remains contaminated. Whereas in the United States and Great Britain environmental impact statements are required for each pipeline, the Nigerian government requires no such study and the companies gladly skip this step. This carelessness leads to much leakage and destruction. Many of the spills are not cleaned up; the sites are simply abandoned once the fuel supply is exhausted. Any protests by native tribes for monetary compensation and a change of practices have been met with military repression. The oil companies have willingly accepted the military's assistance in silencing these voices by jailing and killing protesters. Some of the oil companies claim to have changed their policies to be more environmentally sensitive; however, you have seen little evidence of this. A Shell spill from 1970 is still leaking, although Shell reports it has been cleaned up twice. Mobil Oil claimed that it would compensate victims of a spill for the loss of their traditional fishing livelihood and is now suggesting that villagers are lying about the extent of damage.

Although this most clearly impacts the people of the Niger Delta, this issue is not just limited to environmental destruction there. All over the world, oil companies are destroying our rain forests, polluting our waters, killing our fish, making land poisonous. The lack of environmental laws result in cheaper gas and oil prices for developed countries around the world; because prices are cheap, consumption is not a hotly debated topic and more of the world's resources are depleted. The average driver in America may not see the connection between his consumption and our planet's devastation, but the connection is clear. This cannot continue forever. Unless international companies are required to comply with the strictest environmental regulations of the most developed countries, our planet will be destroyed.

Human Rights Observer/Activist

You have traveled around the world but mostly in Africa investigating charges in human rights abuses and waging education campaigns against governments who violate the Universal Declaration of Human Rights (UDHR). You believe that we all have a responsibility to protect human rights. You have been invited to provide testimony that advocates for the rights of all human beings, particularly those of the people of the Niger Delta. You will first highlight the human rights abuses that have occurred as a result of the relationship between the oil companies and the military dictatorship in Nigeria. But you must also convince the other participants that the responsibility for protecting human rights goes beyond individual governments that are actually violating the human rights—it must also be the responsibility of those who participate in a system that tolerates and often benefits from these abuses. This includes corporations. In fact, corporations, because they make a profit off the people being abused, have an even greater responsibility in ensuring human rights. You want to take the moral high ground. And there is good reason to do so in this case.

All individuals have a right to be free from fear and to be free from want. In Nigeria, the government and the oil companies have taken away those rights from the people of the Niger Delta. All the profits from the oil go to the government in the North or to the oil companies, and no benefit is seen in the delta. Villagers there seldom have running water, sanitation, usable land, passable roads, medical care, decent housing. Meanwhile, oil company facilities are equipped with everything people need for health and comfort. The Niger Delta environment is destroyed, and the peoples' voices are silenced. Whenever they have protested conditions in the delta or asked the companies to intervene on their behalf, villagers have been met with arrest, torture, and death. And the oil companies still keep making money. In several cases it appears the oil companies have not only benefited from the government repression, but initiated and paid for it as well.

So who is responsible and what can be done? Although the United States has not signed on to the UDHR, it is a member of the United Nations and first of all, it seems clear that any member nation has a responsibility to ensure human rights. You believe that any member nation should refuse to purchase goods (in this case oil) from companies doing business in and with a dictatorial government. A boycott of oil from the Niger Delta might get the Nigerian government and the businesses to clean up their act. If governments took this stand, oil companies would soon realize it is in their own best interest to defend human rights or they would have nowhere to sell their oil. It is in the best interest of industrialized governments to have a stable oil source outside of the Middle East; but only if human rights are guaranteed will Nigeria be a stable source of oil—just look at the problems going on right now.

If countries won't take the lead, you must convince business that stability is in their best economic interest. Businesses are more successful in stable countries. Where there is repression, there is revolution. Where there is torture, there is protest. Shell and the other oil companies are well aware of the financial damage done by protesters. The companies have had to abandon many sites and have lost quite a bit of revenue. Currently a third of the country's oil production has been shut down by unprecedented acts of resistance. Clearly the people of the delta will take no more abuse. It is time to change business practices.

Companies have stated in the past that it is not their place to interfere in the government of the countries with whom they are doing business. It is not their place to meddle in political problems. However, these same companies have never hesitated to use their influence to lobby for reduced environmental restrictions, lower corporate tax rates, and lower wages. It is obvious they will get involved if it meets their financial needs. So you must convince them that working for human rights meets their financial needs.

Times have changed, and companies are now beginning to recognize that they need to respond to these allegations of human rights and environmental abuse. However, much of this response is superficial. It is no good for a company to commit to environmental protection and then deny all the destruction it has caused. Mobil claims that it has responded to issues of environmental destruction; Chevron admits wrongdoing in its relationship with the Nigerian military. Shell has also claimed that it has changed. It insists it asked the government to stop the execution of Ken Saro Wiwa, but they asked too late. One phone call does not a stand make. Shell is offering to clean up oil spills and committed $500,000 for community and environmental projects this year. But $500,000 is a drop in the bucket. Shell makes nearly $500,000 a day in the region. And there is little evidence of even that $500,000.

The companies need to put their money where there mouths are—in terms of developing the region and in terms of threatening the governments with pullout if human rights abuses continue.

Although you realize the importance of working within this forum to achieve an agreement, if the groups are unwilling to sign off on an international business practice standard that protects human rights, you will launch a public education campaign that encourages a boycott of oil companies that do business in the region. Such a boycott has convinced Shell to change its business practices in other regions; you think it can work again.

Oil Company Representative

> We're much more likely to see other companies as collaborators rather than adversaries. . . . We aren't so much competing with each other as we are competing with the earth. And maybe that's a healthy way to look at it.
>
> *George Kirkland, Chevron Nigeria*

You have lived in the delta for five years as an operations manager. You have been chosen to be here because you are so familiar with the region and its issues. The job can be a hassle with all these protesters and sabotage, but the pay is good and the benefits are great. You will be able to retire early, and you get to see a little of how the other half lives.

Today you represent the interests of several oil companies in the region, including Shell, Mobil, Chevron, and British Petroleum (BP). In the past, oil companies have made it clear that it is not the role of a company that is a guest in a country to tell that country's government what to do. You still believe this. After all—who's to say a government is going to listen to you anyway? If you take too strong a position, the company may be forced out of the country. Then what help can you be to a disadvantaged people?

When activists blame you, they are ignoring the reality that 70 percent of the profits from oil production go straight to the pockets of the Nigerian government. It's the government's job to spend this money where it sees fit. It's not the responsibility of business to tell the Nigerians what to do with their money. If the Niger Delta wants money and development, they should ask their government and stop whining at your door. However, you realize that staying neutral is no longer suitable for your public image. Consumers want to see you care about the environment and about human beings around the world. So you are changing your policy and your public image.

In the past you have worked with the military to protect your economic interests, but now the situation is blowing up in your face (literally). Sabotage, protests, and oil fires have shut down a third of production in Nigeria. The rebellion in the Niger Delta is becoming more organized and more effective. If something isn't done soon, the instability may turn into a civil war and you will have to pull out entirely. But that doesn't mean you feel companies bear the responsibility of protecting human rights. It simply means that right now it would be to your advantage to solve the crisis in Nigeria.

To do this, you want to talk up the things you are doing in the region—you are willing to compensate villagers when there is proof of environmental damage because of company negligence. You have committed funds toward development projects. You are reconsidering the role of the military in protecting sites during acts of resistance and sabotage. Most of these commitments, admittedly, do not take a huge chunk out of your profits in the region; you do have a responsibility to stockholders to maintain profits.

One thing you want to make sure the people at this forum understand. These resisters are not just innocent political protesters, they're criminals. They're fanatics. You set up a water pump, and they just shut it down and then blame you. The villagers need to make a commitment too. After all, their acts of sabotage are responsible for many of the fires and spills. You will not take the blame for that. In exchange for further actions on your part, MOSOP and those other radicals have to stop the violence. They need to work with you, not against you. They cannot use terrorism. They cannot take oil rigs. You must work together. In fact, Shell has already had one meeting with MOSOP and will agree to have more in order to address its concerns.

At this point, you feel as though your response has been adequate and are a little irritated to be attending a hearing where a coalition of interests are determining actions your companies must take. An international compact that links human rights to economic policy and practices is going too far. The heart of capitalism lies in free trade. Regulations should be voluntary. Otherwise our whole global economy is threatened. Let's face it: Consumers want low prices. Low prices come with lower wages, lower environmental regulations, and less attention to sticky political issues. It is your duty to provide oil at a low cost to the driving public and, in so doing, provide jobs for the region. Where's the harm in that?

Nigerian Government Official

You are from the North, of course, and managed to survive the recent government turnover. As a former military officer, you eventually became part of Abacha's advisory cabinet. You work in the Industry and Development Office and have been working hard to attract and maintain business in the region.

You are excited to be part of this international forum. Ever since the Ken Saro Wiwa disaster, the international community has shunned your government. Of course, its members still buy your oil, but you want to have a voice too. Now is your chance. The first thing that must be made clear is that, although this is still a military government, it is not Abacha's regime and it is merely transitional. It is the intention of General Abubakar to hold elections very soon. He is as eager as the rest of the world to see Nigeria as a stable and productive member of the international community.

Although you are thrilled to be here, you are not interested in any kind of international compact that links human rights and economic policy. After all, what right do other countries have to tell you how to treat your people? Isn't this how all this trouble got started in the first place—when the imperial powers came in here and told you how to run things? As if other countries care about your people anyway! How would the United States feel if you told it what to do? It is just as guilty, if not more so, of human rights abuses in its own country and around the world, but no one would ever dare suggest to stop doing business with it. The United States is the wealthiest nation on earth, but its human rights record is questionable: The gap between the rich and poor is extreme, universal health care is not provided, the political system has been bought and sold, the death penalty is a common practice, and citizens can't walk the streets in safety. You don't refuse to do business with it. Even if U.S. government officials walk into this forum with shining words about the necessity to protect human rights, you know that they are doing business with your country because you offer something they need at a price they like.

These companies came into your country without your permission when you were still a colony of Britain. They set up their operations and established their practices without any concern for what you might say or what the people of the region might need. You are maintaining this relationship because of the desperate need your country has for revenue. After all, colonization depleted Nigeria of its wealth, leaving it dependent on outside corporations. What else could you do? Besides, you have a big house, servants, and a Swiss bank account. You feel lucky, and you know your wealth and comfort depends on the success and large profits of the oil companies.

Still, you realize that you need to put a better face forward to the international community and to your own people. You have promised democratic elections in the near future, you have released political prisoners, you are committing money to the region, and you want to guarantee free speech rights. However, this sabotage and violence on the part of the Ogoni and the Ijaw and others must stop. It is not free speech to capture the property of another. It is not free speech to siphon gas, leading to oil leaks and fires that further damage the delta communities. This activity must stop, or you will be forced to make it stop. It is the duty of the government to protect all residents.

You are tired of being the only bad guy in this story. This repression is not just a function of your government. It is a function of a global system that preys on inequalities. You recognize that your power in the North is a result of the unequal status set up by colonialism; you don't want to shift this power. But you want the rest of the world to know you are doing something to reduce the tensions between the North and the South. You are planning a series of summit meetings designed to address issues concerning all parties.

You would be eager for the oil companies to promise some of their profits toward developing the Niger Delta, but don't want to see your government take an economic hit as a result of any policy agreed to here.

MOSOP (Movement for the Survival of the Ogoni People) Activist

> Be proud, Be proud, Ogoni people be proud. We shall no longer allow the world to cheat us.
>
> *Ogoni Song*

> We either win this war to save our land, or we will be exterminated, because we have nowhere to run to.
>
> *Ken Saro Wiwa*

You are an Ogoni from the Niger Delta. Your brother has been jailed for active participation in MOSOP. Your family lives on a farm that is too contaminated to grow crops. Your sister works for Shell because there are no other job opportunities, and it breaks her heart to see their sloppy, careless treatment of the earth you have held sacred. You love your tribe, your family, and your land, but you hate the oil companies. To Shell and the other oil companies, Ogoniland is just another place to make money. But to you it is your home, your livelihood, your very survival. You are passionate about this issue because you feel you have no other choice. You and other tribal communities have been chewed up and spit out.

Through the exploitation of oil, the Ogoni livelihood—their land—has been poisoned. Spills, leaks, and fires have ruined your earth, your water, your air. Even after the endless spills are "cleaned up," irreparable damage has been done. You cannot grow food. You cannot drink the water. You cannot afford to buy oil. The average annual salary is only $300. You have the highest infant mortality rate in Nigeria and no hospital. Your people and the other tribes in the region are dying. Oil fires have killed hundreds. Some people called the recent oil fire a crisis. But it is not a crisis. "Crisis" implies a short-term problem. This fire and all the other environmental and human destruction are the result of long-term policies and practices. It is time to put an end to these "drilling and killing" ways.

You blame both the oil companies and the Nigerian government for the human rights abuses that have occurred. The oil companies and Nigeria have destroyed the earth and are killing you. The environment is destroyed because there are no government regulations and because of oil companies' careless practices. The political oppression—the executions, the violence, the torture, the arrests—are the direct result of the military dictatorship but are fueled and financed by the oil companies. You are not just saying that the oil companies' cooperation and silence encourages the government; you are directly accusing them of participation and involvement. After all, when Ken Saro Wiwa called for a boycott of Shell and asked compensation from the company, he was framed for murder and executed. Shell chose to wait until the last moment to plead your leader's case. They could have stepped in much sooner and forced the government to change its mind. After all, Shell and the oil companies hold the financial key to the government. Chevron admits requesting and hiring the military that shot the protesters who wanted to negotiate for clean drinking water, electricity, environmental compensation, employment, and scholarships. Mobil's need for headquarters resulted in hundreds of homeless villagers. These companies are not innocent bystanders. These companies are guilty of murder.

You have tried to work within the system (even as the system was hunting you down, throwing you in jail, and killing you on the streets). You supported government reforms and even voted in the last fair election (which was annulled by the military). You have fought back on your own. You have organized with other resistance groups. You have used the courts. You have tried to negotiate with the oil companies. You have appealed to the international community, but your voices continue to be muffled by the roar of the oil fires, the whir of machinery, and the vroom of the oil-guzzling cars around the world.

A boycott of Nigerian oil is vitally needed. You know the oil companies have claimed they really want to work this out. They are running scared now, but their measly efforts are not enough. Strict limits and controls are not even enough. It is time they left Ogoniland for the Ogoni. They have done enough damage. And continuous pressure on the Nigerian government must be kept up until Nigeria is fully democratized. You know that the current government promises free elections and has released some prisoners. But until free speech is restored, until a full and fair election is held, until the Constitution is amended to guarantee equal rights, until restrictions prevent the government from sucking the life blood from the delta— the international community must stop funding the Nigerian government. That means it must stop buying oil. An international condemnation of the government is not enough. Only sanctions and a boycott can influence the government now. Your lives depend on such action.

An international compact that links human rights to economic policy is sorely needed in our modern global economy. If oil companies will not voluntarily pull out of the region to put pressure on the Nigerian government to change its policies, then the governments in the rest of the world must help. If nations refuse to buy oil from the region, both the oil companies and the government will change their practices. You want an agreement, but with the delta resistance movement becoming more effective and more organized, you won't compromise. Your group and others have successfully shut down a third of oil production in the country. It is time they listen to you for a change.

Representative from the U.S. Trade Secretary's Office

You've been appointed as an assistant to the U.S. Trade Secretary during the current administration. Although you work for the U.S. government, you also see yourself as an "ambassador" for U.S. business. You love this job. You love to travel, see the world, and meet people. You believe the United States is the best country in the world—a place where businesses can grow and, as corny as it may sound, where people can go from rags to riches. After all, you started out as a graduate from a state college with no money in your pocket—and now look at you!

Although you think a World Economic Forum is an excellent idea and look forward to removing some trade barriers, you believe this is not the time or the place to be discussing human rights issues. Economic policy has no business being linked with human rights. It is only because these activists have the media wrapped around their little fingers that they were invited to this summit in the first place. And it is just taking up valuable time that could be spent on trade issues.

Besides, it is clear from the progress China and other countries have made toward democracy that the only sane approach to human rights is constructive engagement (continuing to do business and gently urging governments toward political reform). Making threats and demands against other countries only builds up resistance. And what would pulling out of Nigeria do? We'd end up having no influence over there. And a boycott? Well, that would only hurt the poor people of Nigeria, who need the revenue. And it would hurt the people of America too if oil prices went up. Doing business with and in other countries—no matter what their human rights record—is a win–win situation. We make money, and they move toward development and democracy.

These environmental and human rights extremists want to blame the situation in Nigeria on the oil companies. They want to point a finger at the "big bad businesses." But you know that it is because of these oil companies and the global marketplace that these countries are moving from poverty to prosperity. Human rights are *not* being violated because industry is moving into these regions. Human rights are being *elevated*. Jobs are provided, quality of life is enhanced, and most importantly, information is exchanged. What is democracy, after all, but the free exchange of ideas and information? Because we are now a global economy, even the remotest jungle in the darkest of Africa is connected to the rest of the world. Through that connection, the Africans can learn about democracy and can strive toward improving their lot in life.

You must convince the other participants in this conference that it is the duty of the oil companies to stay in this region, in spite of the hardships the people endure. The businesses must be a shining example of capitalism, democracy, and success. How else will these people ever know what is possible?

You are committed to the idea that a corporation's role is economic, not political. It is not the place of a company to legislate or dictate how a government should treat its people. Different societies have different needs. You are sensitive to the fact that one culture should not pass judgment on how another culture treats its community members. You know the United States would not like it if Nigeria started telling Congress what laws to pass. And what if some Japanese company came to the United States and started pressuring you to change your policies and practices? Nigeria has every right to run its country on its own without interference from the rest of the world. And businesses have every right to drill for oil. After all, 70 percent of the oil revenues go to the Nigerian government. That is a pretty fair deal. It is up to the Nigerian government to respond to the needs of its people. It is up to businesses to continue expanding this global marketplace so that prosperity can reach every corner of the earth. Any international compact will destroy the delicate balance of free trade. To attract investment capital, businesses must be free to make decisions without any hindrance. More regulations mean less profit. Less profit means less investment. Less investment means less growth. And that could lead to global economic disaster.

APPENDIX D:
NIGERIAN OIL CRISIS:
Globalization and Human Rights Postconference Reflection

1. Write a second internal monologue from the voice of your character that explores your feelings about the decisions made at this economic summit. Be specific and detailed in your reflection. Respond to at least one quote or statement made during the summit by another group.

2. What parts of this summit were realistic? Unrealistic? Explain. (Who would have been invited, not invited? Who would have been listened to? What kinds of decisions would probably have been made?)

3. Agree or Disagree (and explain your position): A World Economic Forum held this year invited international labor organizers and human rights activists to participate in the discussion of globalization and international trade policy. This is a significant step toward reshaping the immoral face of globalization. This is a first step in linking human rights to economic policy. There is hope that multinational corporations are changing the way they do business to take into account their effect on the environment and on human rights.

4. What would likely be the long-term impact of the decisions that were made at this summit? Be specific and detailed in your response.

5. Set your role in the summit aside. How would *you* answer the question about what a business and foreign governments' responsibilities are toward human rights? In other words, should human rights be part of economic decision making and trade policy? You can give your opinion on the questions the summit considered or the resolutions your role drafted.

6. What would you do as an Ogoni or environmentalist or a human rights observer to influence international policy on these issues? List three strategies—be specific.

7. Review the following quotations from the film *Globalization and Human Rights*. Analyze, discuss, and respond to two of them.

Globalization and Human Rights: Can Money and Morality Coexist?

The essence of globalization is subordination of human rights, of labor rights, consumer, environmental rights, democracy rights, to the imperative of global trade and investment. This is world government of the Exxons, by the General Motors, for the Du Ponts.

Ralph Nader, Consumer Advocate, 1996 Presidential Green Party Candidate

This [Economic Summit] Meeting is an enormous sort of cocktail party—a lot of contacts, people meet. It is actually symptomatic of the age because you have presidents and prime ministers courting the financiers and the industrialists.

George Soros, billionaire investor, philanthropist

It is a worrisome phenomenon when people, who have not been elected except by their capacity in the marketplace, become sort of a shadow government of the world.

Ariel Dorfman, Chilean author and activist

I think it [globalization] is helping human rights because what it's doing is giving jobs to people at salary levels that they never would have had access to before. So in time I think it will become more self-corrective.

James Robinson, Ex-head of American Express

If this global economy cannot be made to work for working people, it will reap a reaction that may make the twentieth century seem tranquil by comparison.

John Sweeney, AFL-CIO President

They need some new rules for the game. . . . Those rules are there. They are in place, and should be applied. There *are* international labor standards. There *is* a universal declaration of human rights that needs to be applied in this global economy because they're simply not.

Phillip Jennings, Britain
President of International Labor Federation

These rights have to be universally applied if we want to live in a world of peace and justice. . . . Unless globalization proceeds with a determination to implement human rights standards everywhere in the world we are going to face catastrophes.

Pierre Sane, head of Amnesty International

I think there has been a lot of progress on human rights but I don't think linking trade and human rights is a very productive process.

Robert Hormats, International Vice Chairman of Goldman Sachs Investors

There are other needs in society that cannot be fulfilled by the market and those needs are neglected. So there is some market failure but much greater social failure—in fact a failure of the political process.

George Soros, investor and philanthropist

In many parts of the world, large corporations are operating in countries where basic fundamental human rights and worker rights are undermined, are not enforced, are violated. And so companies in a sense become complicit with governments, with dictators, with violators of these basic rights.

John Cavanaugh, policy analyst and author

Raising human rights issues . . . is a difficult and delicate task. . . . We are learning as we go. So are we doing all we can? Yes, I think for the moment we are because nobody else is saying and doing these things. Do we need to do more? Quite probably we do.

Alan Detheridge, Shell Oil Nigeria adviser

Shell and all the other oil companies have the collective power. They could play positive roles. They have declined to do so. They have been called on to intercede with the regime with respect to political prisoners . . . they have largely declined to do that.

Gay McDougall, U.S. human rights lawyer, antiapartheid activist

Those that argue that if Shell just withdrew from the country that would bring the regime to its knees, I'm afraid are mistaken. . . . We can't withdraw the oil wells. We can't withdraw our pipelines and our facilities.

Alan Detheridge, Shell Oil Nigeria adviser

It's going to happen that ultimately, the oil companies there, for instance, will see that it's far better to be on the side of the people, to be on the side of justice, to be on the side of freedom, and not kowtow to the powerful—who are powerful only for a moment, and then they become the flotsam and jetsam of history.

Archbishop Desmond Tutu, Nobel Peace Prize Winner and Chair of South Africa's Truth and Reconciliation Committee

We do not expect business to become a human rights defender. We know that if business adopts a human rights language and behavior, it will be as a means to the long-term objective of securing greater and greater profits. . . . There [are] some tactical alliances that we can develop.

Pierre Sane, head of Amnesty International

Companies like Shell have a role in promoting human rights . . . certainly within the communities in and amongst whom we operate.

Alan Detheridge, Shell Oil Nigeria Adviser

There has been an explosion of human rights organizations all around the world that are now in touch with each other and are now beginning to talk more and more about common problems and common strategies.

Gay McDougall, U.S. human rights lawyer, antiapartheid activist

APPENDIX E: INSTRUCTIONS FOR NIGERIA AND OIL WORLD ECONOMIC FORUM ROLE PLAY

Materials:

1. Class set of Nigeria Fact Sheet [Appendix A]

2. Class set of Student Instructions [Appendix B]

3. Six copies of each role—one for each group member [Appendix C]

4. Class set of Postconference Reflection guidelines [Appendix D]

5. Six placards—paper or cardboard that can be folded to stand on its own

6. One copy of PBS documentary *Globalization and Human Rights* (optional)

Preparatory Work:

1. Students will have done prior work on colonization and its effects on current African country governments, economies, and so on. They may have read *Things Fall Apart* by Chinua Achebe. They should also have some previous study of neocolonialism.

2. We encourage you to have students engage in prior lessons on the Universal Declaration of Human Rights.

3. You could assign Internet assignment to search for these issues and look at some websites including those of Shell and CorpWatch. Could do long lecture or reading on Nigerian history.

Background

1. Read Nigeria Fact Sheet together and discuss along the way.

2. If you have it—show Nigeria and oil section of *Globalization and Human Rights* video (PBS). The section is only about 13 minutes, from minute 17 to minute 30. Discuss.

Role Preparation

1. Create six groups of 3–5 students each. Each group will represent one role. Pass out Student Instructions and copies of their role only to each group. Assign the internal monologue (see Student Instructions). Finish internal monologue and Instruction questions for homework.

2. Have students all read their internal monologues out loud. If pressed for time, have them share in their groups and then read two from each group, or you could jigsaw them (so each role is represented) and have them read them in groups. Can conduct press interviews at this time.

Forum Preparation

1. If you have it, have students watch the beginning of the *Globalization and Human Rights Video* (minutes 1–12) and ask students to listen for good quotations they can use in their role-play.

2. Students will get in their groups and make their placards with their role name on each.

3. In their groups students will share their thoughts on the Instruction questions and agree on points. Have recorder take notes.

4. Students should then draft specific resolutions on the issues as a group.

Negotiations

1. Students appoint negotiators to lobby and form alliances. At least one person must stay at the group's home base for other roving negotiators to visit with.

2. Students will send their negotiators to other groups to form alliances. Traveling negoitators cannot meet with other traveling negotiators. Allow only 10–15 minutes.

3. Students return to groups and rewrite resolutions based on alliances.

Summit/Conference

Tell students that they should record at least three provocative comments from the conference because they will need to discuss them during the debriefing.

1. Ask for a group to volunteer a resolution and put it on the board or overhead. Or have groups pick a number for random selection. After each resolution is voted on, get another group to offer one. Spend only twenty minutes on each resolution. The entire summit can last one to three class periods.

2. The group that offers a resolution will summarize arguments in favor of that resolution. You can then do one of the following:

   a. Ask for arguments pro and con alternately, then open it to debate, and then eventually vote.

   b. Ask each group in turn to state its position on the resolution, then open it for debate, and then vote.

   c. Ask for five minutes of arguments in favor and then five minutes against and then open it for debate.

3. Make sure you have a permanent record of the resolutions passed.

4. Ask for some final brief closing statement from each group at the end of the summit.

Debrief

1. Provide students with Postconference Reflection.

2. Students write up debrief homework or in class.

3. Have a debriefing discussion using the questions as a basis. Do not skip this part. No matter how the role-play goes, the discussion about the outcome and the process is key to the students' learning experience.

After All This

1. Have students take the roles of human rights activists or environmentalists or Ogoni and work up a campaign using posters or skits or songs or petitions or strikes or boycotts.

2. Have a speaker come. Is anyone in your area from the region and involved in the issues?

3. Research effects of oil in another region.

4. Have students engage in some activist activity—write a letter to an oil company or to a newpaper, start a boycott, make a webpage, have a teach-in, and so forth.

14 Teaching What's Not in the Book
The Lives of Migrant Farmworkers

Dirk Frewing

My parents took us on a driving excursion just about every weekend when we were young. My sister and I would pile into the backseat, and our family would escape the green suburbs of Seattle for long, hot forays into Oregon, Idaho, and the dry plains of the eastern half of Washington. My mom always said she had to find some sunshine. We usually found it east of the Cascades.

My dad would consult a guidebook, and we would drive for hours to go hiking, camping, or stay in motor hotels from another era. We stayed in places like Yakima, Wenatchee, Chelan, or Bend. It always looked like my idea of Kansas or Nebraska in the 1950s. The rural, agricultural landscape out the back window of the car was certainly different from the one I was accustomed to at home.

I remember watching all the apple orchards and wheat fields. I would take breaks from mercilessly teasing my younger sister about the line across the backseat and gaze out the window. I saw tiny white shacks on dusty frontage roads next to the highway, and I remember my parents explaining about the hard lives of the people who worked picking fruits and vegetables in the sun. I also remember being amazed that people lived in the white shacks, which looked almost identical to the shed my grandfather used to store his lawn mower (with which I was well acquainted) and yard tools.

Years later, when I was still mowing my grandfather's lawn and in high school, we got the traditional social studies curriculum. In U.S. history class our junior year we memorized all the presidents in order and learned that "civil rights" was something that happened to African Americans between the Korean War and Vietnam. I remember watching black-and-white footage of Klan marches, lunch counter beatings, and fire hoses in Birmingham. It seemed that these things had happened a million years away from my own life in the comfortable, prosperous suburbs of Seattle. I had absolutely no idea that migrant farmworkers were suffering many similar types of abuses just across the mountains in the sunny orchards and fields of the Northwest.

In high school I learned about Martin Luther King and Malcolm X, but I didn't know a single thing about migrant farmworkers. My official introduction was during a literature class in college through a book called *Plum Plum Pickers*. After college I visited work camps and fields around Woodburn, Oregon, through a friend that was working with the farmworkers union PCUN (Piñereos y Campesinos Unidos del Noreste). My Spanish language skills and interest in the subject have allowed me to work with many migrant students and families in two different high schools and one elementary school summer program. During this ten-year period of discovery and learning, I remained astounded that the desperate working and living conditions were so accepted, unchallenged, or unknown. I am not naïve, but it just didn't seem to make sense.

My observations in secondary U.S. history classes during the past few years confirm my assumption that ideas of civil rights and social justice are still addressed in the same straitjacket manner. For teachers to talk about issues of civil rights and ignore the struggles of migrant farmworkers is ridiculous. As Daniel Rothenberg notes in his book, *With These Hands: The Hidden World of Migrant Farmworkers Today,* the social and economic costs of modern agriculture in the United States demand that we take a second look at hard work, opportunity, and certainly social justice.

I believe that any discussion or study of civil rights and social justice in secondary social studies curriculum needs to include a look at the lives of migrant farmworkers. Students are afforded a rich opportunity to explore issues of social justice, economics, history, and immigration. In addition, migrant farmworker issues can introduce students to concepts such as a "dominant" society, the idea of "marginalization" and exclusion from an established set of values and expectations. The plight of migrant farmworkers is a socially invisible problem, yet the nature of their work binds them intimately to our own lives.

Farmworkers were not included in many of the basic federal worker protections enacted during the New Deal. To explore notions of freedom and equality in the United States, secondary social studies students should have a sense of the human sacrifices made by workers in the American agricultural system. Today, migrant workers are intimately and fundamentally connected to everyone who eats fruits or vegetables. They are an integral yet socially invisible component of U.S. society that works in desperate conditions so that large-scale agribusiness can provide low-cost fruits and vegetables to consumers. The vast majority are desperately poor immigrants who harvest nearly every piece of produce that ends up on our dinner tables, yet suffer from lack of access to basic health care, shelter, education, and resources that would be unimaginable in any other industry in the United States (Rothenberg, 1998). Students should also explore the relationship between immigration and the modern agricultural system to see how labor supply affects working conditions. Study of migrant farmworkers can lead to discussions of perceived equality and social justice in the United States. It can also open a discussion of the relationship between immigration, oversupply of labor, and the working conditions of migrant farmworkers.

I did some background reading that provided a historical outline and foundation for a migrant farmworker unit in my U.S. history class. Agricultural labor shortages as a result of U.S. entry into World War II led the War Manpower Commission to form a Special Committee on the Importation of Mexican Labor in 1942. The first Mexican agricultural workers arrived in California later that same year as whites left the fields for jobs in the new wartime economy. In 1943 Congress officially approved the passage of Public Law 45, which set up what is known as the Bracero ("farmhand") Program. Under the Bracero Program, the U.S. State Department, Department of Labor, Immigration and Naturalization Service, and Department of Justice created an organized labor system that would permit more than five million Mexican braceros to be contracted to agricultural interests in the United States until the termination of the program in 1964 (Calavita, 1992). Growers and ranchers were supplied with a guaranteed supply of cheap Mexican laborers, who were willing to accept the difficult working conditions in the United States. Once the seasonal harvest was complete, geography and public policy made it easy for the labor force to be returned to Mexico. Since braceros could be sent home at any time, they were unlikely to complain or try to organize for improved working conditions (Rothenberg, 1998). It is interesting to note that similar "guest worker" legislation has been proposed during two recent legislative sessions in Oregon.

The lasting legacy of the Bracero Program is evident in the reality that the overwhelming majority of migrant workers today are either from Mexico or are of Hispanic origin. Patterns of migration and settlement continued long after the Bracero Program was terminated. Social and economic links between Mexico and the United States were established during each harvest as migrant laborers returned to work. Many families eventually left the migrant "stream," or traditional pattern of following the fruit and vegetable harvest, and settled permanently in the United States.

Concepts of equal treatment under the law and notions of civil rights are not difficult to sell to adolescents. As students read Malcolm X or Martin Luther King, Jr., they can relate to the realities of being excluded, treated disparagingly, or required to comply with curfews. Unfortunately, most high school classes do not enlarge the scope of the study of civil rights and justice in the United States to include issues related to migrant farmworkers. Our U.S. history textbook this past year contained just three sentences related to Cesar Chavez and the Hispanic/Latino struggle for equality.

I wrote a unit plan for the study of migrant living and working conditions in the United States and taught one week worth of block periods on migrant workers at a large suburban high school. My students were primarily Anglo-Americans from homes with two parents. They came to school with notebooks, dividers, pens, and some vision, however limited, of their place in a larger world beyond high school. They rarely missed class, and for many, a trip into Portland was a large event.

Students read firsthand accounts of farmworker life in Daniel Rothenberg's book, had discussions, looked at photographs, and watched *The Fight in the Fields* from PBS. Students were very attuned to the colorful news footage in the film and seemed particularly affected by one of Cesar Chavez's hunger strikes. This seemed to be the detail of the film that had the greatest impact on my class. As we were discussing the film, most of the questions seemed to be related to the scenes of police with nightsticks breaking up striking workers or the fact that Cesar Chavez stopped eating to draw attention to his cause. Students kept saying, "You mean he didn't eat anything? At all? Did he drink water?"

The introduction to our study of migrant farmworkers begins on a sunny afternoon on which most students seem to be focusing their attention out the window, daydreaming of summer and not anything related to social justice. My student teaching supervisor sits in the corner of the room, typing quietly on her laptop. Perhaps subconsciously inspired by Bill Bigelow's soccer ball exercise, I have brought a slightly worn Red Delicious apple and a large stalk of broccoli to class. I ask students to sit in a circle. There is not enough room, so the class turns into a large U-shape. I ask them to pass the apple and broccoli around, observing, feeling, and smelling each item.

"Somebody brought you something better than an apple, huh, Mr. Frewing?"

Their comments are primarily related to the smell of the broccoli, which is beginning to show some signs of wear.

I then ask the students to list all the things that went into the production of this fruit and vegetable. A few students look uncertain and ask for clues. I give them five minutes to come up with their own list and then record their contributions on the overhead projector. The students list the following: water, sun, seeds, sugar, chlorophyll, fertilizer, pesticide, time, labor (planting, picking, shipping), trucks, boats, planes, plastic, wax, soil, air, vitamins, store workers, nitrogen.

I ask the class to think about the price of an apple. Someone offers, "They're cheap."

I share with the students my rationale for our study of migrant farmworkers; those human beings on their list who pick, among other things, the apples and broccoli in this country. I tell them that when I was in high school history class, "civil rights" was something that happened between African Americans and Anglo-Americans for a short time period between the Korean War and Vietnam. I have discovered that the students in my classes this past year enjoy hearing about my own high school experiences, especially when I tell them that we will now get to examine some things that were left out when I was in high school. I also share with them the fact that as residents of Oregon, they live in a state that employs a great number of migrant farmworkers. The class gets very quiet as I tell them that there are families in the neighboring town of Hillsboro living in houses made out of blue boat tarps and two-by-fours.

I next ask the class to think about their parents and any talk of grocery bills they might hear or be involved with at home. I ask the class, "What percentage of yearly income after taxes goes to pay for food in the United States?"

The class starts to lose focus somewhat, as they are somewhat unclear about the question. Attention shifts to the sunlight outside. Someone asks, "What's the question? In a week, month, or year?" We refocus, and I explain the question again. I call on several members of the class, and all guesses are above the 30 percent range. By the looks on their faces, this is a difficult concept for some students.

"OK, let's look at some other countries."

We move down a list on an overhead transparency I have prepared. India, 50 percent. China, almost half. Mexico, 31 percent.

"In the United States, we spend roughly 10 percent of our after-tax income on food. What does this mean? What does this have to do with anything?"

A student offers, "We have more money to buy other stuff."

Someone else adds, "They [migrantworkers] work for cheap. We don't have to pay them very much so our food is cheap."

"Why not?"

"Because they're illegal or not citizens or something like that."

In our discussions, students seemed to return to the idea that citizenship and legal status were almost permissible reasons for working conditions to be so bad. For my class, notions of social justice or inequality were overshadowed by paperwork and legal status. The lack of official documentation based on official pieces of paper or cards mitigated the gross severity of the living and working conditions of migrant farmworkers. Students seemed to justify or explain the poor and desperate conditions of migrant families by repeatedly reminding me that the migrant workers were not "legal" and not entitled to expect the same levels of pay, conditions, or housing. I guess this is not surprising considering that adolescence is a time period defined by official papers that carry power and authority. Perhaps students can easily identify with the idea of being excluded and the power that is carried by a driver's license, hall pass, transcript, traffic ticket, or signature. I think it is difficult for them to imagine the connection that transcends paperwork or political borders on a map—the fundamental connection between human beings who produce food in desperate conditions and human beings who consume the same food.

I attempt to demonstrate the power of farmworker union organizing during one of our discussions. I tell the class to imagine that I am a prospective employer rather than their teacher. They immediately stop talking and sit up in their seats.

I say to the class, "I have a job that is not particularly dangerous or terrible but it has to be done soon, and I will pay $14 an hour for someone to do this job. Who will work?"

Hands shoot up across the room.

"Pick me! Dude! Right here! I'm ready to go!"

I am delighted to see some of the more reticent and reluctant students waving their arms in the air and smiling animatedly. Students laughed and looked at those around them, laughing. I continue to lower the hourly rate of the job until I reach a level equal to minimum wage in Oregon. A few of my students work in restaurants, so they are quick to inform me of the current rate.

I walk around the room, loudly announcing each new pay rate and asking the class, "Who will work?"

At each lower pay rate, fewer and fewer hands stay up. I finally am left with only one hand up; only one student willing to work for minimum wage.

I then ask the class, "Suppose you had all gotten together before I came in the room and agreed that no one would work for less than $8.50 an hour. I need this particular job done. I am still the boss. I sign the paychecks. Do you as workers have any more power? Does your agreement that nobody will work for less than $8.50 change the equation?"

Several students reply that yes, they had more power as long as I couldn't go and bring in any other workers.

I add, "Now imagine that one-third of you have to leave the room every fifteen minutes and be replaced every time you agree that no one will work for less than $8.50. You have to explain what is going on to the new arrivals while I, the boss, am trying to find workers.

"What is the only power that migrant farmworkers have that permits them to try to gain better working and living conditions?"

A student in the back offers, "Not to pick the fruit."

Someone else adds, "Or to agree on their pay."

"Exactly. That's the idea behind a union."

As we are discussing the similarities between African-American and Hispanic/Latino civil rights movements in the 1960s related to farmworker strikes, I begin to use a word that I immediately realize the students are not quite clear about. When I start to use the term *marginalized,* many in the class begin to make the face that tells me we need to slow down in order to define and clarify this idea. I have come to make some relatively astute judgments about how a class is going by the looks on faces. As in playing cards, it is possible to gauge your next move by examining a simple facial expression. We talk about the idea of societal values, expectations, and opportunities for different groups in the United States. They laugh as I ask if any have heard the terms "The Man" or "The System."

As I look on the overhead transparency that displays my outline notes on Hispanic/Latino history, I ask the class where the most important information is located on the page.

"In the middle where all the writing is."

I draw some dots on the edges of the overhead.

"Here's the margins. What's going on in the margins? Anything good?"

"No."

"So what does it mean to be marginalized?"

"Left out of the good stuff."

There are so many statistics in social studies classes, and to the collection of numbers I add a few more. According to Rothenberg's book, fruits and vegetables in the United States are a $28 billion-a-year business. The average migrant farmworker makes $6500 a year. As this last number goes up on the board, many students gasp audibly and a girl in the back says in an awed voice, "I make more than that." Class time has run out, but students who were squirming in their seats at the beginning of class are now mildly inflamed. There is a request to go and visit a migrant camp. One girl says we should do a project or somehow help them. I mention a few churches and local groups that work with migrant farmworkers, but looking back I realize that I make a mistake by not capitalizing on their interest. I notice for the first time that the teacher's enthusiasm can easily carry over to students.

I feel like I did such a thorough job presenting the incredible hardships and numerous barriers faced by migrant farmworker families that my students felt nothing could be done about the plight of migrant workers. I had too many statistics and bleak firsthand accounts of life in the fields. Students told me they felt that nothing had changed following all the hard organizing work and strikes. All the statistics and the large-scale nature of agribusiness seemed too daunting to address. Students told me that, as with many uncomfortable or unfair aspects of life in the United States, "That's just the way it is."

Although they felt that there is still a great deal of racism and discrimination in our society, students stated that they could see a difference in the condition of African Americans in the United States. One African-American girl wrote in a later paper that she was allowed to go to a "nice" school with her classmates thanks to the earlier struggles of other African Americans. Students can see that there are no longer public signs directing certain groups to use separate water fountains or restaurants. They cannot see that same level of improvement in the condition of migrant workers, so they might feel that nothing can be done to improve living and working conditions. I didn't set out to preach to my students, only to make them more aware of an invisible problem that is troubling and uncomfortable to acknowledge. Perhaps I should have preached a little more. If I have the opportunity to present this topic in a future U.S. history class, I will get someone to come in and speak or arrange a field trip.

Throughout the year, I constantly asked students to think about the relationships among success, hard work, and opportunity in the United States. I would ask them to think about whatever their idea was of an "American Dream" or what they considered successful. I then asked them to think about what assumptions are made about those who achieve success in whatever terms they chose: money, position, power, or status. What kinds of assumptions are made about successful people? Students agreed that those who were successful had undoubtedly studied hard, worked hard, and generally exerted a great deal of effort to achieve their successes. On one side of the dry erase board, I listed the student descriptions of what it meant to achieve success and the personal qualities needed to be successful

On the other side I asked students to list qualities that defined being "unsuccessful" in life. Students identified qualities such as poverty, a low-status job, or receiving public assistance. I asked students to make the leap and think about the assumptions they had formulated about successful people; if we assume that those who have "made it" according to whatever criteria they used, what do we then assume about those who are unsuccessful?

It usually takes a minute but someone will offer, "that they're lazy."

"Think about all that you have seen related to migrant farmworkers. Do the workers you have seen strike you as lazy? Why is it possibly dangerous to make assumptions about hard work and opportunity? Are there any things that might be changed to improve opportunities for groups such as migrant farmworkers?"

I took great delight all year in reminding students that social studies was the most dangerous and inflammatory class on their schedule because I could teach them a whole semester of events and people they had never heard of. Students always liked this, but I think beyond the shock appeal there is excellent room to discuss the idea of a hidden curriculum and what material is deemed appropriate for inclusion in history textbooks. I was repeatedly asked to "Teach us something that isn't in the book." By spending several days exploring migrant farmworkers, I feel that I was able to do just that.

I was somewhat concerned that the students would leave the room with the impression that everyone who spoke Spanish and only those who spoke Spanish picked fruits and vegetables. We talked about trying to avoid falling into stereotypes and the importance of not making assumptions based upon stereotypes. In a nondiverse, affluent suburban school, this type of dialogue is often more necessary than anywhere else. It struck me again and again that my students were very sheltered and limited in their experiences each time we talked about relations between language or cultural groups.

I taught this unit as a student-teaching intern. It was without a doubt the best thing I taught all year. Students were more engaged than during any other time during my first semester of teaching on my own. I felt like I had to do a little pushing with my supervising teacher to change the traditional chronology of the semester and devote a few days to migrant farmworkers. After seeing the results, I know now that after all the enthusiasm and interest that emerged from the classes, I could have done a much better job discussing actions that could help ameliorate such desperate conditions. Although my classes had some excellent discussions, I failed to capture their reactions and reflections in any writing of any length. Next time I will have students do more writing and also include a more experiential component; perhaps a field trip or guest speaker.

It seems like a long time has passed since I passed the worn broccoli and apple around to a room full of puzzled faces. This year, as I sit at my desk after a long day at my first teaching job, I look at the names on the attendance sheet and I get a true sense of the size of the chasm between two very different schools. When I was teaching about migrant farmworkers, I was in a suburban school that had bento (a Japanese-style box lunch) as a cafeteria choice and an enormous parking lot full of new student automobiles. This year, migrant students and the sons and daughters of migrant farmworkers are not confined to the pages of a book or scenes from a video but sitting in the graffiti-scarred desks of my basement classroom.

References

Calavita, Kitty. 1992. *Inside the State: The Bracero Program, Immigration, and the INS.* New York: Routledge.

Rothenberg, Daniel. 1998. *With These Hands: The Hidden World of Migrant Farmworkers Today.* Orlando: Harcourt Brace.

15 *What Does Justice Look Like?*

Andra Makler

The power of the imagination comes from our ability to entertain alternatives to what we have experienced or been told. . . . If we were not able to imagine the world as other than it is, then taking an active role in change would be unthinkable.

Herbert Kohl, *Should We Burn Babar?*

G rowing up in Mount Vernon, New York, I never thought much about how white my neighborhood was, or wondered where all the black people in the library, on the bus, or on the streets in the downtown shopping area lived—until one of our neighbors called a special meeting to discuss the pending sale of a house on our street to a black family. The reaction of our neighbors, and the discussions between my parents, confused and disturbed me. Why were people shouting at each other about property values? What about all the stuff we were always hearing about brotherhood? What about *our* anger when we were told "No Jews allowed!"?

My high school was a converted World War I factory. Every time we ascended the front steps, my friends and I were greeted by a bronze statue of Teddy Roosevelt and groups of teenagers who clearly belonged to social cliques that none of us had encountered in our junior high schools. Everyone in town went to A. B. Davis High, but there were separate tracks. We were divided more by class and family values than by color or religion: If you were expected to get a job right after high school, you took commercial and business classes; if your parents believed the world would end unless you went to college, you didn't. Walking through the halls of my high school, I suddenly realized that my mental picture of my hometown didn't include most of the people walking through the halls with me. I also learned that not everyone in town went to Davis: there was a vocational high school, in the "colored" part of town, located in a building that had been condemned for use as the city jail.

In her novel about the civil rights movement in the southern town of Turner, Thulani Davis located *1959* as the pivotal year for understanding the dynamics of racism.[1] For me, 1957 was that year: my sophomore year, the year after Linda Brown's family challenged the school system in Topeka, Kansas. That year, I learned to sing folk songs at hootnannies in New York City with Odetta and at concerts with Pete Seeger, who was prevented from performing at the high school when men from the American Legion charged that he was a Communist who would brainwash us with his songs. In my synagogue youth group, I was reading about "justice and Judaism" and pondering the prophet Micah's frightening challenge: "What is required of thee . . . is to do justly, love mercy, and walk humbly with your God." In "psychodrama" exercises, we role-played encounters with our parents in which we announced we were going to date a black person. My friend Danny played us a new song on his guitar as the civil rights movement heated up our TV screens: "If you're brown, stick aroun'; if you're black—get back." My Norman Rockwell picture of America suddenly held too many pieces that did not fit together.

I believe that this book actually began that year, in 1957, though I know that other experiences, other stories, also shaped this project.

Why am I calling this book a project? This is the language of existentialism: As one of my favorite authors, Maxine Greene, skillfully reminds us in her introduction to another book on teaching about justice, living requires choice.[2] To see wrong and not to act is a choice—a poor choice. Thus, she writes, Camus creates the sanitation squad to try to alleviate the suffering caused by *The Plague*. The task is beyond human capacity, but it is the task we must choose, if we are to affirm our humanity. And here is my connection to the prophet's charge—to do justly and love mercy, and walk humbly. . . . It is a task at which we must fail, for it is by its very nature always work in progress; but it is work that we must choose, if we are to affirm our humanity.

Researching the Teaching of Justice

I am a student of teaching along with my students, who are prospective and experienced teachers. I have observed literally hundreds of classes. About ten years ago, I realized that—despite claims to the contrary—I rarely saw students engaged in discussions of justice. I wondered why. I wanted to know how the teachers I observed understood their own work. I wanted to check my perceptions as an out-

---

[1] Thulani Davis, 1992, *1959* (New York: Grove Weidenfeld). I am indebted to Susan Wentland for giving me this book.

[2] Green 1998, in *Teaching for Social Justice,* ed. W. Ayers, J. A. Hunt, & T. Quinn. (New York: Teachers College Press).

side observer against their perceptions of their own practice. In 1991, I therefore embarked on a multiyear qualitative research study to find out how social studies teachers (who typically want to motivate their students to become adults who care enough for the condition of the world to work for positive change) conceptualized the idea of *justice*, if and where in their curricula they believed they helped students to explore issues of justice, and finally, what meanings their students derived from their classes.

From the eighteen middle and high school social studies teachers I interviewed, I learned that although each believed it was important to teach about justice (or "for justice," a construction several preferred), all were reluctant to explicitly frame materials as instruction about justice. Instead, they used lessons about injustice (such as the treatment of minority groups in U.S. history, treatment of women in other cultures, court cases about civil liberties, news accounts of inhumane treatment of people all over the globe). I also learned female and male teachers' concepts of justice were more alike than different, encompassing concerns about fairness, care, and right and wrong.[3]

For the next phase of my research, I chose two of the interviewed teachers, a male and a female, deservedly recognized as good teachers, who described themselves as explicitly and overtly teaching about issues of justice in their curricula. With their permission, and permission from their principals and students, I spent a full semester observing one of their classes on a regular basis, sitting in on small groups as students did their work, reading student papers, and talking with students formally and informally about their understandings of justice and whether, and how, what they studied in class influenced their ideas about justice.[4]

What I saw in class both pleased and disturbed me. Both teachers appropriately used a mix of whole-class discussion, small-group work, direct instruction, and highly participatory activities such as debates, role-plays, and mock trials. Students explored controversial issues and were guided and challenged to state opinions supported by evidence; both teachers were scrupulously careful and even-handed referees of discussions. Students learned worthy information and skills. But in each class they learned more about injustice and problems with the U.S. system of government, including our jury system, than they did about justice or the relationship of justice to the ongoing construction of a pluralist democratic society in the United States. Discussions in both classes often explored issues of justice (for example, should Native Americans be compensated for a historical wrong? In our legal system, to protect one human right we often violate another). But these issues were not explicitly labeled and presented to students as issues of justice.

---

[3]This study is described in Andra Makler: "Social Studies Teachers' Conceptions of Justice" *Theory and Research in Social Education,* 22 no. 3 (Summer 1994): 249–80 and "Through Teachers' Eyes: Teaching about Justice and Injustice" *Update on Law-Related Education,* 18 no. 1 (Winter 1994): 15–20, 49.

[4]One class was a required U.S. history class (honors level) for juniors; the other was an untracked elective class called Human Rights and the Law.

After lessons that explored issues of conflicting rights or compensation of vulnerable groups for wrongs suffered as part of the history of their relationships with the U.S. government or European-American settlers, I reviewed students' written work and my notes on their comments to peers and to me. Their responses showed that they got the point of the lessons they experienced, but they also exhibited confusion and discomfort. For example, when students were asked, "Do you see a connection between human rights and justice?" their written responses fell into one of three categories.[5] Responses in the first group expressed the idea that the connection between human rights and justice is an ideal that never has existed and is often violated: "To get justice society violates a human right in order to preserve human rights"; "In my opinion, they are not connecting and they need to. . . . Certain rights are protected more than others, which is not fair." Responses in the second category connected punishment to justice because "this protects your human rights." I found no connection between the two concepts in the third group: "I think it is more of a reversal . . . human rights are being exploited for political gains"; "No, because people say justice should be served, but it never is."

In their roles as legislators at a simulated "hearing" to decide whether the state of Florida should compensate Seminoles today for the historical taking of their lands, students argued that it was offensive to hold them responsible for wrongs committed in a previous century. They made a strong case that present-day Seminoles were not entitled to ask for special treatment, and that providing such treatment would be discriminatory to other minority groups such as refugee Cubans. Those charged with presenting the Seminole claim argued for redress and monetary compensation. They claimed that Seminoles were disadvantaged by the decrease in their population, which was a direct consequence of government policies, and that redress—such as a voice in policy to correct for having had no voice earlier in U.S. history—was owed. In the debriefing following the role-play, the majority of students remained unconvinced by any of the arguments presented in the hearing; the class position was that neither side was "right."

The Taught Curriculum and the Evaded Curriculum

The teacher made no attempt to help the class examine the conceptions of justice that implicitly framed any of the arguments presented in the role-play, or to engage them in discussion of what they believed would be "right" or just in this case. In a conversation with her, she described her quandary this way: "I am reluctant to lay [an issue] out there as 'a justice issue.' I want it to come from the kids, but sometimes it's pulling teeth and I wonder why I don't just lay it out for them. That's a

---

[5]All student responses in this chapter are quoted as written, without correcting spelling.

real conflict for me." She then challenged me to "describe an opening where justice could have been discussed."

When I commented to the teacher of the law and human rights class that "students seem to be thinking more in terms of legal/illegal than about justice/injustice," he disagreed: "No, any time they're questioning a [legal] decision—was it right?—they're thinking about justice." But the diagrams students drew ostensibly to show how they were connecting their learnings about law and the court system to their ideas of justice, did not provide visible evidence that they were making such connections. Rather, these diagrams showed students learned what was explicitly taught; they showed an increased understanding of legal concepts, specific cases, and the operation of the courts and legal system. A comparison of their statements and diagrams made in March with those they made in June showed students focused their attention on legal terms related to cases studied in class, rather than on human rights or ethical considerations such as fairness or right and wrong.

Student Realism and Relativism

At the end of a semester of study in the law and human rights class, students articulated the following conflicting conclusions:

- "It's like human rights is a totally different thing than justice."

- "Human rights are a way of promoting equality between people, which in my mind is a just concept."

- "I think everyone has a different idea about the definition of justice and of human rights. . . . No matter what we do someone's rights are being violated by trying to protect someone else."

One student, who stated in March, "In order to obtain justice, human rights have to be protected," wrote in June, "Justice is when you have accomplished what you wanted to accomplish through a law suit. Justice is served when you win your case. . . ."

To get a sense of the U.S. history students' emerging concepts of justice, I asked them to "imagine a just country" and then compare its characteristics to the United States. Some students exhibited marked cynicism:

- "What imaginary just country? There never was one and never will be."

- "It is impossible to provide justice for everyone; I believe the U.S. tries to provide justice for the people it cares about (the influencial, powerful people). Individuals may provide justice for the lower-class people, but the country as a whole does not."

Students in the law and justice class expressed cynicism in their writing: "If you do something that you know is wrong, expect to suffer the consequences. If someone does something wrong to you, hope that they too will be punished, but don't count on it." One young woman in the U.S. history class wrote poignantly:

> There are too many stereotypes and "ism" issues. People are insecure, phony and pessimistic as well as close-minded. Nobody dreams anymore—they just look for nightmares. Leaders . . . don't believe in thier true beliefs. No one listens because they're all too busy arguing or they're caught up in themselves. Each out for only themselves—survival of the fittest—not the whole.

Students in both classes echoed the realism and the relativism of this written response:

> The US is as close as it comes to this imaginery country. In the US there is freedom of opportunity. That is all that is possible. It is not possible to keep people from doing unjust things but it is possible to control the unjustice doers from doing it. It is a very foggy issue. Justice is different for everyone.

Correcting a Missed Opportunity

It is appropriate for social studies teachers to encourage students to analyze and criticize official U.S. policies and pronouncements, to reflect on whether we live up to our ideals historically and in the present, to pay attention to different value positions articulated in magazines, classroom texts, and national news media. Criteria of excellence in scholarship in the social sciences and history require examination of case and countercase. It is not a matter of "political correctness" that teachers encourage students to explore different points of view about current politics and policies, or different interpretations of the historical record. But disciplined study is grounded in good theory; a good theory helps us to frame questions and provides criteria for evaluating the soundness of our answers. Although one class studied some political theory, all the teachers I interviewed said they made a decision not to provide any explicit theory of justice to their students. I think this is a missed opportunity.

Adolescents need help in constructing a value system. It is part of the school's explicit mission to engage the young in learning about the world and their place and role in it. In this country, we reject the idea that students' destinies are predetermined; it is part of the American creed that our lives are what we make of them. Commitment to "fairness and justice for all" also is part of that creed. Thus, it is critically important that schools join with families and religious groups in engaging young people in the key developmental task of constructing an ethical system of values in which to ground their choices of actions and their relationships with other human beings.[6] It should be part of our teaching to move students beyond the incapacitating idea that justice is so relative a concept that it is impossible to set criteria (or policies, or procedures) to implement it. This is one of the ways we can help to sustain our society's commitment to democratic ideals and values. If it is impossible for people to achieve a shared understanding of justice, there is no point in working to obtain it.

I began my research believing that justice was a cultural universal and expecting everyone to share my idea of justice. I was surprised to find that my colleagues had ideas very different from my own. I was surprised that so many students believed that justice was so abstract and relative that it was pointless to believe it could ever exist. I realized I had to ask myself, Why am I surprised? What do I think justice is, that this surprises me? One of the teachers, a former student, asked for my ideas about how to do this thing called "teaching" toward justice, reminding me in the same breath not to be so concerned about influencing teachers: "We won't necessarily follow what you suggest, you know!" That remark was humbling. Also liberating and challenging. I am indebted to her for that reality check!

Pondering the responses of colleagues and students, and my own conclusions, I came to understand that although every language may have a word for justice, the meaning that fills in that concept is culturally constructed and colored by class, gender, and the moment in time. Although this may seem obvious, it took me months to come to this realization. That realization was important to the shaping of this book; I would therefore like to explore this idea for a moment, drawing on ideas from philosophy and political theory.

With Justice, It's Not *E Pluribus Unum*

The dominant paradigm in Western political science and philosophy equates justice with fairness. However, the conceptions of both justice and fairness within this—our—tradition have changed over the centuries. For example, Plato's *Republic* shows us a just social order premised on the idea that individuals know their place and act accordingly. Plato believed that people were born suited by their natures to fulfill one of three social roles—artisan, soldier, or political leader. Thus, a person who displayed certain personality traits was suited only to be a soldier and was expected to fulfill that role, quite apart from any personal desire to do so. Only the few males who demonstrated the requisite personality traits of leadership should aspire to, or

---

[6]A leading scholar in the field of social studies education, Freeman Butts is just one of the voices reminding us that education for democratic participation requires opportunities for students to consider moral and ethical choices, including questions of justice, as the grounds for action. See Butts, 1990, "Democratic Values: What the Schools Should Teach," in *Citizenship for the 21st Century,* ed. W. T. Callahan, Jr., & R. A. Banaszak (Boulder, CO: ERIC Clearinghouse for Social Studies/Social Science Education).

be educated for, roles as lawmakers or societal leaders. Women, by definition and by nature, did not possess the personality traits of any of these roles; they were fit only to serve men and bear children. A society is "well ordered" and just if it fulfills these criteria. Today, we reject Plato's ideas about women and "nature" and believe that, in a just society, individuals freely choose their adult roles and occupations.

But we still do not have agreement about the features of a just society or even whether it is possible to achieve a state of justice in a real-world human society. Philosopher John Rawls also equates justice with fairness; like Plato, he wrote a book describing a just society.[7] Rawls pictures a just social order as one that individuals would choose from behind a "veil of ignorance," if they did not know what their place, status, or role in that society was going to be. His theory has been criticized, especially by feminist philosophers, on the grounds that such conditions are manifestly not real-world conditions and therefore not helpful as guideposts to justice in the world we live in.

There also is disagreement about whether justice ought to be equated with fairness, and whether fairness should be regarded as a principle to which we owe allegiance as a duty (the position expounded by Kant). Carol Gilligan, Nel Noddings, and others challenged the equation of justice with fairness as a male construct, rather than a universally acceptable definition of justice. Drawing on research with women, Gilligan and Noddings say justice sometimes requires departure from principle in order to be responsive to individual circumstances and include an element of caring.[8] Noddings believes that just relationships include an element of reciprocity in which individuals are able to be both the one caring and the one cared for. Arguing from example, they claim that responsiveness to the particular context of a situation, including the relationship of the persons in the situation, is more likely to lead to a just outcome than invocation of a rule or principle. Canadian philosopher Debra Shogan has proposed a theory of moral motivation that links benevolence to justice. She says each is incomplete without the other.[9]

Shogan believes that justice must encompass both fairness and compassionate concern (care for and about others). Her work offers us a bridge between the public domain of law and more personal considerations of ethical treatment of others. For example, she notes,

> Because we live in a society in which race has often been used by adjudicators to exclude people, it follows that to be blind to race would be to favor those who have benefitted from racial exclusion. Personal features such as race, gender, class, and

---

[7]Rawls, 1970, *Theory of Justice,* (Cambridge: Harvard University Press.)

[8]See, for example, Carol Gilligan, 1982, *In a Different Voice,* (Cambridge: Harvard University Press); and 1987, "Moral Orientation and Moral Development," in *Women and Moral Theory,* ed. Eva Feder Kittay & Dana T. Myers (Totowa, NJ: Rowman and Littlefield). 1987. Nel Noddings, 1984, *Caring* (Berkeley: University of California Press).

[9]See Debra Shogan, 1992, *Care and Moral Motivation* (Toronto, Canada: OISE Press).

disability are far from being irrelevant in decisions in which bias toward people with certain features is either blatant or hidden. . . . To ignore distinguishing features is to see everyone as a generalized other rather than as a particular, concrete other with a concrete identity; consequently, to be impartial in this way is to risk being guilty of injustice. (p. 23)

Other philosophers, however, are uneasy about equating justice with particularistic responsiveness to specific features of a situation. Philosopher Alasdair MacIntyre, for example, rejects the very possibility of justice in a truly pluralist society; he believes there would be no way to reach the consensus required to actually implement and sustain justice in such a society. He sees diversity as a source of discord and argues that pluralistic liberal democracy that treats opinions as preferences has no standard by which to decide among competing conceptions of justice.[10] From a global perspective, MacIntyre's position seems quite sensible, if troubling.

Philosopher Brian Crittendon rejects MacIntyre's claim that the liberal democratic political tradition that honors diversity is by definition relativist. His concept of diversity does not require us to accept all positions as equally good or all differences as equally compelling. Crittendon believes it is possible to articulate a standard for deciding among competing conceptions:

What liberal pluralism defends is the recognition that, in addition to rules of logical coherence, there are public criteria, independent of the conceptual perspectives or interests of any particular group, against which beliefs and values can be assessed as more or less rational. . . . The most thorough development of these characteristics is found in the collective intellectual traditions that we call the disciplines. Modes of systematic rational thought also apply, in a less precise way, to significant human practices such as moral conduct, the law, government, the economy and education.[11]

The comments of Crittendon and MacIntyre show that high school students' view—that because everyone holds a different idea of justice, there is no way to attain justice, or a just society—merits serious examination and reflection. Students are grappling with central issues of any concept of justice, but they lack the sophistication of professional philosophers. Middle and high school students find it hard to understand the role of dissent in a pluralist democracy. Aware of maxims equating democracy and equality, many conclude that justice requires all voices to be given equal time. Nearly a quarter of the students in my study believed that harmony—defined as the absence of discord or difference—is the enabling condition for jus-

---

[10]MacIntyre's ideas can be found in his 1988 book, *Whose Justice? Which Rationality?* (Notre Dame, IN: University of Notre Dame Press).

[11]The quotations from Crittendon are taken from (1994) "Conflicting Traditions and Education in a Democracy: Can Liberalism Provide Defensible Common Values?" *Curriculum Inquiry,* 24(3), 317–18.

tice. They wish to be fair and honor difference. Like the college students described by William Perry, they are trapped in the thicket of relativism, unwilling and/or unable to judge one person's opinion better than another.[12] One of the brightest young men in the history class wrote in September: "I am constantly pondering justice, law and generally Man's self-governance. I have been struggling with questions about the moral justifications and ethics of a society having laws of any kind for quite some time." By December, he had decided on the following social conditions as prerequisites of justice:

> In this [imaginary] country, all the citizens are the same color, race, gender, and sexual orientation. We have no outstanding characteristics that make us different from each other, so the government finds it impossible to discriminate for or against any person or group of people. Because we are all the same there are seldom any disagreements.

Other classmates agreed with him. One wrote,

> Agreement between the people and government, in the government, and among the governed, is vital. If you can structure a society in which no factions exist, then you are well on your way to either an indestructable community of people who need not be governed or to total failure. Possibly both.

Re-examining the "Face" of Justice

My research shows that high school students currently are engaged in study of topics and issues that require systematic examination of the features of justice. Teachers' reluctance to articulate clearly the issues of justice embedded in discussions of injustice perpetuates students' confusion and leaves them to wander out of the thicket of relativism on their own. Students' oral and written comments show that they are trying to construct a conceptual framework for thinking about justice and that they need help.

Although social studies teachers agree that justice is an important topic that should be part of the curriculum, their own education rarely includes coursework in political theory. Teachers believe that through study of historical and contemporary examples of times when justice was not served, students somehow derive or develop a coherent framework for thinking about justice. I can find no evidence in the research literature, or in students' responses, that this belief is warranted. It is relatively easy to engage student interest at the level of empathy and outrage that

---

[12]William Perry, 1970. *Forms of Intellectual and Ethical Development in the College Years* (New York: Holt, Rinehart & Winston).

Rousseau believed was the necessary starting point for the development of a sense of justice. It is far harder to take the next step and conceptualize curricula that explicitly support such development. Teachers clearly need some help.

The work of legal scholar Judith Shklar has helped me to understand that justice is not merely the mirror face of injustice.[13] Justice and injustice are separate, though connected, concepts. Shklar's concern is, however, the mirror image of mine. Examining the writings of Plato, Aristotle, Mill, and other thinkers to whom the Western tradition pays homage, she finds that legal scholars, political theorists, and philosophers traditionally build models of a just society but fail to give *injustice* its due. I find that social studies teachers provide many and varied opportunities for students to ponder the injustices of the world in the absence of systematic consideration of the features of a just social order.

Let's Question Traditional Conceptions of Justice

In my classes, I want prospective and experienced social studies teachers to understand the importance of theoretical models. I want them to understand that a map is a model of the world, and so is Adam Smith's famous notion of a market. A model is a representation of how things look, or ought to look. We all have implicit models of how things ought to be. When something happens that violates our sense of how the world should work, we notice. But all too often no one is there to ask us to examine our assumptions, and we may not even recognize that we are operating from an assumption that is not shared by others around us. Thus, settlers believed Oregon to be "empty country" and European colonists believed that African peoples lacked "culture." The consequences of our failure to examine our implicit models are rife and often dire.

John Dewey believed that schools should be a model of "associated democratic living" because he thought that schools should educate the young to participate in the real work of sustaining a democratic society. That work involves consideration of the features of a just society, along with recognition of injustice—and a commitment to act in ways that do not perpetuate injustice. Cicero claimed that justice was the province of the citizen. Judith Shklar claims, "It is not that people really want matters to be as they are but that they are wholly unable to know themselves and the way to order their lives for happiness. So they settle for the injustices of normal justice."[14] Social studies classes are the appropriate place for students to study this model of "normal justice" and to ponder whether they, like Shklar, find the model

---

[13]See Judith Shklar, 1990. *The Faces of Injustice* (New Haven: Yale University Press).

[14]Shklar, p. 23.

deficient (riddled with injustice), and what a better (less deficient) model of justice might look like.

Teachers often shy away from theory, especially political theory, on the grounds that it is "too abstract" for adolescents. My research contradicts this: Students are very interested in issues of fairness and justice. By presenting students with a conceptual framework for thinking about justice—such as the traditional three-part division of justice into procedural justice, corrective justice, and distributive (social) justice—and by examining issues and ideas related to each, teachers could begin to shift the concept of justice from the evaded to the taught curriculum. For example, they might ask students to generate criteria for just punishment of wrongdoers. Should we still use Hammurabi's code of "an eye for an eye?" What would constitute just compensation for a parent's loss of a child by murder, or by accident? They might also ask students whether they believe justice is more likely to ensue when there is a system of rules (laws) to follow, or when a wise king (such as Solomon, perhaps) decides. They might pose situations in which one idea of ethical behavior (to treat all equally) conflicts with another (the obligation to take special circumstances, such as blindness, into account). They might ask when it is fair to treat a close friend or relative the same way we treat a stranger, and when it is not. What is the relationship between caring, justice, and mercy? What should justice look like in *this* situation?

At the root of all conceptions of justice is some sense of an appropriate ordering of social structure and relationships among persons. Neither philosophers, kings, nor ordinary people agree on what the proper order, or balance, of benefits and harms across individuals and groups should be, but many wars have been fought to establish one version as dominant over another. However, the eighteen teachers I interviewed about their concepts of justice all agreed that justice is fundamentally "about right and wrong." They saw justice as connected to the way we treat other human beings, to our desire not to deliberately cause harm to humans or the natural world, to our willingness to speak out when we see others wronged and to act to right wrongs, whether we ourselves have committed them or not.

The teachers in this book have invited us into their classrooms to view the way they execute the "millions of intricate moves" that engage their students with the real-world complexities of issues of justice. As these chapters demonstrate, there are fissures in the familiar stone image of a blind goddess of justice holding a set of scales. The image of justice that emerged for me is that of a Picasso face, deconstructed into many acute angles and planes, challenging us to set aside our notions of linearity and corporeal substance for a more complex image of the many conflicting parts that form our social and personal selves. Thus, David Molloy helps his students to understand the importance of rules of order, behavior, and procedure in a system of justice predicated on fair treatment of all involved. Jessie Singer, Dirk Frewing, Sandra Childs, and Amanda Weber-Welch, Theresa Kauffman, and Kim Stafford write about different facets of a just response to a difficult situation; they show us how cultural context and historical moment shape our understandings of the situation and our ideas about how to respond. Mary Burke-Hengen and Greg Smith require their students to personally engage homeless people as well as the paradox of homelessness in the world's wealthiest country.

Despite the peer mediation program's success, Geoff Brooks and Russ Dillman write of their sense of failure because students from all the ethnic and social groups in the high school are not using the program's services. Like Theresa Kauffman, Linda Christensen, and Bill Bigelow, they worry that "fairness and justice for all" may require moves more intricate than they, or we, can devise. Paul Copley, in contrast, encourages his students to use the tools of economics to pose just solutions to the social ills that result from cases of market failure. And Michael Jarmer asks the teachers he works with to consider whether there is any justice in war.

Adolescents already know that individuals have different ideas of justice. Systematic study of the evolution of Western notions of justice, accompanied by cross-cultural comparison, would provide adolescents with coherent frameworks against which to test and refine their own evolving ideas. Asking students to articulate the features of a just situation, or to discuss what would have to change to make a particular unjust situation just, might help them to see that human choices—to act or not to act—make a difference. Meaningful teaching of participatory citizenship cannot evade the question of how a democratic pluralist society should organize to sustain itself over time.

"Millions of Intricate Moves"

This book is our collective effort to provide some guideposts for teaching toward participatory citizenship, and to acknowledge the difficulties of teaching toward justice. Kim Stafford inadvertently provided an organizing metaphor in his selection of a verse from his father, the poet William Stafford. He also sets the tone for the book in another important way: He shows how our childhood experiences may come to frame our adult teaching choices. Ruth Hubbard and I believe that this is the meaning of the phrase "We teach who we are." Even if unconscious or subconscious, these links are nevertheless significant. Similarly, the learning experiences we construct for our students will become part of their personal history and frame their choices in ways we cannot predict. One of the hardest parts of teaching is learning to acknowledge the uncertainty within which we work.

This book provides pictures of the possible, grounded in real teachers' efforts in real classrooms. We hope readers will find these stories inspirational and that they take ideas and adapt them for their own classes. We provide different approaches to teaching, appropriate to the methods of inquiry encompassed by middle and high school social studies curricula, to show the "millions of intricate moves" creative teachers employ. The teachers in this book are realists who know how to imagine "possible worlds." They choose to act even though they do not know all the answers. They honor us by showing us how they trust their students to join them on the difficult journey of envisioning a more just world.

I would like to thank Peter Seixas for helpful comments on an early draft of this chapter.

CONTRIBUTORS

Bill Bigelow has taught high school social studies in Portland, Oregon, since 1978. He's written several curricula, including *Strangers in Their Own Country* (1985, on apartheid in South Africa) and, with Norm Diamond, *The Power in Our Hands* (1988, on labor history). He co-edited *Rethinking Columbus,* 1998 and *Rethinking Our Classrooms*, 1994 and is an editor of the education reform journal, *Rethinking Schools*.

After teaching integrated English and social studies at the middle school and high school levels, **Mary Burke-Hengen** came to Lewis & Clark College to teach and work with beginning teachers. Although Mary loves her work and the opportunities it presents, she misses the community service work of her public school years and so developed the course with Greg Smith described in their chapter. Co-editor of *Building Community: Social Studies in the Middle School Years* (1995) and author of several articles and chapters on teaching and learning, Mary plans to continue to write about her work as an educator interested in community activism.

Geoffrey N. Brooks is employed by Portland Public Schools as an Integration Coordinator for Franklin High School, where he also teaches an African-American/U.S. history course and coordinates a Peer Mediation/Conflict Resolution Program. Mr. Brooks is married with one teenage daughter and is an educator with twenty-eight years experience. He is also adjunct faculty at Lewis & Clark College and at Portland State University. He holds an M.A.T. in Liberal Studies from Lewis & Clark College. Geoffrey's passion is challenging Americans with the truth about race, class, and the miseducation of American youth.

Sandra Childs first tasted the fruits of resistance in southern California at the age of twelve. She sneaked out of her house to join a UFW picket line in front of Safeway to promote farmworker rights. After getting her B.A. from Reed College in Oregon and her J.D. from SUNY Buffalo, she renewed her commitment to social justice by working as a labor lawyer. She then realized teaching was *the* tool for change and and got her M.A.T. at Lewis & Clark. She teaches social studies and language arts at Franklin High School in Portland, Oregon, where she, as her daughter Emma Sophia puts it, "teaches kids to read and write and ask questions." Emma has taken on the family tradition and has been seen at various Portland Area Rethinking Schools Meetings shouting, "Power to the Toddlers! Power to the Toddlers!"

Linda Christensen teaches in Portland Public Schools, co-directs the Portland Writing Project, and co-edits *Rethinking Schools.*

Paul Copley chairs the Department of Social Studies and teaches AP economics and twentieth-century history at Sunset High School in Beaverton, Oregon. He is also adjunct professor at Lewis & Clark College and Portland State University. A previous work, *"The Productivity Factor": Comparing Japanese and U.S. Modes of Production,* was published in 1985.

Russell Dillman currently teaches social studies at Franklin High School in Portland, Oregon. He is the co-founder and co-director of Law and Public Service Program and co-director and founder of Franklin's Conflict Resolution Program. Russ earned a B.A. in Physiological Psychology from Central Washington State University in 1972 and an M.A.T. from Lewis & Clark College in 1988. Born in Tsingtao, China, his varied career includes mental health counseling, wine sales, restaurant service, and teaching in Portland Public Schools since 1988.

Dirk Frewing has worked with Hispanic students in Oregon high schools for the past four years. He is currently teaching high school ESL (English as a second language) classes to the sons and daughters of migrant families in North Portland, Oregon.

Daniel Gallo is currently teaching in the International High School program in Eugene, Oregon. In his classes, he continually makes the effort to illuminate the social values and conflicts that shape different periods in history. Through values exploration, and the underlying attempt to understand the passions that undergird human experience, he believes that all members of the community in a classroom are afforded the opportunity to deepen their humanity. He is also a devoted smoothie drinker, guitar player, cyclist, and lover of music.

Michael Jarmer teaches high school language arts at Rex Putnam High School in Milwaukie, Oregon, and, is an adjunct faculty member at Lewis & Clark College. He is a fiction writer, poet, and musician; he sings and drums in a Portland pop band called Here Comes Everybody.

Theresa Kauffman continues her lifelong passion for teaching middle school students at the Hill School of Fort Worth in Texas. She became involved with Law Related Education in 1982 and has taught numerous workshops and college courses on a variety of social studies and language arts topics. She has served on the board of the Oregon Council for the Social Studies, on the Oregon State Bar Association's Law Related Education Committee and is currently a consultant for the State Bar of Texas. She has written several professional articles and authored a chapter about using mock trials with students in *Building Community* (Heinemann, 1995).

David Molloy earned both a B.A. and an M.A.T. from Lewis & Clark College. He teaches eighth-grade language arts at Jackson Middle School in Portland, Oregon. When he grows up he wants to be a filmmaker or write the great American novel.

Jessie Singer teaches English in Portland, Oregon. She is a member of the Portland Area Rethinking Schools Steering Committee and co-leads a support group for new teachers. In her free time, she enjoys writing, yoga, and her cat, Gus.

Gregory Smith is an associate professor of education at Lewis & Clark College. One of his central professional concerns is finding ways to strengthen the link between formal education and the community contexts in which it takes place. He is the author of *Education and the Environment: Learning to Live with Limits* (1992), editor of *Public Schools That Work: Creating Community* (1993), and co-editor of *Ecological Education in Action: On Weaving Education, the Culture, and Environment* (1998).

Kim Stafford is director of the Northwest Writing Institute at Lewis & Clark College, where he teaches writing. He is the author of *Having Everything Right: Essays of Place* (1987) and *A Thousand Friends of Rain: New and Selected Poems* (1999).

Amanda Weber-Welch teaches social studies and language arts at Gresham High School and is currently on maternity leave with her daughter Madelyn Rose. In addition to writing curricula on her own, Amanda finds that collaborating with colleagues interested in social and economic justice helps to strengthen her own work with students.